MW01106871

Project
Management

Charles C. Martin

Project
Management

HOW TO MAKE IT WORK

A DIVISION OF AMERICAN MANAGEMENT ASSOCIATIONS

Library of Congress Cataloging in Publication Data

Martin, Charles C   1923-
    Project management.

    Includes index.
    1. Industrial project management. I. Title.
HD69.P75M37   658.4'04   75-37884
ISBN 0-8144-5408-9

© 1976 AMACOM

A division of American Management Associations, New York.
All rights reserved. Printed in the United States of America.
This publication may not be reproduced, stored in a retrieval system, or transmitted in
whole or in part, in any form or by any means, electronic, mechanical, photocopying,
recording, or otherwise, without the prior written permission of AMACOM, 135 West
50th Street, New York, N.Y. 10020.

Second Printing

Preface

Project management is a powerful tool whose more extensive use in business and government would measurably increase efficiency and improve the ultimate chances for success of many undertakings. I wrote this book in the hope of stimulating a wider—but appropriately selective—use of project management so that such improvements could be realized.

The central ideas of project management are simple and direct. Unfortunately, in the earty and mid-sixties, an excessively complex implementation of its techniques by the Department of Defense, which forced the complexity on its contractors, caused many executives to regard project management as unsuitable for commercial undertakings and therefore to shy away from it. Still greater caution was engendered by some writings on the subject which concentrated on elaborate control techniques that are not inherently a part of project management, and are applicable only to large projects. Project management is basically straightforward and takes on complexity only when used in large and complex projects. Properly used, it can be effective throughout business, government, and other institutions.

The basic principles and techniques of project management, properly applied, fit projects of all sizes, but in this book I have particularly wanted to emphasize the applicability of project management in small organizations, and for small projects in organizations of any size. Some of its greatest payoffs will come from such applications, at costs that are only a fraction of the gains in efficiency and performance.

I have observed organizations manage a large project well and then manage the next one ineptly. This suggests that they once hit fortuitously on the right approach but did not really understand the basic principles. Considerable effort has been made in this work to sort out and present these principles.

Success in project management depends very greatly on the decisions of the general manager of the organization, but the actions of other senior executives also exert important influences. Therefore, this work is addressed to the general manager and his immediate subordinate executives as well as to the project manager and the other managers on his team.

I have had the good fortune to be associated, in one way or another, with several dozen projects. They ranged from very small to very large, from early conceptual planning and proposals to final production and deployment, from straightforward design to developments pushing the state of the art, from in-house information systems development to production under a formal fixed price contract. I have worked at project management from the view of the government, the prime contractor, the subcontractor, and an organization completing an in-house project. To my colleagues on all these exciting projects, extending over more than twenty-five years, I offer thanks for the exchange of ideas that stimulated so much of the thinking that went into this work.

I owe thanks to several people for their help in completing this work. Jenelle Lyon made a major contribution in organizing material, typing a large part of the manuscript, and maintaining order during the whole undertaking. If my role was that of project manager, she was manager of project control.

I am also indebted to Philip Reed, who commented on several parts of the manuscript and contributed valuable thoughts on how to tell the project management story to an intelligent reader not already steeped in its lore.

Sharon Einck also made a major contribution in typing part of the manuscript. Barbara Martin helped by reading two versions of the text and making numerous suggestions for greater clarity. Finally, I must acknowledge the quiet but companionable encouragement of Blossom Martin throughout the entire project.

CHARLES C. MARTIN

Contents

1

Project Management— A Powerful Tool

WHAT IS A PROJECT?

Project management is a highly effective management tool. Let us see what a project is.

A project has a single set of objectives; achieving them represents completion of the project. These objectives often involve research, development, design, manufacture, and construction and/or installation of hardware, but they may also include completion of a study, development of computer software, or similar activities not involving hardware. Activities centering on hardware may be treated as a separate project for a while and then included in the normal stream of business; for example, the market research, design, initial production, and initial market launching of a product may be treated as a project, after which the project organization is disbanded and the product is managed as a part of normal activity. A project has a finite and fairly well defined life span. It is not an activity that will go on and on as a normal part of the organization's existence. It is well to keep in mind that although project management disciplines and practices are part of managing any continuing organization, all individual projects come to an end. They may be replaced, but always by projects that are equally distinct. Many projects have exceeded their useful life at unnecessary cost because, at the outset of the project, general management did not ask the highly relevant question, "How can we tell when it's finished?"

A necessary feature of any reasonable project management approach is the appointment of a project manager. He must be assigned responsibility for the success of the project and sufficient authority to achieve it. However, in large projects it is often not enough to designate a single manager with a potent charter; in addition, other key managers on the project team must be assigned appropriate responsibility and authority.

A project has a team of people committed full time or at least primarily to project work. They come from different parts of the organization and are required to work closely together to fit their diverse activities together to meet project goals.

A project imposes a unique set of requirements on the organization. Techniques and practices that work in the normal or mainstream flow of business are not adapted to accomplishing project tasks; an example would be the design, construction, and start-up of a new research facility. It is true that some organizations, in such fields as construction and advanced hardware development, conduct the major part of their business as projects, but the criterion of a "unique set of requirements" applies because each project is different in many ways from those that came before and will come after.

Finally, an activity is not a project until top management thinks it is. Only when the senior managers controlling the resources necessary to accomplish the assignment are willing to consider it a project and make the necessary delegations of authority is there likely to be a useful application of project management.

The fundamental requirement in organizing, staffing, planning, and controlling a project is that it be viewed as a single entity. Management regards the project as an integrated collection of efforts by all affected parts of the organization; it cannot consider organizations one by one, noticing in passing that each plays a contributing role in the project. Authority for making project decisions is clearly defined by top management and communicated conspicuously enough that all concerned understand clearly the intent to treat the project as a single entity.

Staffing a project team is of obvious importance. The manager must appear to his team as a competent leader, and to functional departments as a competent line manager. All key members of the team must have similar competence and credentials.

Planning for the project must start with a set of project goals, requirements, priorities, and criteria. Then the contribution expected of each functional area can be determined and assigned. Project planning should be precise; it should not be based on summing the contributions each participating department head finds it convenient to make. Specifications of desired performance requirements, schedules, and budgets must be made clear to the organizations that make up or support the project team. This is a prime function of the project manager.

Controls for the project should be oriented toward the project and its component tasks. Controls on overall departmental efficiency are usually not adequate for evaluating each department's contribution to the achievement of project goals.

The implication is clear: Project management requires a change in the fundamental way an organization functions, for an organization previously unaccustomed to the procedure cannot suddenly embrace it without making some changes in its way of doing business. Indeed, many cases of disillusionment have come about because top management thought it could adopt the name *project management*, change practically nothing, and still enjoy the benefits of project management.

On the other hand, introducing project management does not mean that all project requirements go suddenly to the top of the priority list, that functional organizations are subordinate to projects, or that existing departmental controls are abandoned in favor of project controls. It does mean that a new dimension is added to management decision making in the areas of concern to the project. Conflicting policies, requirements, and demands for resources are readily brought to the surface, and an orderly means is established for resolving such conflicts in the organization's decision-making process in accordance with the overall goals and priorities of top management.

Who uses project management?

Leaders in the building industry use the project management approach as a matter of course in their major construction projects.

Companies involved in the development of major equipment in the capital goods industry use it for each new project; conspicuous examples are aircraft and computers. Companies in the consumer goods industries use it in the form of product managers for new products or product lines.

The Department of Defense and NASA require the use of project management in all their major new systems developments and in many of their smaller ones. When they procure a significant development effort from private industry, they will make the award only to a company that has proposed the use of strong project management and has demonstrated its ability to apply the technique successfully. In many cases the project management approach may also be required of the major subcontractors by the winning prime contractor.

The success of project management in the Department of Defense, and the recognition that it is the only practicable way to bring off some complex projects, has led to its extension in the federal government. The Departments of Transportation and of Housing and Urban Development are among successful users of project management. In turn, they require it of their contractors in many major procurements.

Both industry and government have had difficult, costly, and sometimes unsuccessful experiences in the design and implementation of complex computer-based management information systems. Project management principles have turned out to be the best way to achieve success with these systems.

The academic community has recognized the relevance of project management in the solution of its administration and business management problems. The general need for additional skills in project management is recognized by courses offered by academic institutions, the American Management Associations, and consultants. The Department of Defense has established a first-rate service school to train some of its top career officers on the subject.

Project management is a modern and efficient management tool that shows promise of further effective use in many organizations and situations where it has not yet been used.

General management should look on project management as the newest extension of its influence on the management of the organization, aiding it in its complicated coordination of a large number of separate functions and divisions, each with its unique disciplines, expertise, and practices.

Problems that cut across many departmental lines provide the major challenge to, and indeed the need for, a project manager. They are similar to the problems of general management, but at lower levels of the organization. There is also a greater sense of immediacy in making decisions that cut across division lines; the project must go on. Thus general management's priorities and interdepartmental policies are, in fact, being implemented by project managers. It is essential that general management recognize project management to be an extension of itself, and provide guidance to the project manager so that his on-the-spot short-term decisions are consistent with its longer-range objectives.

The project manager should have a general management outlook. He is concerned with today's problems at the grass-roots level. Thus he can make decisions that extend and intensify the policies of general management. If he encounters departmental execution that is inconsistent with top-level desires, he can expose them for corrective action. This is not to say, however, that he is an inspector-auditor-spy; rather, he is an organizational extension of general management charged with ensuring that its policies are followed in all phases of the project.

In many situations, general management has exercised the project management role. In the earlier days of the aircraft industry, when each division developed and produced only one model at a time, the general manager acted as project manager in addition to fulfilling his other duties. In fact, many companies started with one facility and one product; the chief executive was the project manager. Today, the title Assistant General Manager—Project X, found often in progressive companies, attests to the recognition of the general management nature of project management. The project manager is given top executive authority in the operation of his project.

It is often instructive to listen to the reminiscences of executives who look back to the "good old days" when Model I was designed and built; there was no paperwork, no bureaucracy, only unimpeded action toward getting Model I in operation. Their description of how wonderful things were is a good prescription for the working environment we should create today. True, Model VIII has nearly a hundred times as many parts as Model I; it requires ten times as many engineers to design it; and it is pushing the state of the art far more than Model I did. Nevertheless, if management has learned enough during the period between Model I and Model VIII, it can harness better theory, practice, and information systems to provide an environment as conducive to success as that of decades ago.

In major projects, the top executives of the organization are concerned, so that in this context *general management* means the president, the executive vice president, or the team of top executives making the fundamental decisions for operating the enterprise. Although the greatest payoff from project management exists in larger projects that are the immediate responsibility of these senior executives, the principles of project management have wide application at lower organizational levels: in a product-oriented division, in a functional division, and indeed in a large department. Therefore, when the term *general management* is used, it applies to the senior executives of any organizational entity—whoever can charter a project that requires coordination among a number of subordinate departments.

What project management is not

Establishing a committee is not project management. Just about everything that characterizes committees is prejudicial to good project management. First of all, people in an organization are unlikely to respond very usefully to the requirements of a project if they think they are in fact dealing with a committee. A committee generally spends its time working out compromises that accommodate the desires of all organizations represented on the committee, or that at least minimize and equalize the pain.

On the other hand, project compromises should be among costs, schedules, and product performance, regardless of the parochial desires of participating organizations. A committee is oriented to recommendations; a project is oriented to results. About all a project and a committee have in common is the joint participation of different organizational units, and the human problems of getting people with diverse backgrounds to work together.

Appointing a project manager is not, by itself, establishing a project. A project manager must have authority. Without it he will not be effective. A potentially good project manager will try to achieve results, but without authority all he will do is upset himself, other managers, and the organization in general. In addition to assigning him decision-making authority, top management must assign the project manager control over the resources to do the job.

Nor do sophisticated control systems alone amount to project management. They can be a desirable and efficient tool, but even a control system that extracts data with marvelous subtlety, data never available before, is worthless if those data go unused. Someone must read the data, make constructive interpretations of them, and have the authority to act on them.

One of the saddest of management self-delusions is to adopt the jargon of a management technique, do little to implement the technique, and then believe it is in use. Project management is no exception. Disillusionment with project management often stems from lack of sufficient executive action to make the approach useful.

Project management and its synonyms

"Project management" has been selected somewhat arbitrarily for the management approach described in this book. "Program management" is certainly equally respectable, and for the purposes of this book "project management" and "program management" are completely synonymous.

In the construction industry the term *project* is used more widely. This is probably true throughout industry in general. Exceptions are the aerospace, electronics, and ordnance manufacturers who tend to follow the nomenclature of their Department of Defense customer and use *program management*. The term *project engineer* has wide usage even in organizations that have program managers.

In the government, project management was probably used earlier, as evident in the title "Manhattan Project." Currently in the Department of Defense, the term *program management* and certainly *program manager* are used much more widely. However, Department of Defense directives frequently address the subject of Program/Project Management, indicating the commonality of the concept. Sometimes *program* or *project* has had hierarchical implications, that is, one of them is a subdivision or lower-level implementation of the other. No such connotation is implied here.

Systems management has also been used to describe the development and deployment of very complex or very large systems. Sometimes the term has emphasized the technical control of the development. However, the project management principles and practices discussed in this book can be applied with equal effectiveness by those who like to describe their efforts as systems management.

Product management and particularly product managers are frequently found in large consumer-oriented manufacturing organizations. The emphasis here is particularly on the relationship of the product to the market. However, the principles of project management apply here quite generally.

A host of other activities in various organizations—academic units, businesses, government agencies, nonprofit enterprises—are similar to projects. These are described variously as study teams, task forces, working groups, ad hoc groups, research teams, and so on. Here, too, the principles of project management may be usefully applied to the management of their activities.

The term *project management* was selected for use in this book because it seemed to have the widest application across the American business scene. However, the name is not the important thing. What matters is that some effective principles have been derived for managing any of a multitude of activities similar to the "projects" discussed in this book. Also, these activities occur in a wide spectrum of organizations, large and small; business, government, and nonprofit; any of which can apply project management to good advantage on the right occasion.

SOME SPECIAL FEATURES OF PROJECT MANAGEMENT

Every project has a "customer"

Thinking about project management is clarified if one adopts the concept that every project has a "customer." This is obvious enough when the project is undertaken under contract, as in the case of a construction project, the development of a unique piece of hardware, a study project, the installation of a management information system, or the customization of processing machinery. The customer is clearly identifiable, with his specifications, his schedule requirements, his funds, and his reporting requirements.

These concepts are almost applicable in the case of launching a new commercial product, but here the problem is complicated by the need to determine fairly accurately who the customer really is, what he really wants, how much money he is willing to spend on the product, and how soon he wants to get his hands on the product. One must also find out how much more he is willing to pay for a better product, or perhaps distinguish among different classes of customers who have different value preferences for product quality.

But the point is that the success of every variety of project depends primarily on satisfying the well-defined needs of the customer along with a host of desires and preferences that may or may not be formalized, not on satisfying the desires, preferences, or imagined needs of the inventive and creative people in the engineering department who have scores of product ideas they want to see realized, or the desires of the people in the manufacturing department who would like to have the comforts of a perfectly balanced manufacturing line.

When a project is undertaken to achieve an objective internal to an organization, it is easier for people, including the project team, to lose sight of the customer. If a project is established to build a new manufacturing facility, then the new plant manager is the customer, not the facilities manager. If a project is established to design and install a new information system, then the division chief using the system is the customer, not the data processing director. The project manager, assigned to carry out such a project, should orient the efforts of the project team to meeting the requirements of the customer and to keeping him happy in the process.

However, the coin has two sides. The customer should be required to clearly define his performance and schedule requirements at the beginning of the project and to ensure that enough funds are provided to meet them. When the customer wants changes in performance or schedule in the middle of project execution, he should be prepared to pay for them.

Project management affects nearly everyone

Accepting the premise that project management creates change, one may ask, "Who notices the change?" The answer: "Nearly everyone who comes in contact with the project," especially in a large project that uses some resources or skills from most of the departments in an organization. But even in a smaller project that operates totally within the confines of a division, the difference will be evident internally.

The project affects people all the way to the top of the organization. Division heads accustomed to managing their function and accountable only to general management suddenly find themselves receiving direction, not just requests, from the project manager. Division heads committed to optimal division performance now find themselves facing requirements that disturb this *suboptimization*. Certainly a new framework has been created for decision making, and in most organizations the innovations will be looked upon as a change in the power structure.

These tremors are quickly transmitted down through the organizational structure of the functional division. The manager most profoundly affected will be the functional manager responsible for directing the division's effort on the project. Regardless of whose payroll he is on, he will have two superior managers giving him direction and will have conflicting loyalties, both long-term and short-term. Even if the project consists only of a dozen or two professionals from different organizations, the change will be felt by each of them.

Executives on the staff and in the line feel pressed as well. Projects are often established because existing policies are not appropriate to achieve project success, or existing systems are not responsive enough to meet project needs. Inevitably the staff executive will be confronted with alterations or exceptions to policies to expedite the conduct of project business. Or, if he is not so fortunate, he will find that the policies and systems he has generated are being ignored by the project. At this point he can take either the coward's way out and abandon the whole thing, or the more constructive route of approving appropriate changes where warranted.

Because the project was originated to create an organization better suited than the existing one to meeting project requirements, it will place unusual demands on service groups. If these groups are to help the project, such demands should always be met unless they are grossly uneconomic or unreasonable. Managers in the service and support organizations certainly will notice the change.

General management will also notice the change—an unexpectedly effective management scheme for coping with a unique set of requirements and conditions. But less welcome will be the added burden of the greater number of decisions and even conflicts referred to them for resolution. Besides the fairly stable relationships among the functional divisions, they will now have to manage the relationships between the project manager and each division head, and others of greater complexity involving the project manager and several division heads.

The introduction of project management certainly has widespread repercussions throughout the organization. Even in organizations accustomed to project management, the introduction of a new project will produce a momentary imbalance. Most new projects bring new requirements and new environments that necessitate changes in the normal way of doing business. All these changes must be managed.

Introducing project management involves change

Many organizations that have introduced project management, perhaps partly in name and partly in fact, have completely missed the point that introducing a new set of management ideas and techniques will involve change. After effecting changes, including at least adoption of the name *project management*, they have expected things to go on as before—but with improved performance. They may have gotten better results but with surprising changes; or no results and no changes; or, when such an approach is tinged with naiveté, more problems, many changes, most of them unwelcome, and results no better than before.

A situation warrants project management only if such a procedure can produce overall net gains in management effectiveness and efficiency. If the organization continues to function as before and produces good results, then the supposed project techniques are merely ornamental, bringing with them cost complication and opportunities for future problems without really being project management at all.

Project management involves several kinds of change. It creates a strong leader and his team primarily oriented to achieving the goals of the project, rather than optimizing the performance of individual departments. It creates a new decision-making process. It creates complicated interpersonal relationships and new organizational interfaces. All these changes are complex and, to a degree, disruptive, but they are tolerated because of their contribution to overall effectiveness and efficiency.

Concept of project phases

In organizing and managing a project, it is useful to think in terms of sequential phases. This helps to ensure that all decisions are made and all resources allocated to permit going ahead efficiently into each succeeding phase. It also provides a framework for a series of in-depth project reviews with an opportunity for management to provide redirection or corrective action if required, and adds the psychological benefit of having management make a periodic positive restatement of its support for the project.

Specifically, the phases of a project may be defined as the concept phase, the organization phase, the operational phase, and the completion phase. Other schemes have been used to divide the project into sequential parts, but they all arrive at basically the same ideas. In the concept phase, management establishes goals to be attained, makes a rough estimate of required resources, and decides to establish a project. During the organization phase the organizational approach is defined, key appointments are made, the objectives, tasks, and resources of the project are defined, and a plan and a schedule for the operational phase are completed. During the operational phase the major work of the project is carried to completion; frequently this phase is divided into several subphases, for example, design, construction, and activation. During the completion phase all commitments of the project are liquidated, continuing activities are transferred to other organizations, and project personnel are reassigned.

As a convenient generalization, the foregoing phases may be assumed to follow each other sequentially with no overlap. This may indeed be the case in projects that are small or relatively simple. If in the execution of large and complex projects, phases considerably overlap at times, or different parts of the project go through these phases in different time frames, the concept of sequential phases nevertheless remains useful in reaching the decisions required for project management.

ESTABLISHING A PROJECT

Specific decisions and actions are assigned here to particular phases, not arbitrarily but because experience suggests that a certain set of decisions should be made and articulated before work on the project is allowed to continue. The discipline resulting from adhering to these principles is productive; it forces needed key decisions that could otherwise be more comfortably postponed.

Of course, most projects will contain key steps that can be performed more rationally in a phase other than suggested here; these decisions should be made as managerial common sense dictates.

The decision making, planning, communication, and action described below may at first seem too ponderous for a smaller project, but this is not the case. Note that nothing is said about the form of documentation or action; the emphasis is rather on decisions. For a straightforward project, a meeting of key people followed by a single memorandum signed by the right decision maker may be the best way to accomplish all the things required for that early phase of the project. Decisions are important; form is not.

The concept phase is a convenient label for describing all the activity leading up to the decision to organize and implement a project. At the completion of the concept phase it should be possible for the organization phase to begin immediately. The concept phase may begin as a special-task-force study of the output of normal staff planning, as the resolution of a board meeting, as the conversational planning of appropriate executives, or as a specific decision by a key executive.

A principal product of the concept phase is a statement of the goals of the project. This should give at least a rough estimate of the time and cost required to achieve the project goals. There should also be a fairly firm estimate of the resources required to complete a plan dependable and attractive enough to convince the organization to see the project through to completion.

There is, of course, the decision to establish a project. Organizational details need not be addressed, but the general organizational approach should be defined; for example, ''The project will be a separate department'' or ''The project will operate in our normal matrix mode.'' A senior executive should be assigned the responsibility for successfully completing the organization phase of the project. The senior executive who decides to establish a project in the first place (the chartering authority) may himself want to continue to direct the activity through the organization phase (that is, perform the activities of the review authority and directive authority).

The end product of the concept phase is then a directive chartering the project. It can take the form normally used in the organization for significant communications of management decisions, but it must not follow an administrative channel from press to file with merely a low-level administrative review. The document must receive the attention of the key executives and middle managers who will be concerned with the project.

The organization phase of a project begins when upper management has decided to establish a project to achieve certain objectives. During this phase the organizational authorities and responsibilities should be clearly established. The major goals and tasks of the project and the desired time frame should be stated. Resources to be allocated to the project should be defined; those required before the planning phase is entered should be made available. The project manager and key personnel should be appointed; direction for the assignment of other required personnel should be issued.

During the organization phase, a plan should be made for the operational phase. It should give management a clear understanding of the goals, the costs and schedules, the manner of operation, and the end products of the planning phase. The plan should be presented to the designated reviewing authority; approval, with revisions as directed, constitutes the completion of the organization phase.

This phase would typically last a month. For a smaller project, a week might suffice. A large and complex project calling for the mobilization of resources from a number of organizational elements or different locations might require as much as three months. If an organization has a project management philosophy that is well understood by key executives, and has a history of past successes using project management, the organization phase can be shorter than the typical elapsed times noted above. Chapter 3 is concerned primarily with this phase.

One may ask, ''Why take so long to organize the project?'' Often in the enthusiasm to get on with the project immediately, these initial decisions are left incomplete. However, a substantial number of projects fail or run into serious trouble because the basic organizational structure was not thought out, or was at least not communicated to all concerned. Or the project team is authorized to proceed, stimulated by the alluring prospect of the end results, without being given sufficient funds to do the job right.

The operational phase is the largest part of the project activity. Chapters 4 through 6 describe this activity in detail.

The completion phase is primarily concerned with fair and effective reassignment of the project team. It is discussed in Chapter 7.

Project management and the classical management model

Even though project management has special features discussed above, it does not fly in the face of accepted management theory. Presumably, any useful model of project management should fit somehow into the classical management model of planning, organization, staffing, direction, and control. The one proposed thus far does in fact fit into it quite well. This is true in terms of general management, of how the project is established and its performance assessed, and of how the project manager views the project and handles its internal activities.

At first, project management attracted attention because of its use of new control techniques. Writing on the subject concentrated on detailed execution and control of project tasks. Often the larger organizational issues were passed over lightly, without well-defined concepts of project management. A review of papers given at recent professional or training sessions shows that this is still the case, though to a lesser degree.

Among its other concerns, general management planning addresses the development of new products and the provision of new capabilities. In the new products area it is appropriate to consider whether a project management approach is needed to develop and launch a new product. In some industries such as construction and aerospace, a decision to compete for new business usually automatically includes a decision to establish a project organization. When a major new facility is planned, a part of the planning must be directed toward the organizational responsibility for its design and construction, and this too may call for a project organization. Similarly, plans for introducing a major new management information system involving changes in policies, departmental operating procedures, and computer software may include plans for a project to manage the design and implementation of the system.

But no matter when the plans are made for a project, the principle remains the same: They should define its scope, its objectives, and the amount of resources to be allocated to it. After a decision is made to proceed with a new product, to compete for a new project, to develop a new facility or management system, or to undertake any other activity requiring a project approach, top management must devise and staff a project organization. This is probably the most important *general* management contribution to the *internal* management success of any project.

Staffing begins with the crucial selection of the project manager. Project success is unusual without a highly competent project manager. Next the key managers assigned to the project in the functional areas need to be selected. If the project is a sizable one, a process must be established that will enable the project manager to get the right quantity and quality of people assigned to him from these areas.

Finally, direction to establish the project should include statements of project goals, criteria to be used in making project decisions, and an adequate allocation of resources to complete the project. With these in hand, project direction can be confidently delegated to the project manager. Thereafter, only in case of crisis or the need for major changes in project concept should general management need to take an extensive directive role.

Control by general management is as necessary for a project as for all significant activities of an organization. However, internal management of a project already includes its own control systems. Where project management is not a way of life, general management will often specify the control systems to be used in the project, but having done this, it requires only a summary of the control information developed by the project team in the course of performing its own management task. Only if a project gets into trouble should more information have to be developed.

Now let us examine the role of the project manager in the model of management activities. Internal project planning is an extremely important project management function, and it may take on a dimension not ordinarily present in the planning of an organization. Although key organization and staffing of the project are usually accomplished when general management initiates the effort, some detailed organization of the project team and staffing at the lower levels may be delegated to the project manager. Finally, direction and control are important tasks of the project manager; after the initial planning phase of the project is completed, they constitute his principal functions.

To summarize: General management plans and initiates the project and is principally responsible for its organization and staffing. Direction and control are exercised on a continuing basis, but take less general management attention than organization and staffing because, once selected, the project manager is responsible for planning the internal activities of the project, for issuing necessary direction, and for maintaining effective controls over its progress.

It should now be clear that project management fits within generally accepted management principles. Keeping this in mind, one should be wary of any schemes advanced in the name of project management if they seem to violate respected management doctrine. A possible exception occurs in the successful implementation of a matrix scheme of management, in which a manager can be said to have two bosses—a project manager and a functional manager—whereas two bosses were previously considered a forbidden practice. But this complex subject will be addressed later.

THE PROJECT MANAGEMENT PROCESS

After the project has been organized and staffed by general management, it will operate under the direction of the project manager. The following discussion describes the project management process during its operational phase.

Project management functions are discussed here more or less as though they take place sequentially, and for any given project task they do take place that way. For any single segment of the project no one activity should take place before its predecessors; project direc-

Figure 1.   Project management functions.

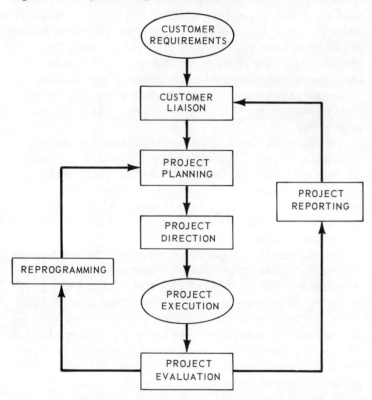

tion should not start before planning of the activity has been completed. On the other hand, after a project is launched, all the activities are likely to be going on simultaneously, but for different parts of the project. The model shown in Figure 1 is a useful way of looking at and thinking about project management, and of bringing order into its execution.

Customer liaison

"Every project has a customer." It is essential to find out what he really wants, and to let him know what he really is getting, when and how he will get it, and how much he must pay for it.

To accomplish this most important communications assignment is a key task of the project manager. If general management really wants him to manage the project, then they, not anyone else, will tell him what they want and how they want it done. Only then can he carry out the project to their liking. Furthermore, if he is really their agent, as he so often is in larger projects, he must know their viewpoint so that he may reflect it accurately in his management of the project.

In short, the project manager must lead the liaison with the customer. If the project is done under contract, and the identification of the customer is obvious, the necessity for assigning the project manager the responsibility and authority to communicate with the customer is, if anything, even greater.

The primary objective of customer liaison is to reach clear agreements on what is to be done on the project, a definition of the characteristics of the project end products, key schedule dates, and the associated funding. Nearly as important is that all parties understand any constraints that appear in the conduct of the project, and the criteria that should be used in choosing between alternative ways of managing the project.

A word of caution: although it has been asserted that customer liaison should be assigned to the project manager, this does not mean that all other members of the project team should be excluded from customer liaison procedures. On the contrary, their selective participation should be encouraged on a controlled basis. Particularly in matters of contract administration, procurement specialists in the customer organization should work closely with the contract administrator of the project team. Similarly, technology specialists in both organizations should communicate directly.

Certainly the project manager should have the authority to establish the project position before such contacts are made and should be given full information about them, and agreements reached in these discussions should have his approval in advance or else be considered tentative until he approves them. In projects conducted within an organization, the project manager has principal authority for liaison with the internal customer, and his office should be the primary channel of communication. But this does not preclude contacts by other members of the team.

As in all business transactions, successful execution of a project is much more readily achieved when there is clear agreement in advance about the intended scope and results of the project. The project manager should have this responsibility.

Project planning

Effective planning is essential for the success of a project. An activity that warrants the application of project management is normally complex enough to require careful integration of its component tasks and coordination of the organizations that will execute the work of the project. Planning ties the project tasks and organizations together. Some projects can succeed without planning, with a "make it up as you go along" management approach, but planning is necessary to achieve efficiency as well as success.

The project planning process is portrayed here in successive steps, but in practice it involves constant interactions back to earlier phases. This is not only an observation of how things work in the real world; it is a prescription for achieving proper integration.

The first step in project planning is one of definition. What exactly are the objectives of the project? What is its desired end product? What are the criteria for making project decisions? What constraints limit the project, including available resources? This information should be obtained from the project customer.

In many projects, particularly those involving hardware development or construction, a preliminary design phase must be undertaken to define the characteristics of the end product so that it can meet the specified requirements of the project. The output of this effort should be sufficiently detailed to permit project planning to proceed.

The next step is to develop a statement of the tasks that must be completed to accomplish the overall objectives of the project. These should be defined first in terms of the end products of the tasks, then according to the role each participating organization will play in each task. As parts of the work statement are completed, schedules and budgets can be developed for the corresponding tasks. These two activities can proceed more or less in parallel.

Finally, functional plans for execution of the project should be made. These outline how to accomplish the tasks defined in the work statement, and should be detailed enough to give confidence that the project goals can be achieved on schedule and within budget. Each plan should concentrate on the nonstandard demands of the project and how these relate to other project plans, rather than on the details of fairly routine activities.

The project manager is responsible for project planning. He is the leader of the team. He may have his own immediate staff to integrate the planning, but the people who will head the project functional organizations must be fully active participants in the planning.

To summarize, the project manager and his team produce project plans that contain a work statement, end-product specifications, budgets, schedules, and implementation plans that will be the basis for project execution.

Project direction

The project manager should have authority to direct all members and organizations in the project team. The nucleus of this direction is a statement of the required project tasks and schedules for their completion. In addition, direction usually includes funding authority and budget constraints and, in the case of technical or hardware-oriented projects, a definition of the project end products. Constraints and ground rules are also part of project direction.

Ideally, project direction is merely an extension of project planning; the project manager simply issues the project plans with a directive to execute them. In real life the matter is not that simple, for it is often desirable to issue direction for only a part of the period covered by the plans. Furthermore, it often turns out that project direction should be more specific and more detailed than corresponding sections of the plans.

The nature and depth of the project direction delegated to the project manager is a major issue in the organization of a project. Primarily, the project manager should concentrate on end products and related schedules and budgets—the *what* and *when* of the project. He should be less concerned with *how* the tasks are executed, or the techniques and detailed resource allocations used to do them. Often his directive authority on how to execute a project will be simply an approval of an organization's own plan to meet project objectives. However, when there is a definite need, perhaps a contract requirement, for a specific method of project execution, he of course issues such direction.

The appropriate depth of project direction is determined by two factors: success and efficiency. Obviously, project direction should be detailed enough to ensure that the objectives and goals of the project will be met. If all project direction has been complied with, and the end products do not meet its requirements, then the direction has been faulty.

Efficiency and proper resource allocation are the other keys to determining the optimal depth of project direction. In a complicated project, the tasks of the various organizational units must be coordinated very carefully; failure of one department to complete its task on time may put all the others in an inefficient mode of operation. Thus, tasks must be accomplished in the manner most efficient for the overall project; good project direction must ensure this.

In most cases, project direction should be issued through the normal authorization channels of the organization, where it will be more readily understood and not regarded as a complicating overlay system. In some instances a streamlined direction system may be required to permit the degree of flexibility the project was established to achieve. But in whatever manner it is given, project direction must be clearly visible and understood by all.

A project manager should not be in a position to issue rapid-fire directions in a helter-skelter manner without enough formalization to permit accountability for performance. On the other hand, the project manager needs the authority to issue emergency direction in any manner he deems appropriate, with the requirement that he follow it up rapidly with confirmation through the normal system.

Project execution

Execution of project tasks takes place after planning has identified their scope and direction has authorized their accomplishment. During these phases the tasks have been identified in such a way that they can be assigned to the departments of the organization. It is the responsibility of the individual department managers to manage and supervise their particular project tasks within schedule, within budget, and in accordance with definition and specifications.

The project manager assigned full line authority over the departments executing project tasks has full responsibility for the efficient performance of these departments in all things including those tasks. In more complex yet often more efficient matrix organizations, the manager is still responsible for the successful completion of project tasks, but he must work through the department heads and their superiors.

Project evaluation

Evaluation is the continuing process of assessing the progress of the project. The word *control* is often used in this same sense, but sometimes that word takes on a fiscally oriented and short-term flavor that makes it less appropriate than *evaluation* to describe this important part of the project management cycle.

Evaluation is primarily concerned with the progress of the project in meeting its principal objectives. It assesses status at the moment, but also extrapolates from that assessment to forecast ultimate project success. Separate assessments should be made about schedules, budgets, and technical performance. The reasons for the variances should be identified, not only by the people who generate the variance data, but also by those responsible for doing the job. Managerial judgment should then be applied to combine them in developing forecasts regarding total project goals.

Ideally, project evaluation consists in comparing existing conditions and current results with project plans and with the specifics of project direction. Any deviation represents a possible problem that should be highlighted, analyzed, and understood. This guideline should be followed as the primary canon of project evaluation.

In practice, however, many problems appear that are real, potentially troublesome, but somehow unconnected with the quantitative variances produced by the control systems. These anomalies, particularly when associated with the judgments and interpersonal relationships of key project team members, may be more demanding of solution than more formally stated variances.

Project management is sometimes associated in executives' minds almost exclusively with the use (or misuse) of various control systems (CPM, PERT, and so on). This essay takes as its premise that successful project management is far more than new control systems. On the other hand, the project management evaluation function will be considerably more effective if it judiciously uses the right mix of controls. And while the right set of control systems certainly varies from project to project, it also does so within the life cycle of any given project.

Successful evaluation of project progress should provide for both formal examinations of data from control systems and informal assessments by project team members. The leadership qualities of a project manager are most important in this phase. He must carefully scrutinize the assessments both of his team and of his control systems, and only then should he form his evaluation of how the project is doing.

Reprogramming

After its evaluation phase, project management usually requires changes in the project plan, in the basic resources assigned to the project, or even in the basic project concept and objectives. Encountering this need for change is not a reason for despair or inaction. Projects are set up to cope with situations of uncertainty and complexity. Project management is as much concerned with keeping the project moving after it is started as it is with the initial planning. Reprogramming is the term used here to designate this part of the project management cycle.

Reprogramming proceeds directly out of the evaluation phase, in which accomplishments to date and estimated future progress are compared with project plans and directives. Variances are analyzed during the evaluation activity to determine their magnitudes and causes. Then reprogramming can take place to correct them.

A first approach to correcting variances may be to call for better performance on the part of an executing department, perhaps bringing this about by eliminating misunderstandings concerning what is desired, or it may be to ensure the availability of intended information and resources. This is simply a matter of clarifying direction and improving performance so that the original plan can be followed.

If it is simply not possible to carry out the details of the original plan, then the subplans must be made to conform to the original plan. If there is a schedule problem in a department, it may be permitted to extend its schedule by reprogramming the downstream work that depends on its output. Or if it is a budgetary problem, additional budget may be provided out of reserves or by transferring funds from some other less critical part of the project. In these solutions the original project objectives are maintained, the project plans change.

If the problem is a major one, it may be impossible to meet all the project objectives: cost, schedule, and end-product performance. Then the program must be replanned to meet the most important project objectives, while minimizing adherence to the others. In doing this, the clear understanding of criteria, discussed above, is most important.

Another reason for reprogramming stems from customer liaison rather than evaluation. The customer almost always requires some change in the project after it is planned and executed. Each change should be defined carefully and its impact on project plans analyzed in the general sequence just described.

Changes in project planning and direction should be accomplished as changes or additions to existing plans and direction, not through different means. It is imperative that the communications and administrative channels used for initial plans and direction be used for changes. Failure to follow this procedure will result in chaos.

Project management is often looked on as a complicated planning exercise followed by a period in which the project manager and his team sit around half-occupied, waiting for results. This is very far from the truth, for coping with the constant changes in the project as it proceeds is often the biggest challenge to project success.

Project reporting

The project manager is responsible for reporting on project progress to the customer and to others outside the project who require information about its status. This is consistent with the project manager's responsibility for customer liaison. In a project done under a contract with an outside organization, the project manager is responsible for reporting both to the customer and to his general management.

It is important that the internal management and external reporting of the project be based on a common set of data. Maintaining more than one set of books is uneconomical and leads to misunderstandings among those who should be working together cooperatively. This does not mean that every piece of data available to the project manager should be given to the customer, but it does mean that the data in reports to the customer should be summaries clearly traceable to project data. Further, it does not mean that every early indication of project difficulties should be reported immediately and in detail to the customer, but does mean that no false or misleading impression should be created by the omission of data in reporting. The nature of arm's-length commercial negotiations may influence the timing and detail of the data released to a customer, but they should never influence its basic honesty.

The project manager's data for reports should be based on any special project control systems, on the information systems of the overall organization, and on reports from departments executing project tasks. Departmental reports to the project manager should be based directly on the data the department uses to manage its work. In the case of a matrix organization, any departmental reports to higher functional management that reflect on project tasks should be made available to the project manager. Assessments should concern themselves with departmental tasks and status, and should not be independent judgments on overall project status.

Although reporting is logically the outcome of the evaluation and reprogramming activities, it really takes place from the very beginning of the project, and should be approached on a positive basis by all members of the project team. It should be looked on as a constructive opportunity to describe project successes and to get understanding and help for project problems.

SUCCESS WITH PROJECT MANAGEMENT

Project management gets it done

The most conspicuous characteristic of successful project management is its consistent ability to get things done. It also reduces costs and improves efficiency. But the main reason for its widespread growth is its ability to complete a job on schedule and in accordance with the original plans and budgets.

Good project management focuses on goals; other considerations are secondary. Such a single-minded concentration of resources greatly enhances prospects of success. Also, its ability to react to problems and effect needed changes minimizes the delays and cost overruns that often plague development efforts.

In some cases, organizations are simply not able to complete complex projects within their normal mode of doing business. Perhaps so much time is required that the project falls hopelessly behind a more efficient competitor's. Or certain interdepartmental study efforts may not be undertaken because experience has shown that these always straggle on without achieving any results useful to the organization. Project management properly applied can turn around such negative situations and bring about positive results.

Good principles have contributed to the success of thousands of small- and medium-size projects; many of their managers never heard the term *project management* but have used the principles nevertheless. A wider application of these principles will also help smaller organizations achieve success.

An example of inability to cope with complexity has occurred in small organizations trying to take advantage of modern data processing methods. A great deal of time and money is spent trying to install a computer-based system; finally, after repeated failures to get it working, management abandons the project as being beyond its capability. Using project management techniques, another similar organization installs a comparable system successfully, without ever having heard the term *project management.*

On a larger scale, the ballistic missile programs deemed necessary for early deployment in the 1960s owed their success to project management. At first their spotty development history led some to believe the task simply could not be accomplished at all. Others thought it could not be done within the desired time frame. After a reorganization that applied a strong project management philosophy, overall success was in fact achieved. And indeed, the relative success of the different missile systems in the overall program is directly attributable to the quality of project management that was applied.

All the above comments about the successes of project management are predicated on the assumption of *good* project management. Many horror stories are told about projects that used project manage ment techniques and either floundered or failed completely. Almost without exception such cases are characterized by ineffective project management. The point of this book is not to urge project management as a universal solution to all management challenges, but to show how to succeed in the complex task of using it properly.

Project management improves efficiency

Besides making things work, project management can make them work more efficiently, either by lowering the total cost of the project or by achieving a superior level of end-product performance, given the amount of the total expenditures.

Costs attributable to using project management usually run between 1 percent and 5 percent of the total project cost. The percentage is usually relatively larger on smaller, or more complex, projects. Management is willing to accept this apparent cost increment because total project cost would in most cases have been higher by much more than 5 percent if project management had not been used.

A project typically consists of a number of related activities, many of which cannot be started until one or more other activities have been successfully completed. A problem with one activity can cause delays in several others; people dedicated to the project wind up charging time to the project without having any really useful work to do. The result is schedule slippage and increased costs.

Project management minimizes the damage of such mishaps by getting an early idea of the problems and anticipating their impact on other activities and organizations, then replanning the work sequence to minimize the amount of time lost waiting for the problem to be solved. Problems that cut across departmental lines are solved more rapidly by project management than by normal interdepartmental coordination.

Another example of cost savings attributable to project management occurs in technically complex development projects. Here several different technologies are involved, and several different technical subsystem problems need to be resolved. Funds are allocated to each subsystem based on estimates of the difficulty and technical uncertainties of the job. In practice, some jobs turn out to be easier than expected and others get into trouble. Those in trouble require additional funds, while those with early success go on to do an even better job, perhaps better than is needed. The project manager can examine project progress on a periodic basis and reallocate funds and other resources in a way that best uses them for project goals.

The principles have wide application

Project management has a wide potential range of application—far wider than its present use. Its principles are applicable to activities in business, government, and the nonprofit private sector; to large-, small-, and medium-size organizations; and to tasks lasting several weeks, several months, or several years. The intent of this book is first to clarify the principles that apply to all projects, then to provide a basis for selecting the various techniques required for different project scopes.

Project management principles are widely applicable to smaller projects in both large and small organizations. Some of the success stories about large projects have doubtless prevented managers from trying the approach on a smaller scale by leading them to believe it is only for the big and the rich. Project management can be the salvation of a smaller project in a large organization where only large endeavors receive senior management attention; it can make it easy for that smaller project to get the priorities it needs for successful execution. It may enable the smaller organization to marshal its resources effectively to focus a management approach and use techniques not otherwise affordable.

Project management is applicable not only to defense and construction projects, but also throughout government—at the federal, state, and local levels. Increasingly urgent demands on government agencies to solve complex energy and environmental problems offer prime opportunities for its use. Where multiple agencies are involved, differing in government level, function, and geographical division, project management is needed to coordinate their joint planning and execution efforts.

Use project management well or not at all

Project management is an effective management technique, but it must be used skillfully and carefully. Although simple in its concepts, it can be complex in its application, particularly in its initial appearance in an organization. Although primary stress has been on the profits to be realized from the intelligent use of project management, it is essential to discuss potential problems so that the manager may have fair warning that management attention is required to achieve successful end results. It is also appropriate to point out that horror stories about project management usually reflect on the user, not on the technique.

Ineptly conceived or poorly executed, project management can be much worse than no project management at all. It is not quite like some other management techniques; for example, partial scheduling, even when not very well done, is probably better than no scheduling at all. Unless it is carefully planned and managed, however, project management brings with it the potential for organizational conflicts and confusion and additional costs. A decision to use project management should imply a commitment on the part of top management to see that it is done right, and indeed done right from the very beginning.

Project management has fallen into disrepute in some organizations for several reasons. The first can be attributed to poor organizational arrangements by general management. The degree of authority delegated to the project manager and the scope of his decision-making powers are not clearly defined. The result is organizational confusion and a consequent deterioration of relations between the project manager and other executives on the team.

Another source of difficulty stems from inadequate staffing. The role of project manager demands good judgment, experience, and executive skills. Underestimating the level of competence required of the project manager is almost sure to guarantee mediocre project management. Temperamental and leadership shortcomings are particularly likely to be fatal. The organizational complexities of a project environment require an especially high level of interpersonal skills, even compared with other executive positions. On a large project, these observations apply equally for the other key members of the team.

Project management has sometimes been held responsible for failures that are basically attributable to general management. Sometimes an organization confronted with problems of incompetence in functional divisions or an inefficient organizational structure will assign the remedial job to a project manager and then be unhappy with his mediocre results. This occurs, of course, because general management has given the project manager problems it could not solve itself—while giving him authority considerably less than its own. His failure is predictable, but it should not be charged against the account of project management.

To summarize, executives of an organization should not use a project management approach unless it appears to be the best solution. They should not permit a haphazard, misunderstood use of project management principles. If they do decide to use this technique, they should expend the time and effort necessary to ensure that it is planned and executed properly. This requires a commitment of time, decision-making responsibilities, and executive skills—but such a commitment will pay off handsomely in the right situations.

General management is responsible for successful project management

Project management is useful, among other reasons, because it can coordinate several diverse units, enabling them to work together more interdependently than usual. The new relationships it creates between divisions demand a kind of cooperation more complex than is necessary in the ordinary flow of work from one unit to another. Any organization chart is based on the idea that general management alone has ultimate authority over all the divisions, departments, and parts of the organization, many of which must be directed, shaped, improved, and perhaps changed to accommodate the ideas of project management. Since the best results always come from leadership at the right level, the success of project management always depends initially on good general management.

The project manager has only the authority that is delegated to him by general management. This authority may, quite properly, be restricted and subject to review, but a project manager cannot act effectively without it. On the other hand, if top executives are going to delegate enough authority to get the job done right, they had better thoroughly review how this authority is being used.

Success in project management requires the wholehearted sincere, constructive support of all the functional executives in the organization. Perfunctory announcements and directives about a project will not achieve this. It takes direct personal signals from the top executive to the other top members of the team to convey the message that the project *will* succeed, and that all members of the team *will* be measured by its success.

Project management is a complex mechanism introduced into an organization because it will get the job done better. It does not come free. It pays off for general management, but requires planning, direction, and conscientious surveillance to achieve its promises of success.

2

People and the
Project Environment

SPECIAL FEATURES OF THE PROJECT ENVIRONMENT

Good people make a project successful

Only good people can make a project successful. In the long run this is true for any organization, but failure to assign good people to a project will result in disaster much more quickly than in an ongoing organization. Furthermore, the disaster is apt to be much more serious in a project, perhaps even leading to total failure. On the other hand, the payoff may well be greater because the project environment provides a better, more flexible milieu in which to bring forth the full exercise of talent.

Of course, good people alone cannot guarantee project success; a project that is poorly conceived, badly planned, or provided with inadequate resources has little hope for success. But even if there is only marginal hope, an excellent team will be far more likely to bring the project off than a mediocre one. On the other hand, if the team is not up to the job, no amount of brilliant planning and lavish use of resources will save the situation; elaborate control systems will only highlight the inevitable and accelerating approach of doom.

It is easy to say that a project needs good people, but harder to answer the question, "Who are good people?" Some requisites are discussed in later sections, but in a nutshell the project team members should have forward-looking, professional competence, an ability to get along honestly and constructively with other people, and an attitude that is both positive and flexible.

While these attributes are desirable for project assignees and are a dominant issue in the selection process, they are not the whole story. The project, affected in a big way by personnel policies and administration, must continue to provide an environment where people can utilize their good qualities and even improve them.

Great stress is placed here on the selection of good people: a project can too easily become a dumping ground for misfits. Equal stress must be placed on maintaining the right environment, for it is tempting to walk away from the personnel challenge after a good selection job. General management must be continually alert to its important responsibility for requiring excellent performance from the people selected.

This discussion on the interaction between the project environment and the behavior of people in the organization was introduced at this point because it provides significant useful background for the discussion of project organization in the next chapter and, indeed, for all aspects of project management.

Project personnel problems are special

Right from the beginning, general management must recognize that establishing a project creates special problems for the people on the project, for the rest of the organization, and thus for the top managers themselves. This does not mean that a project demands a completely new set of personnel policies; it simply means that some new problems must be faced. After all, project management implies change; it is used because there is something to be gained by departing from the normal functional way of doing business. It would be surprising if people, an organization's most important asset, were not affected by the changes.

Necessary and desirable changes in personnel policies and procedures must be recognized at the outset of the project. They should be an important part of early planning, and should be defined and implemented before very many people are brought aboard. The later the appearance of the problems, the more disruption they will cause and the more people they will affect. Personnel problems have brought many a project to a wasteful and embarrassing halt; meanwhile, costs and schedules have gotten out of control. Often the project suffers for some time after the breakdown because of organizational turmoil and deteriorating relations among members of the project team. Personnel problems should be prevented by careful, early planning; if they do occur they should be solved as fast as reasonably possible.

Change—the way of doing business

When project management is first employed in an organization, it produces many fundamental changes. The project manager, a new, powerful, and not universally welcome player, appears on the scene. The existing authority of other managers is changed, usually by curtailment in selected areas. Policies, procedures, and approval cycles are changed. New methods of decision making are introduced. Established power structures are altered. Mutations occur in the informal organization. Personal relationships and methods of doing business with customers may be changed. Old absolutes disappear.

All is chaos—changes occur everywhere—or so it may seem to people throughout the organization. Faith in previous value systems is shaken. Insecurities set in, some of them well founded. Many of the doubts, frustrations, irritations, and forebodings are concealed, but they are there. The impact on people is usually greater than general management anticipates when project management is introduced on a major scale, and is more persistent than they perceive it to be as the whole thing unfolds. All this challenges management in several ways:

- Things will never be quite the same again.
- People who don't like change, even very good people, are going to be less comfortable.
- A situation that is changing is more difficult to manage.

Change—the frenetic project atmosphere

Normal organizational behavior tends to optimize and stabilize a steady-state operational process. A bureaucracy is particularly and affectionately devoted to achieving this placid goal. Most managerial decisions are regarded as necessary to cope with aberrations in the smooth flow of events; one must "put out the fires" (even when these fires are evidence of creativity). Change is acceptable only if it results in an orderly modification of the steady-state process. A world that lacks that steady state is viewed as untidy and unacceptable.

On the other hand, a project typically has no steady state—unless turbulence is regarded as its steady state. It consists of a series of related but dissimilar phases. Surprises occur constantly. Plans are important, but must continually be changed to conform to the realities of the moment. Soon after one phase begins running smoothly, it is time to finish it and get on with the next, while planning the one after that. Creative research and development activities, in particular, follow this unchartable voyage of constant change. That is one reason why they thrive so often in a project approach.

The tone of a good project is always a bit frenetic, hyperactive, more vivid than life. If too much so, it is suffering from deficient prior planning or decision making; if not enough, it lacks good leadership. But the complex structural relationships and the constant changes that complicate matters in another dimension lead to a very special, lively, challenging environment. A member of a project team feels rather like a capable four-ball juggler who knows he must now also keep that fifth ball in the air and under control.

The frenetic changing project environment has all sorts of individual psychological implications. First of all, the person who loves stability will be miserable. The person whose job is to fine-tune and perfect the system will be frustrated; each time he has the system optimized and stabilized to cope with the input and the environment, the environment and the input will change. People who like orderly hierarchical relationships will be offended by a situation where the identity or rank of the project hero of the day remains unknown until each day is over.

The two-bosses problem

A new organizational environment is created in projects by the simultaneous activities of the project manager on the one hand and the functional heads on the other. As noted above, project management selects this organizational complexity only because it is a more effective way to get the job done; it permits use of superior technical judgment and expertise, but focuses its special leadership attention on the tasks and goals of the project. The intricacies of this arrangement are more apparent in the matrix project, but they also occur in task forces and rather heavily "projectized" organizations.

Most conspicuously affected by this phenomenon is the project functional manager, the man assigned full time to the project and responsible for managing all his function's project activities. He reports simultaneously to two bosses: the project manager and the senior functional head. The priorities of these two senior officials are frequently at odds, even though each executive may be genuinely concerned with both the immediate success of the project and the long-term health of the entire organization.

This situation calls for exceptional balance and good judgment on the part of the project functional manager. Not only must he find a way to satisfy both men, but he cannot do so by adopting a shabby short-run compromise that really satisfies no one in the long run. If one of his bosses clearly misunderstands the problem while the other is unquestionably right, he must have the courage to stand up for the right decision and convince the misguided party. He must scrupulously avoid the coward's choice of telling each superior what he wants to hear. In particular he must never play one boss off against the other; that is sufficient cause for his being replaced forthwith.

When doing his job really well, the project functional manager is an important communications link between his two leaders. Each time he finds them disagreeing, he brings them together to resolve the problem. If particularly judicious, he will either anticipate troublesome issues or foresee their evolution and arrange discussions that will prevent them from ever becoming controversial. If one of his bosses is far more unreasonable and mercurial than the other, he must not succumb either to pique or to intimidation and thus tilt his judgment accordingly. All this requires perceptiveness and the ability to communicate well. Even under the best of conditions it produces occasional strains.

The project functional manager is not the only one subjected to special emotional pressures; his two bosses experience them as well. Particularly when project management is a recent innovation, the functional head may feel a very real sense of personal affront and deprivation of authority. His frustrations may range from open hostility to subtle attempts to sabotage the project by withholding the best talent and advice, or he may undermine confidence in the project by his own sophisticated "viewing with alarm." To him the project manager is an unwelcome interloper.

The project manager may also undergo traumatic shocks. By nature he does not suffer fools lightly and is not even very patient with wise men. He bristles when plans for his project are questioned, and sometimes harbors the secret wish to execute bearers of bad news about project progress. He is offended by anyone who might slow down the expected immediate and total response to his direction. Under these conditions he is unlikely to regard functional heads as heaven-sent aids to his project or to seek them out for advice and counsel.

Other project personnel are subjected to the tensions associated with the two-boss problem, although not to the same degree. The social scene is more complex in project management than in a normal organization. Why put up with it at all? Because often the advantages far outweigh the disadvantages.

Impermanence of projects

Projects are impermanent. The clearly identifiable goals that mark the success of a project also mark its end. The engineering division, the financial division, the manufacturing division all go on and on, but the project will end. Many projects end in a year or two, and even the larger ones complete their work in five years or so. True, some project teams go on to other similar challenges—a wise use of unique resources—nevertheless they do not have the certainty of enduring.

Many competent people simply do not like the chancy project environment. Some of them are highly talented and creative professionals, perhaps a bit insecure, who have found their special niche in a functional division. Through hard work and superior intellect they have achieved a status in an environment that is congenial. Accepting a project assignment means going into a hostile environment populated by a few of one's peers and abounding in all sorts of odd types with inferior academic credentials. Particularly obnoxious will be the ject manager, a rather loud type surrounded by bright but uncivilized young aides who harass one with inconsequential questions about money and schedules, with no appreciation of ever-challenging technical problems and elegant responses.

Another respectable member of the organization for whom a project assignment is a potentially traumatic experience is the tidy, methodical manager. He is probably a man devoted to duty, of better than average intelligence, with an excessive fondness for apparent order and a dislike for change. He has built his success on conformity, on intelligent compliance with policies, on making the status quo work well. He appreciates procedures more fondly than is necessary. He runs a department of excellent efficiency. He is appalled at the prospect of deserting the superbly functioning environment he has created to join a project. His labors in perfecting a nearly unchanging process of unparalleled smoothness will be unappreciated by a project manager whose goal is to start, bring to a full run, and stop production. Such disorder, connoting instability and inefficiency, is unlikely to turn out well.

People who fall into the patterns described above are not ideal candidates for project assignments. However, if their presence is required, they are likely to feel much more at home in a matrix than in a project management type of organization. Particularly for the professional specialists, having a stable organizational home makes a project assignment far more acceptable. That is one reason why the matrix approach is preferred in many projects of high technology.

Projects and creativity—the chance for glory

Projects daringly conceived and imaginatively executed offer great opportunities for talented people. Indeed, the freeing of creative people from inhibiting rules and bureaucratically restrictive environments can be the best reason for establishing a project. When a project achieves the delicate balance between bringing out the best of inventive thinking and providing adequate controls to ensure that efforts are directed toward project goals, then it is headed for a striking record of success.

People sense that a really good project is an opportunity to excel. Goals are clearly visible, freedom of action is greater, and superior performance will be applauded and rewarded. Under enlightened leadership, this environment can stimulate creative talents to achieve goals that had seemed hardly attainable. Projects must be managed to achieve this extraordinary success.

PERSONNEL POLICIES AND PROJECT MANAGEMENT

When general management recognizes the importance of the idiosyncrasies of people in project management, its job has just begun. Next it must think out and communicate its views to the rest of the organization. It must establish clear policies that preclude personal frictions between project and functional personnel throughout the organization, and that prevent the project's stated intentions to achieve change from being frustrated in a web of bureaucracy. Personal direction is, as always, paramount; but formal direction is more important than usual.

The perceived need for a project can arise suddenly, but even where it is under consideration for some time it may be rather closely guarded information. Announcement of a project may burst on the scene as a surprise to most of the people in the organization, and an unwelcome one at that. Changes, and surprises in particular, lead to speculation and suspicion. Rumors flourish. Failure to define policies clearly can be interpreted as a cloak-and-dagger scheme to give the project carte blanche. Jealousies and resentments thrive. Anyone disliking the project can interpret a lack of policy as an intent to exploit the organization. (Anyone on the project will get undeservedly rich; therefore, ostracize him!)

When policies are carefully thought out in advance, as they should be, it is appropriate to announce them soon after the project charter is published. This eliminates misunderstandings and quells rumors. It puts everyone on a common basis of understanding.

Even more important is the elimination of the false starts that occur in the absence of policy. Well-meaning managers may assume that existing policies still apply when, in fact, significant changes are in the making. Or worse, noting that policies are nonexistent or existing policies obviously don't apply, each of a number of different managers makes up his own version of what a reasonable executive would issue as policy.

All versions may well be reasonable, but chaos ensues when people are given different versions of the policy. This problem is usually blamed on the project rather than on the personnel executives who are most responsible for it; the project is "all mixed up." Clear direction makes for efficient execution of the personnel function on the project.

An equality principle

A reasonable test for personnel policies used in a project environment is this:

> *After reassignment at the end of his tour on a project, a person should have the same compensation level and the same prospects for the future that he would have had if he had performed equally well (or badly) in a normal assignment not connected with the project during the same period.*

Like so many fine principles, this one is easy to understand and difficult to apply. First of all, who knows how well off he would have been if he had stayed in his old environment? Nevertheless, this problem is not as difficult as it might seem. Comparison with the progress of the people who were his peers when he left to join the project gives a good insight; if they have, on the average, received 30 percent additional compensation since that time and have been promoted one organizational grade, that is an appropriate baseline for him. Difficulties arise, but this guideline works pretty well.

Project experience brings out the best and the worst in people. It may give someone a chance to display previously hidden flashes of leadership genius, so that he may now look much better than his old contemporaries, or it may create pressures that bring out a flaw in character, a failure to perform under stress that damages a reputation permanently. Yet such instances do not really negate the principle; they are situations peculiar to the project, and their consequences for particular individuals are particular consequences. This occurs all the time without any proximity to project management; some people are lucky and others are unlucky in getting jobs that highlight their best features or their worst.

The most difficult situation—the exception that proves the rule—occurs when management makes an obvious error in assigning someone to a project. He may be too rigid, too resistant to change; the job may create personal or domestic strains; or it may simply be a case of mismatching the job and the man. Under these conditions an inept or even miserable performance on the project may be forgiven, the unfortunate individual may be returned or assigned to a job at a level with his old peers, and the project interlude should then be forgotten by all concerned.

The principle proposed is basically long term in nature. Good judgment must be exercised in equating the shorter-term benefits and comparable disadvantages of being on a project. But excessive preoccupation with sterile computational schemes to achieve equality is usually not helpful. Good experienced judgment in the short run and application of the equality principle in the long run give the best results.

Standard policies and special policies

Whenever a project is initiated, there is a great temptation to believe that personnel policies can be left alone, and that perhaps it will be enough to cope with exceptions merely by overriding executive direction expressed informally. Yet this in effect ignores the problem completely. To yield to this temptation on a major project is to invite misunderstanding and unnecessary interpersonal irritations.

Standard personnel policies exist presumably because they represent the best and fairest way of dealing with people in the organization. They are frequently formalized to a high degree by union agreements in the private sector, by civil service procedures in the government sector, and by academic and related practices in the nonprofit sector. Every effort should therefore be made to live with existing personnel regulations.

However, when there is a clear need for a special policy or a deviation from standard policies, the matter should be faced squarely. The project manager, the head of personnel, and affected division heads should be asked to present recommendations, hopefully jointly agreed upon. However, any disagreements should be defined clearly and presented to general management for review. If necessary, a decision can be made and communicated informally to the interested executives. Even an executive decision that there will be no special arrangements is not a waste of time; it is rather a positive decision that clears the air and discourages continuing efforts to tinker with policies.

Next, the decisions for changes should be put in the same form and issued through the same channels as those used for normal personnel policies. This can be done either by making an amendment to each affected policy or by issuing a single policy statement covering exceptions applicable to the project.

This black-and-white approach to personnel administration at the beginning of a project saves much time later on. It lets everyone in the organization know of executive intent. It immediately stamps out any widespread feeling that project people are using cloak-and-dagger methods to gain all sorts of concealed benefits for themselves. What differences exist are there for the world to see.

PERSONAL QUALIFICATIONS OF THE PROJECT MANAGER AND HIS TEAM

Leadership

It goes without saying that leadership is an essential quality for any successful executive. It is crucial for a project manager. No effort will be made here to define the term. One can use any of the serviceable prescriptions and definitions formulated by the many excellent writers on the subject, or use a concept that appeals to oneself particularly, but in either case the principle applies.

Leadership is especially important for the project manager because he must motivate people who have ties both to the project and to the functional organization. He must exercise his leadership subtly so that he stimulates eager and constructive support for the project and the project team without causing attitudes toward home departments to weaken. Indeed, the best type of project leadership fosters strong positive loyalties both to the project and to the functional organization.

All this is more difficult in a project environment than in the simpler world of normal departmental entities. The transient aspect of projects further challenges the project manager to motivate people to perform well, even though they know their stay under his direction may be rather shorter than a normal tour. This condition is particularly pertinent in short-term task forces where a team of committed individuals must accept leadership willingly to gain the benefits both of synergism and of the various individual talents.

A complex project requires a team of widely different players and departments: researchers, planners, engineers, fiscal experts, logisticians, production managers, and still others. The project manager must have a leadership style acceptable to all. It is a problem to lead electronics, propulsion, structural, and civil engineers in a common cause, but at least they have a somewhat common view of how things should be done. It is a bigger problem where managers of wide-ranging departments are concerned.

Leadership is more difficult in a project than in the normal type of organization because a project is freer in form and more involved with change. The head of a department or division has a challenging leadership task, but on his side he has an ongoing team, a set of practices for doing things, and an established set of interpersonal relationships. Moreover, motivating people to perform well is made easier for him because the environmental framework for doing this is generally readily perceived and well understood. On a project, on the other hand, people are strangers, things are different and change faster, and the future is uncertain. Leadership is a larger and more complex challenge here.

Honesty and integrity

Honesty and integrity are desirable in all executives. Theoretically, no respectable company will appoint and retain any executive who clearly lacks these qualities. Nevertheless, and regrettably, some managers with technological, marketing, or other specialized skills are tolerated even though their interpretations of honest behavior and their handling of ethical problems can euphemistically be described as unorthodox.

If one starts with the premise that all the executives in an organization are honest, then the project manager should be conspicuously honest, and it is helpful if he has this reputation throughout the entire organization. The project manager is entrusted with the delegated authority of general management; this alone would seem to demand a particularly high brand of integrity. He is placed in a number of complex situations where getting people to trust each other and work together is a key condition for success; if he himself is regarded as completely honest, his decisions resolving disagreements between different organizations in the project will be far more readily accepted by those whose views are not sustained. He will be regarded as having made the decision that best serves the interests of the project, and harmony will prevail.

When people are being recruited for a new project, many good men, uncertain about the vagaries of project life, will be persuaded to join because they personally trust the project manager. Dealing with the customer is another area of his responsibility where integrity is important; projects or their successors can extend over many years, and nothing ensures a lasting constructive customer relationship better than a history of open honest dealings.

It is easy enough for a fast-talking, sharp operator to draw attention to himself as a potential project manager. His strategy is simple: to tell each person what he wants to hear—but not always the same story, of course. The complex organizational and technical environment is a fertile field for this sort of seedy character. True to form, when he encounters difficulties on a project he will conceal them as long as possible from both his customer and his own management. When inevitable disaster finally occurs he is armed at least with an eloquent Pearl Harbor file proving that not he, but everybody else on the project, was at fault. Such dubious operators can succeed in major projects for some time, even years, but they eventually fail and leave behind them serious protracted problems for their organization.

Command of project technology

A project manager should obviously be able to understand what is going on in his project. He must be able to communicate upward with customers and higher management and downward with key technical managers and professionals. It is a delicate question, just how much technical competence the project manager should have. If one has found that rare combination of the best technical man in the field who is also a reasonably competent manager, the answer is simple; but, alas, fate is not always so kind.

On a technically oriented project, the project manager must be able to understand thoroughly not only the major technical issues, but the complex, subtle second-tier issues as well. If he can discuss them effortlessly in the jargon of the experts, this will probably suffice. He need not be highly creative but he must be able to evaluate creative efforts and thereby communicate with an immediate subordinate who heads the technical operation. Only in this way can he assess risks and make the necessary tradeoffs between technical issues, costs, and schedules. This is why so many project managers have an engineering background.

In general, it may be said that both the technical people below him on the project and the executives above him should have confidence that the project manager will see that the right technical decisions are made. That is why the complex matrix organization form is so successful when led by a project manager who can draw on the best technical expertise available. But he must know how to talk lucidly about technical problems.

In the early stages of a project, technology predominates. Rough estimates of future costs, profitability, and reasonable time scales can be made, but these are all dependent on technology. Thinking it through is the main thing. After a project progresses into design and development and later into production or construction, the technical die is pretty well cast and the emphasis shifts to execution. For this reason, a highly technical manager often leads a project in its early phases, later passing the baton to a manager of a broader, less technical competence.

Business management competence

A project manager should understand the basic managerial skills of planning, staffing, directing, controlling, and so on. He need not be able to discuss them in the latest business school terminology, but he must know how to apply them effectively. Project management is a management job like others, but it operates in a highly visible arena and on a compressed time scale.

In the fiscal area, the project manager does not have to be an expert, but he must be able to communicate as effectively with his project control manager as with his key technical people. Fortunately, accounting and scheduling are skills that can be acquired by taking available training programs.

Particularly with technical people, the problem is not to get them to understand accounting and scheduling, but to impress on them that costs and schedules are equally as important as elegant technology. Many a technical expert who understood accounting nearly as well as his accountant has led his project down the trail to disaster because he just did not think that counting those beans was all that important.

Alertness and quickness

A man with the many talents of Figaro and an excellent engineering degree would make the ideal project manager. The frenetic atmosphere of projects and their wide range of problems partly explain why this is so.

Projects must be flexible, though always in conformity with overall project plans. Any project that is not moribund produces continuing changes. The project manager must direct the great variety of changes so that they result in movement toward real project objectives and not random unproductive motions that spend project resources without making any corresponding contribution.

The project manager has or should have conversations with many people on the project, whatever its size. Each person will vary in his enthusiasm for the project, competence to evaluate, ability to articulate, reasons for speaking out, and countless other responses and qualifications, but a good project manager will listen, will recognize the environment out of which the remarks have come, and will gain a lot of information about his project.

A project manager on a large project is exposed to data from many control systems, formal and informal. To identify trends from all bits of data requires quick mental reactions. Inevitably, many inputs of data are not objective, either because of personal bias, the limited horizon of the observer, or misreading of a symptom, but occasionally the misrepresentation will be deliberate, perhaps because of a misguided notion that distortion of the facts is in the project's best interest. Ability to think quickly in relating all data inputs to a baseline of facts is a great asset both to a project manager and to his key subordinates.

Imaginative versatility and honest flexibility

If you enter a room and select the people who have seen everything a business career can show them, you have a mixed bag that includes all the project managers; if you make a second selection and keep those who are willing to see it all one more time, then you have only the project managers.

A project is more complicated than ordinary organizational endeavors. That is one reason why it was established in the first place. It may span the entire spectrum of the enterprise's activities, or penetrate into new aspects of the operation. New situations, new people, new goals, new technologies, new problems, new requirements, and the thousand combinations of all these challenges can lead good managers into present, let alone future, shock. The program manager must have the imagination to perceive the unforeseeable, the unmentionable, the unthinkable combination of untimely, unnerving events and must be able to react to them with versatility. He must comprehend the effect on every part of the project and on every member of the project team, then solve the problem with everything put in its proper perspective.

To repeat, planning is a key element in project success. But external requirements change, or events within the project may change the situation. The best plan of yesterday is often no longer the best way to achieve the goal of tomorrow. New plans are necessary, and these will change too. The project manager must be ready at any time to modify any existing plan for a "better" one. Flexibility does not mean an easy good humor in downgrading project objectives, or a relaxed corruptibility in abandoning good business practices, both of which may look good in the short run; it implies a tough willingness to change plans in light of current realities, always with the best interests of the project in mind.

Energy and toughness

Project management is a demanding business. No executive job can be done in a standard workweek, but project management is particularly stringent and can be brutal in its physical and mental demands on the project manager.

The project manager has to cope with a large number of interpersonal relationships. This means he must be available to many people, alone and in combination. All problems seem to demand immediate attention if not solution. Management by exception is a good idea, but no two weeks are planned to encompass the same events, so all is exception.

Since a good project does not have relaxed schedules, failure to reach a milestone demands immediate attention. If communications are as they should be, customers as well as senior general management and functional executives will want and will receive reports about progress. Eager managers on the project team want help, decisions, counsel, and ratification of their tentative decisions. And even with all this, there must be time to think, to evaluate, and to plan again.

A good project manager must have the ability to cope with the great quantitative and qualitative demands that will be placed on his time, and he must be near top form during most of this time. He must be able to weed out the nonessential demands, but even after he has done this, his schedule will be rigorous. He must have the physical stamina and mental toughness to respond well to both a very busy schedule and a very long workweek.

Decision-making ability

A good project manager makes far more decisions than the ordinary executive at the same organizational level. A functional executive may spend much time and thought on a single decision that implements a policy his subordinates will use in making their decisions. In a project, however, things are too new and change too fast and involve so many unlikely combinations of people and organizations that it is impractical to manage primarily by set policies. Policies should be used wherever possible, but the large part of project business is transacted by means of on-the-spot decisions. The project manager must recognize when decisions need to be made and must be willing to make them.

It has been observed that a project manager will succeed if 51 percent of his decisions are good ones. It is certainly desirable that the manager keep the project moving, if possible forward, with immediate decisions made when needed, rather than stalling it while agonizing over a number of unsettled issues. But the really excellent project manager goes beyond this and makes a very high percentage of good decisions. One may look at a number of successful managers from quite different kinds of projects and with widely varying management styles, and the one thing they have in common is good judgment; they make consistently good decisions.

That is why it is a good idea to go with a known winner. It may be difficult to grasp his management style or analyze his mastery of techniques, but a record of success is evidence that he has made good decisions in the past and is likely to do so in the future.

Desirable qualifications for project people

Competence is obviously a requirement for any assignment, but is more important on a project. In many routine jobs, even those demanding fairly advanced professional skills, a person of only modest competence who has diligence, organizational loyalty, and the knack of getting on with people may do a very creditable job. On a project this is simply not the case.

A project is established because special effort is needed to meet its goals. It presents new problems that must be solved in new ways by creative, intellectual effort, not by reliance on the same old techniques. Good decisions must be made rapidly, and this requires clear and fast thinking. That does not mean each project slot must be fitted with the best man of his grade in the organization; it does mean that the project position should be staffed with bright, creative people, not with second raters.

People assigned to a project should be able to communicate, to get along with others, and to establish constructive working relationships with new colleagues. In a stable organization, long-term operational practices may have been refined over years to the point where they can accommodate all but the most virulent interpersonal relationships. But on a project, where so much is new, there are no standard solutions. Good decisions must be made on the spot, and this requires good people communicating freely, working together to develop a constructive solution that is both good for the project and generally consistent with good management principles. Therefore the shy individual is not usually a suitable choice for a project, even if he has the best of motives and real devotion to the project.

Flexibility is another great asset in project people. A good slogan to apply during the selection process is ''Bureaucrats not needed here.'' Since a project is full of change, people who are uncomfortable with change are unlikely to be productive; people who oppose change are likely to be a menace.

At least a moderate sense of organizational sophistication is also required, particularly when the matrix form of organization is employed. People must not be upset by having ''two bosses.'' They must be able to keep the idea clearly in mind that both the project and their functional organization are best served by project success. Apparent disagreements in methods should be resolved so as best to achieve the common goal.

In addition to needing all of the qualities described above, project functional managers need most of the characteristics prescribed earlier for the project manager. In particular they must have mature judgment, for they are at the focus of the matrix decision-making process. It is no coincidence that managers who have had this experience wind up so often as both functional division heads and project managers.

TRAINING FOR PROJECT MANAGEMENT

Skills required

To do a good job as project manager or as one of the other key managers on the project, one needs the basic skills required of any broadly responsible executive. In addition, an undergraduate degree in the main technology of the organization is important, whether it be engineering, science, economics, city planning, information systems, or sociology. Beyond this an M.B.A. or an executive management course as a supplement to academic training in business management is desirable.

Certain skills are particularly oriented to project management. These include:

Planning: A basic knowledge of how to plan, along with an

understanding of systems analysis (systems engineering in some cases) and statistical risk analysis.

Financial control: Basic accounting, cost accounting, budgeting, cost estimating, learning curves, and estimating the value of work accomplished.

Scheduling: Basic scheduling techniques, critical path methods, and line of balance.

Configuration management: The techniques of administering and maintaining the integrity of an engineering and production or construction release system, and the technique of controlling computer software. These techniques apply as well to projects that address matters other than hardware or software.

Contract administration: The administration of contracts both with a customer and with a supplier, incentive contracting, and risk analysis.

Behavioral science and leadership: An understanding of how people behave in different organizational structures; communications skills; an appreciation of group dynamics; and the development of leadership.

Finally, an understanding is needed of the pertinent basic systems and procedures of the organization. A project manager needs to know how the existing machines run. Wherever possible, he should use these arrangements as they stand; he should develop new systems only when the old ones are inadequate, and he should make sure that key people understand existing policies and procedures well enough to make them work with maximum efficiency. Many a project has bogged down in a morass of new procedures invented by amateurs intending to correct imagined deficiencies in old ones, when the real problem was inadequate control or poor management.

Consultants and training

Consultants can be retained productively by an organization that either has no experience in project management or is foundering in its early attempts to make project management work. Training is an area where consultants have been particularly helpful.

Consultants are useful in training managers and key professionals in several areas:

- Operation and use of specific general control systems such as PERT.
- Understanding and use of control systems to meet the specific requirements of a customer, for example, the requirements for a cost schedule control system in Department of Defense Instruction 7000.2.
- Development and direction of a course on program management designed to describe the specific internal practices of the organization.
- Short, intensive, specific managerial courses intended not to provide expertise for the specialized professional but to give the project manager and his key managers a working knowledge of a professional area important to the project. Several such areas are accounting, contract administration, configuration management, quality assurance, and systems engineering.
- Specific orientation on a new technology unfamiliar to most of the project team but vital to project success.

An organization should retain consultants only after having thought through the training problem well enough to specify exactly what is required. Canned courses can be very effective and economical in the long run, but should be used only where they meet a clear need. The mere plea, "Help me," will usually prompt the consultant to bring forth his standard courses as part of the proposed package.

One of the most effective training courses available to an organization is an in-house program developed by a high-grade consulting firm in conjunction with key managers. Such an approach can deal with the organizational environment, practices, policies, and goals as they apply directly to projects at hand, and it can do so at a very high level of interest and efficiency. Careful development and presentation of such a course is expensive, but if the need exists it is a good investment.

Academic courses, short courses, and seminars

Project management has not ordinarily been recognized as a degree major in undergraduate programs, although in special cases universities have established special programs oriented to project management—often in response to support from the Department of Defense and other government agencies.

However, universities have responded, especially in their professional extension curricula, to interest in education on particular topics that are useful to project management. Certificate programs exist in such subjects as contract administration and procurement management. Courses in PERT and other CPM techniques abound. Courses are often taught at night by managers and professionals who work by day in real projects. In any metropolitan area where aerospace, electronics, and construction companies flourish, worthwhile academic offerings will be available.

A number of short courses on project management are also offered by commercial education firms and consultants. A one-week course on the fundamentals of project management offered by the American Management Associations is a very effective introduction to the subject. Several firms offer more specialized courses oriented toward the management of computer information system projects; these can be particularly useful to people assigned to a key project job for the first time.

From time to time, seminars on specific aspects of project management are offered by a wide range of organizations—for example, professional societies, professional education firms, consultants, and universities. Typical subjects covered are PERT, cost and schedule control, systems engineering, configuration management, and design to cost. Frequently, Department of Defense agencies will make senior management people available to speak at these seminars to inform contractors of the latest policies and regulations of the Department.

Sessions such as these help experienced project people keep up to date on the state of the art and give them a chance to exchange views with managers and professionals from other organizations. The ideas discussed are often helpful to people outside the defense industry as well.

No single source covers all the project management training needs of an organization, but in combination they can be very useful.

Professional societies

The Project Management Institute has emerged as a leading professional society devoted to project management. Founded in the late sixties, it has passed through its formative years to achieve a respectable level of maturity. It publishes a quarterly magazine, *Project Management* (P.O. Box 43, Drexel Hill, Pa. 19026), holds a well-attended annual meeting at which a variety of papers are presented, and holds occasional seminars. Chapters have sprung up around the country with representation from the construction, computer, aerospace, and electronics industries and with active participation by government agencies and the academic community.

All this makes for a broad spectrum of interest that is in no way limited to aspects of DOD requirements. Other professional and industrial associations and societies have occasional meetings devoted to project management or subjects of related interest.

The Defense Systems Management School

The Defense Systems Management School is mentioned for two reasons. First, it offers what is probably the best available formal training for project management. And second, although it exists primarily to serve the needs of the Department of Defense, it maintains ties with industrial and nondefense government communities. It makes its courses available to a few people from other federal agencies and from the defense industry. It is now beginning to do research on project management.

Located at Fort Belvoir, Virginia, near Washington, D.C., it draws a number of senior speakers from the government. Its basic 20-week Program Management Course is directed to people who will occupy intermediate management jobs in program or project offices and related agencies. The instruction is on a high professional level, comparable to graduate school. A three-week Executive Refresher Course covering both basic concepts and new developments in the field is also available for people who will occupy senior management positions in project management or related agencies. In addition, various short courses are available.

Starting at the top, the faculty is experienced and talented, and benefits from attention by senior people in the Department of Defense. The Defense Systems Management School should exercise an important influence on thinking about project management in the years to come.

Managing in-house training

One fundamental task an organization should do in-house is to evaluate its needs for key project management people, the skills of the candidates for the jobs, and the additional training required to achieve the necessary level of skill. This effort should be synchronized with the planning of career paths. An organization just embarking on a major commitment to project management can well use a consultant, but he should be selected for his broad knowledge in the field and not because he has a package to sell.

Developing a complete in-house training program for key project personnel is expensive. It is justifiable only when an abrupt increase in capability is required of a number of people. Even when the program is designed in-house, it will usually be economical to have some of its components presented by outside experts in the field. A month-long program, even on a part-time basis, will produce a marked level of improvement in the competence of key managers.

Case studies based on the experiences of the organization, or of similar organizations, are highly effective in training senior people, and particularly a project team. Although the studies must be of high quality to be effective, and are expensive to prepare, they are worthwhile in many cases—not only for project people, but also to help senior functional executives appreciate more fully what project management is all about. They would be a most useful component of the one-month course just described.

New projects of medium size and larger usually require that people just coming aboard attend a special training session that may last from a day to a week. Topics covered would include the organization of the project, the plans for the project, the organization of the customer and any major subcontractors, an update on the principal technologies and fields of expertise needed for the project, and the systems and procedures to be followed. This training is best done by people in the organization. Such an orientation saves a great deal of time and confusion in getting the project under way.

The general manager and senior functional executives should review any major in-house training program to ensure that the policies presented or implied in the instruction are correct. Embarrassing situations have occurred in which a course instructor taught a philosophy of project management quite different from the one management had in mind. It is particularly desirable that the training program include talks by some of key managers.

GENERAL MANAGEMENT, PEOPLE, AND PROJECT MANAGEMENT

Earlier it was pointed out that honesty and integrity, highly desirable qualifications for all managers, are particularly important in a project manager and must be clearly visible in his style of management. General management must be equally sensitive to issues of honesty and integrity in all matters connected with the project, even more than in its usual activities.

First of all, general management must pay particular attention to this issue when selecting the project manager. Thereafter, it must make clear that the entire organization expects the highest standards of integrity from people on the project in their conduct of project business. This policy must also be made clear to the customer and the major suppliers from the outset, and periodic conversations with general management's executive counterparts must be held afterward to ensure that the proper standards are being maintained. It must also see that commitments made to project personnel are carried out, both in spirit and in letter.

General management must set the tone for constructive relationships among all the people on the project, and between them and the rest of the organization. It is always a challenge to cope with the many complex organizational and interpersonal relationships on a project, but an atmosphere of honesty, frankness, and mutual trust is a giant first step toward avoiding problems in the first place and solving them rapidly when they do occur.

Project experience as professional and managerial development

Project experience is an excellent step in career development. Many former project managers are currently the chief executives of large corporations or their major operating companies, or serve as senior functional executives (for example, vice president— engineering).

A project manager's experience is valuable because he deals with many divisions of the organization. He solves problems that cut across divisional lines, an activity that is a general manager's main function. Although he is responsible for only a limited part of the organization's total activities, the project manager learns to think like a general manager and to practice general management skills on a modest scale. What better on-the-job training situation could be invented?

On a large project, the immediate subordinates of the project manager also see the problems involved in coordinating the various parts of the enterprise and gain many of the same benefits from this overview. Particularly in a large organization, managers may be constricted to viewing the world as consisting of their functional division with occasional and sometimes disturbing contacts with other divisions; but on a project they participate without prejudice in all the operating interfaces with other divisions and thereby get a much better understanding of their problems.

The opportunity for career development on a project is much the same for the professionals assigned to the project. The scale of operations is small enough that they can see the interaction of many functions. They learn to appreciate the effects their own decisions have on other departments. Often the experience leads to the startling realization that people in other departments are also intelligent and dedicated professionals. The financial man is no longer a bean counter, the manufacturing manager is no longer the man with dirty fingernails, the researcher is no longer the gnome on pink cloud nine. Everyone becomes aware of the necessary but unglamorous administrative interfaces that transmit information between departments and permit them to work together, and learns to see the total activities of the organization in better perspective.

Encounters between individuals within the tight project environment can be far more complex, varied, transient, and emotional than is normal in the larger world of the organization. Successful participation in the project heightens one's understanding of such situations and improves one's ability to deal with them effectively. People learn to listen, to integrate personal attitudes into their whole scheme of decision making, and to communicate. All this is a valuable part of professional and managerial development.

Project management as a career path

Project management is now recognized as a career path in such impressive organizations as the Department of Defense, the construction industry, the electronics industry, the aerospace industry, and NASA. It is also receiving increased attention in other branches of the federal government and in many industries with major commitments to research and development.

Career planning for potential project managers should concentrate primarily on selected assignments with appropriate supplementary training. A good career path would start with an assignment or two in a functional department rather than immediate assignment to a project. Demonstrated ability as a line supervisor is a good prerequisite for important project jobs. It is then appropriate to alternate assignments between functional and project jobs, including one as a project functional manager. A hypothetical but typical and highly effective career path for a project manager would be:

Professional design engineer
Engineering group supervisor
Professional, W Project systems engineering and planning staff
Engineering section supervisor
Manager of configuration management, X Project
Project Manager, Y Project (small)
Project engineering manager, Z Project
Deputy project manager, Z Project
Vice president, project manager, M Project

A similar career path for someone having an academic business background with an emphasis on finance would be:

Professional, fiscal planning department
Supervisor, PERT systems
Professional, W Project systems analysis staff
Section chief, cost estimating group
Contract administrator, X Project
Project manager, Y Project (small)
Project fiscal manager, Z Project
Deputy project manager, Z Project
Vice president, project manager, M Project

Finally, a career path for a man having an academic business background with a specialty in manufacturing would be:

Industrial engineer
Foreman, assembly department
Member, W Project cost estimating staff
Section manager, tooling
Purchasing manager, X Project
Project manager, Y Project (small and in the field)
Project manufacturing manager, Z Project
Deputy project manager, Z Project
Vice president, project manager, M Project

All three career paths are typical for many existing project managers, but with one major exception: People ascending the last two ladders will find it more difficult to make the big step to project manager of a large project than will their colleague with the engineering or technical background.

In industry, most project managers have come from the engineering department. This reflects the particular suitability of project management to developing new products or constructing new civil engineering structures. Like it or not, it also reflects the fact that it is usually easier to teach an engineer accounting than to teach an accountant engineering. Though this preeminence of engineers may not always remain so, it has been so in the past. Nevertheless, while one might not be given the job of project manager, the career path that leads to a role as project functional manager on a large project is no mean accomplishment, and this last can easily be the step before the ascent to top executive of a functional division.

Many project managers find successive assignments as project managers throughout their careers. Some find productive roles in less strenuous but very senior staff positions where their knowledge of all facets of the operation are a great asset. As just noted, others profit from the broadening experience by becoming senior functional executives. Finally, the most fortunate become chief executives of an operating component or even of the whole organization.

Decision making in the matrix environment

As we have seen, a matrix organization has many advantages and is often the best way to run a project. It brings to bear the best judgment of both project and functional executives on problems of staffing, planning, and operational decision making. The price for this is complexity in decision making. We have already examined this complexity in terms of organizing the project and getting it started; in the long run it becomes increasingly necessary for general management to make decisions between functional and project managers to preserve a constructive set of relationships throughout the organization.

General management must be readily available to settle issues and disagreements that inevitably arise from a matrix organization. Every encouragement should of course be given to the project and functional heads to work out mutually acceptable and beneficial solutions, but many issues that arise are a symptom that new priorities should be given constantly changing short- or long-range objectives, project demands, or functional efficiency. If general management is not available to make such sensitive decisions, undesirable confusion can mar relations between executives, to the detriment of the project and the whole organization.

If decisions are not made when they should be, key executives spend an unnecessarily long time in conflict or confrontation. If the battle becomes symbolic of a struggle for prestige, it can unnecessarily poison the relation between key players, and between their key subordinates as well. The functional executive is put in a miserable position when his two bosses on the project are feuding, and it may damage his relationships with both of them. Unnecessarily prolonged bickering erodes the spirit of project cooperation that is so important to success. Unhappy and frustrated people do not do as good a job as happy people.

Also, lack of a fast, clearly defined decision-making process can favor the conniving manager at the expense of the constructive one. The message "You men work out these problems" is an obvious signal to compromise—and the best way to resolve many differences of opinion.

The subtle conniver, however, can turn this to his advantage by constantly encroaching on the reasonable prerogatives of his counterpart. Such encroachment creates irritation and then a minor crisis; an artificial conflict now exists, yet under the executive direction a compromise is in order. The forthright manager, reluctant to go against general management, capitulates, and his sneakier colleague has won another round. All is settled, until the next jurisdictional melee is provoked. It is not unlike the "salami" technique so dear to totalitarian negotiators. General management can prevent such personal friction by making the clear-cut decisions that really need to be made.

General management's continuing responsibility for managing people

Throughout this discussion, general managers have been encouraged to manage projects with the undiminished zeal and constant attention that they devote to other parts of the organization. An alert general manager may charter the project, design a reasonably clear organizational structure, pick a good project manager, oversee selection of a good team, approve sensible changes in personnel policies, and then relax in the glorious feeling that his management of project people has been done and done well. In fact, his executive responsibilities have only begun; they continue throughout the life of the project, reduced perhaps in the required frequency of their open assertion, but no less critical for project success.

By opting for project management, and particularly for the sophisticated matrix approach with its unique opportunities for effectiveness, the general manager has established a decision-making process and a concurrent set of executive interrelationships that are more complex than the usual procedures. Thus he must exercise a highly personal surveillance over the project manager and the interfacing functional executives to assure that teamwork exists and that hidden conflicts and subtle hostilities are not undermining the unity and effectiveness of the whole organization.

3

Project-Oriented Organization

ORGANIZATIONAL ISSUES
WITH PROJECT MANAGEMENT

The most important decisions general management must make about project management concern organization and the selection of people. Of the two, organizational decisions are the more difficult because they are more subtle, require more thought, and are more troublesome to correct if done badly in the first place. It is fairly simple to replace a project manager or other key manager who is not succeeding, but it is traumatic to reorganize a project in midstream. Furthermore, it is difficult to diagnose organizational deficiencies. Although they produce such obvious symptoms as failure to meet goals, poor project morale, or interpersonal conflict among executives, it may be some time before the underlying organizational problems are discerned.

Organizational decisions are therefore the most crucial that general management must make when establishing a project. If they are carried through properly, they set a sound framework for solving all other project problems. In a clear organizational arrangement, incompetent managerial performance is readily perceived and can be corrected by coaching, redirection, or replacement. Inappropriate management systems will highlight their own shortcomings so that they can be improved. A mechanism will exist for correcting faulty project plans or indifferent execution of good plans. On the positive side, a sound organization provides the framework for a good team of people to execute project goals in an efficient and effective manner.

Management principles and project organization

Management principles as understood by practicing executives and elucidated by the academic community apply equally to project management. Any organizational scheme that fails to pass the test of accepted progressive management criteria is also likely to fail when applied to a project. Project management is not built on gimmicks.

The matrix form of project organization, in which a functional manager assigned to a project receives direction from both his functional superior and the project manager, may appear to violate the principle that a person should have only one boss. However, no conflict need exist in actuality because the functional manager has only one place to look for direction in any given area of decision making; to oversimplify, he looks to the project manager for what to do and when to do it and to his functional superior for how to do it and with whom.

The situation is analogous to but not identical with the line and staff form of organization. Staff executives, for example, the controller and the personnel executive, certainly have the authority to prescribe the framework in which many things will be done, but the line executive is still responsible for his operations within this framework.

Delegation of authority and assignment of responsibility

The need to delegate authority and assign responsibility creates conceptual difficulties for the organizers of a project. The problem is inherent in all project structures, but is particularly complex when the matrix form of organization is employed. It goes something like this: It is easy enough to divide up authority between the project manager and functional executives, but how does one assign responsibility for the success of the project? More specifically, whom does one hold responsible for project difficulties or failures? Hoping to avoid an unfair organizational arrangement and in effect hoping for the best, executives shy away from making any specific assignment of responsibility or delegation of authority. This practice does not heighten the chances of project success.

A nontheoretical, pragmatic approach to this problem is to delegate specific authority to the project manager, with the reservation that certain decisions will be left to the functional executives. The project can then get on with its work; no time will be wasted debating who will make which decision. If the project is a success, which is more likely with clear delegations of authority, there will be enough glory for everyone. If it runs into problems, there will be time enough then to assign responsibility for deficiencies. Therefore, charge ahead after clearly defining and delegating authority.

A more sophisticated approach, more satisfying to the thoughtful executive but not contradictory to the ideas expressed above, goes as follows: Project management, particularly in a matrix mode, is a deliberate division of authority undertaken to get the best of both possible worlds. Certainly the project manager must be held responsible for the success of his project. However, the executive who divides the authority in the matrix mode is ultimately responsible. If he wishes to share this responsibility with subordinate executives, he may then hold both the project manager and the functional executives jointly responsible. Success in complex projects is in fact dependent on effective performance by both the project manager and functional executives.

Principal organizational issues

Four principal organizational issues of project management may be enumerated:
1. How much organizational independence should be given to the project?
2. Where should the project fit in the organization?
3. How should people assigned to the project be managed?
4. What directive authority should the project manager have?

When these issues are dealt with adequately, an organization has the fundamental groundwork for good project management. Sophisticated techniques of planning and control will further improve performance, but the necessary environment for good project management is there.

Complexity and simplicity

Project management is a complication in the structure of an organization. It is employed not because it is entirely a simple concept, but because it is a better way to accomplish certain tasks, and in some cases the only way.

It should be remembered, however, that the basic idea of project management is simplicity itself: to provide a straightforward operational grouping of the people dedicated to accomplishing a specific task, under a single leader responsible for the success of the task. The object is to provide the project team with a direct and simple environment within which to accomplish its task without embroiling it in irrelevant bureaucratic procedures designed to enable the larger organization to carry out a different set of functions, perhaps not so closely interrelated.

The proper approach, then, is to confront the complexity issue head-on during the organization phase of the project. By solving involved problems early in the process, much of the complexity is taken out of project execution. The project team, and in particular the project manager, can then move in a straightforward way to accomplish the assigned task unencumbered by complex organizational, procedural, and jurisdictional problems.

ORGANIZATIONAL INDEPENDENCE
OF THE PROJECT

A crucial decision in organizing a project is the amount of autonomy to be assigned to the project manager. Different arrangements are of course appropriate for different kinds of projects. At one end of the spectrum, the project may be made a completely autonomous element of the parent organization. Arrangements tending in this direction are often referred to as ''projectization,'' a term used in subsequent discussions. In contrast, in the ''matrix'' arrangement, a project manager is assigned project responsibility but is expected to rely on existing functional organizations. Achieving the right balance of projectization and matrix organization is a central issue in organizing a project. But really, an almost infinite variety of organizational arrangements can be invented for managing a project.

Most currently active project organizations are similar to one of those given below, and listed essentially in the order of their decreasing autonomy. The titles assigned to the different approaches are arbitrary, and are by no means universally understood in the same way. The important thing is not that this or some other name be selected, but that the issue be thoroughly thought through by general management before it establishes the project. Before going into detailed discussion of the characteristics and application of each of these project forms, it may be useful to define the concept of project autonomy.

A concept of project organizational autonomy

Organizational autonomy in a particular area means that the project manager has complete and exclusive control over the people and resources devoted to that particular managerial task. This implies that:

- The project manager is completely and exclusively responsible for the successful performance of the operation in this functional area.
- All people concerned with the project are on the payroll of the project manager.
- The project manager is responsible for the personnel management of the function; this includes evaluation, promotion, counseling, training, salary administration, career development, and termination.
- Standard company policies and procedures apply to the organizational element unless specific exceptions are defined by general management.
- In the defined functional area, the project manager is responsible for compliance with all applicable company policies and directives and with all external laws and regulations.
- Surveillance by staff and functional officers over the activities of the project exists only to the extent that it does in all depart ments;

staff executives do not have extra authority merely because the matter concerns a project.

- The project manager is responsible for the technical excellence of the activities of the project.
- Consistent with delegation from general management, the project manager determines how resources assigned to the project will be used and how the project funds will be spent.
- The project manager is responsible for scheduling the activities of the project.
- The project manager utilizes standard company control systems to ensure effective performance of the project; he establishes or obtains any additional control systems needed to cope with special project conditions.

Completely projectized management

A completely autonomous organization—called "complete projectization"—may be set up to accomplish the objectives of a project. This involves assigning to the project organization all the capabilities normally given to an independent organizational entity, for example, a division of the parent organization. The project manager may be viewed as the general manager of the project organization, or vice versa. Each functional organization in the autonomous project organization is headed by a manager reporting to the project manager-general manager.

This is certainly the simplest organizational concept and the easiest to explain and introduce effectively to people unaccustomed to project management. Although the usual organizational complexities are avoided in this type of project organization, other principles of project management are equally appropriate for managing the affairs of the project in the independent division.

A completely autonomous project organization has several advantages:

- The project manager has maximum control over the affairs, personnel, and resources of the project.
- Supporting organizations are responsive primarily to the needs of the project.

- Procedures and practices may be optimized to meet the special needs of the project.
- The organization can react rapidly to the requirements of a fast-moving and fast-changing project.
- It is easier and quicker for people to understand this type of project organization and to develop effective working relationships.

Several significant disadvantages to the completely autonomous project organization may also be listed:

- Unless the project is quite large, this form of organization usually requires more people and is more costly than other project organizational approaches.
- It may be difficult to find an executive who is qualified both to manage the principal business of the project and to provide general management for all the supporting functions of the organization.
- Organizational independence may encourage the project to depart from proven administrative practices and to indulge in wasteful "reinvention of the wheel."
- Administrative matters may divert the project manager from the main business of the project.
- It may be difficult to staff the project organization with the required number of functional experts. (For instance, the fifth-priority project gets the fifth-best expert, who indeed may not be very expert.)
- It may be difficult to attract first-class people to the project organization because of their concern about their careers and assignments after the project is terminated.
- High costs are encountered because people are retained in the organization as insurance, beyond the time when they can usefully contribute to the project.
- Reassigning project personnel at the completion of the project is relatively more difficult.

A number of situations exist in which the completely autonomous project organization is appropriate:

- The project is to be accomplished at a location remote from the rest of the organization.

- The project is of such importance that it is desirable to give maximum control and flexibility to the project manager.
- Project management organizations are new to the company and project operating techniques must be implemented rapidly.
- The customer providing funding for the project desires an autonomous project organization.
- Different accounting policies and procedures are appropriate for the project.
- Special treatment is to be provided for project personnel, for example, special benefits, special protection from seniority interruptions, and unique labor relations treatment.
- For tax or other fiscal reasons, it is desirable to treat the project organization as a subsidiary.
- The project is a joint venture with another organization, and a jointly controlled project management is desired.

Partially projectized management

To achieve the advantages of a completely autonomous project while avoiding its problems, a partially autonomous project organization may be established. It will be called "partial projectization."

Functions devoted almost solely to the project or of central importance to it are assigned to it; the people concerned are put on the payroll of the project manager. Support functions continue to be assigned to the normal functional organizations, which respond to the requirements of the project manager with their own functional people.

In a large project for developing advanced hardware, the required functions might be assigned as follows:

Assigned to the Project Manager – Projectized	*Assigned to the Functional Organizations – Not Projectized*
Engineering	Accounting
Final assembly	Procurement
Inspection of final assembly	Facilities
Scheduling	Industrial relations
Project planning and control	Fabrication and subassembly
Major subcontract management	Inspection for fabrication and subassembly

Contract management
Customer relations
Field test
Logistics support

Purchasing
Public relations
Laboratories

In a project for developing a major data processing system, functions might be assigned this way:

Assigned to the Project Manager – Projectized	Assigned to the Functional Organizations – Not Projectized
Systems analysis	Computer operations
Programming	Functional requirements
Scheduling	Accounting
Project planning and control	Industrial relations
Training	Facilities
Documentation	Administrative support

The advantages of a partially autonomous project organization are many:

- The first four advantages described for a completely autonomous organization—those pertaining to control, responsive support, optional procedures, and rapid response to fast-changing requirements—are largely present here.
- The project manager can devote his time to the main business of the project and need not be expert in or devote time to supporting activities not related to the central issues of the project.
- Supporting activities requiring expertise remain in the hands of the functional experts, thus maintaining effective performance and avoiding reinvention of the wheel.

The primary disadvantage of a partially autonomous project organization is that in its own autonomous areas the problems of high cost and personnel administration that exist in a completely autonomous organization are also present. However, they are usually less acute in the areas selected for projectization.

Several situations in which it may be appropriate to use the partially autonomous project approach are as follows:

- Projects for developing a new and complex product or data processing system.
- Projects involving a major effort by a number of major subcontractors or supporting organizations.
- Projects of considerable urgency or priority.
- Projects in which the customer funding the project desires a significant degree of autonomy.

In effect, these situations have the same project urgency that leads to complete autonomy. However, given their more particular objective, they attempt to achieve higher efficiency by projectizing only those functions central to program success while obtaining support from functional organizations.

Matrix project organization
with strong project functional management

In a matrix project organization with strong project functional management, the project manager is delegated general management authority in matters affecting his project. Assisted by a small planning and control staff, he defines project tasks and schedules, assigns them to the appropriate functional organization for execution, and provides budgets for accomplishing the tasks. The functional organization head is responsible for executing the project task in accordance with project requirements, in any efficient manner that he thinks will achieve technical excellence.

The phrase "strong project functional management," while somewhat arbitrary and cumbersome, is intended to emphasize the very important concept that each functional organization assigns a manager to the project under the following ground rules:

- He reports to, or at least has direct and free access to, the functional head.
- He reports to the project manager for all project business.
- He devotes full time to the project, or at least has project business as his top priority in cases of conflicting demands.
- He has the authority to make commitments to the project manager on behalf of the functional head and his organization.

- He participates fully in project planning and in all project review and control activities affecting his function.
- He is responsible for ensuring that the project manager is provided the best possible expert and technical advice in his particular functional area.
- He has the authority to issue direction regarding project matters to all people in the functional organization assigned to the project.
- He carries out project tasks in accordance with policies and procedures established by the functional head. In cases of conflict, he is responsible for informing both the project manager and the functional head of incompatibility between project direction and functional policy.

The advantages of matrix project organization with strong project functional management are many:

- In the majority of cases, it is the least costly form of organization for a major project.
- The project manager can devote his time to the complex issues of the project and to coordinating its various organizations, tasks, and priorities without being distracted by details of execution.
- This form of organization retains the expertise and management skills of top functional managers in the execution of project tasks.
- Scarce expertise can be applied most flexibly and efficiently to a number of different projects.
- Matrix project organization is an attractive arrangement for highly skilled professional people who want to work on a new and challenging project but are reluctant to leave their organizational home for one in which their professional skills and attitudes might not be properly respected.
- It is easier to accommodate to changes in project manpower requirements and to off-load efficiently as a project phases down from its peak load.
- The entire management team works toward successfully achieving project objectives with strong feelings of responsibility, interest, concern, and pride.

- General management may more readily perceive and resolve conflicts between project requirements and functional organization policies.

Several disadvantages of matrix project organization with strong project functional management are apparent:

- More effort and time are required to define and communicate a set of policies that will ensure successful matrix project operation.
- In an organization unaccustomed to project management approaches in general and matrix project management in particular, the problems encountered in its initial transient phases may be damaging or indeed fatal to the project.
- Biases of functional division heads may subtly work against the priorities desired by general management.
- In a fast-moving and fast-changing project, the matrix organizational approach may not be able to achieve reaction times that are fast enough to meet project requirements.

Matrix project organization with strong project functional management is more often than not the most appropriate organizational form for a major project in a mature organization accustomed to project management. An organization not accustomed to project management will still find it a very attractive and effective form, provided that top management is willing to take the trouble to organize the project thoroughly, issue appropriate policy direction, and allow sufficient time to introduce and shake down the concept.

Matrix project organization
with normal functional management

As noted above, the project manager of a matrix project is delegated general management authority in matters affecting his project. Given appropriate staff assistance, he defines project tasks and assigns them with schedules and budgets to the appropriate functional organization for execution. In the mode of normal functional management, no significant change is made in the functional organization structure or operations. The special requirements of the project are simply fed into the department along with the routine requirements, and these are met in the normal way.

The outstanding advantage of the matrix project organization with normal functional management is its minimal disruption of the functional organization's operators. In addition, the advantages described for matrix project management with strong project functional organizations also apply here. The outstanding disadvantage of this method of organization is that the project may not be executed effectively, because interest, attention, or priority is lacking within the functional organizations. The disadvantages listed for the matrix organization with strong project functional management exist here also, but usually to a greater degree.

This type of project organization is most adaptable to a situation that requires complicated planning and decision making, but in which the project plan can be broken into relatively unrelated tasks that are normal for the functional organizations involved. To be workable, it requires functional division heads who understand and support project operation and goals.

Project task force

A task-force organization may be established to carry out a project. Here again general management delegates to the project manager the authority to make decisions in matters affecting his project. Personnel from functional organizations are assigned to the task force, on either a full-time or a priority basis, and may operate in different roles. In all cases they continue to receive administrative support from their home organizations.

In some activities, task-force personnel are in effect on loan to the project manager; they operate completely under his direction and management and are not required to operate according to their functional organization policies. In a second mode, while under obligation to the project manager for all project direction, they are constrained to follow their normal home organization policies and procedures.

A third mode adds the further responsibility for representing their functional organizations in the decision-making procedures and other activities of the task force. In cases of conflict, they notify both their functional head and the project manager. In a fourth mode, they are responsible for obtaining additional support from their functional organizations in carrying out project tasks. An individual may operate on a project in all these modes at various times, but it should be determined in advance which role is appropriate for which activity.

The advantages of a project task force are that:

- It can be established very rapidly.
- It is extremely flexible, both in its operation and in its possible modification to meet changing project conditions or requirements.

Its disadvantages are that:

- It is difficult to control the activities of a task force set up for a large project.
- It is not the most efficient way to manage a long-term project.
- It is more difficult to obtain additional support from functional organizations with this approach.

The task-force type of organization, then, is most suitable for small- to medium-size projects that can be accomplished in a limited time, say not longer than a year. It is, however, extraordinarily effective in these situations.

How much organizational autonomy for the project?

One of the most important decisions that must be made by general management early in the life of a project is to select the amount of organizational autonomy to be assigned to the project. If an inappropriate type of organization is selected, the project will be launched in an aura of acrimony or apathy that can dog it for months. Organizational changes made after a period of contention are usually interpreted as a loss for someone, thus further contributing to project disharmony.

An alternative to describing various project organization schemes according to the possible applications for each one is to consider the various characteristics of the project or of the parent organization in which the project must operate.

Length of the Project. It is almost never efficient to set up a projectized organization in a short-term project. On the other hand, a long life for a project does not by itself indicate the desirability of projectization.

Size of the Project. In larger projects, administrative and support organizations may not be inefficient; however, in small projects, such groups may simply be unaffordable. Many tasks require an expert only a part of the time, but a project requires that he be paid full time.

Unique Aspects of the Project. When the business of the project is different from the normal business of the organization, procedures can be optimized by setting up a projectized organization. If a matrix approach is used, the functional organizations either will not or cannot cope with project needs; forcing them to accommodate to the project may force inefficiency in normal business. Personnel, benefits, and union agreements can be made to fit special project situations if the projectized approach is used.

Experience with Project Management Organization. If an organization has a history of dealing with complex projects, it can usually adapt well to the matrix concept. However, with no project background, an organization may find it necessary to projectize to get the project to succeed at all. Sometimes recalcitrant functional heads refuse to support a project and a projectized organization is adopted as the only way to ensure project success; then, with experience, the functional heads perceive the merits of sincerely supporting the matrix concept when the next project is launched.

Stability and Rigidity of the Parent Organization. Some highly effective organizations have a very stable, almost rigid mode of operation that may be optimized to function quite efficiently for normal operations. Managers are conditioned to operate within a clearly defined line organization structure. In this type of environment it is almost impossible to make a matrix project operate effectively. The project manager, and indeed the project itself, is regarded as a threat to the stability and efficiency of the organization. To make a project work in these circumstances, it is usually necessary to use projectization, thereby giving the project manager adequate, effective authority and administrative support.

Developmental and Professional Aspects of the Project. Some projects involve complicated planning and carefully timed execution, but they can be carried out by competent line organization teams. An example is the activation of a new facility. In other projects, development, design, and research are key issues, and researchers, academics, designers, systems analysts, architects, programmers, and other professionals play a key part. For these projects, the matrix approach works particularly well. Professional people are often reluctant to leave their technically oriented functional organizational homes, for they are apprehensive about being assigned to an organization where their technical qualifications might not be recognized and their professional status might be ignored. They find that the matrix organization makes effective use of their talents while permitting them to work and feel comfortable in the professional environment of their home departments.

Past Treatment of People Assigned to Projects. In many cases the staff of a projectized organization has been enticed by such imprecise promises as "We'll take care of you when the project is over." However, their reassignment on completion of the project has received less executive attention than the initial staffing. It is haphazard or may even be left to the individuals. Seeking positions with their old functional organizations, project assignees have been treated as "disloyal" or as "deserters" and have wound up worse off than before they joined the project team—even to the point of working as subordinates to people they formerly supervised. Such a situation becomes immediately well known throughout the organization. A new project will find it hard indeed to attract capable people, and functional department heads will often send their undesirables to the project. Here a matrix approach is preferable.

Visible Top Management Attention to the Project. The perceived attitude of top management can play a major role in staffing a new project management organization. If that attitude is clearly enthusiastic, good, aggressive people will want to join the organization. Functional heads will want to send good people to it, or at least will not want to be identified as having sloughed off second-rate people to a project so strongly backed by top management.

On the other hand, if top management shows that it is not very interested, the new projectized unit will probably wind up being staffed with rejects and second-raters. Lacking genuine enthusiasm, general management would be better advised to proceed with a matrix organization, where functional heads can be held responsible for their respective performance, rather than some poor project manager who does not have the resources to do the job.

Physical Location of the Project. If most project activities are to be carried out in a location remote from the main operating center of the organization, there is much to be said for projectization. A project manager who does not have full control over the local functional units will lose a great deal of time coordinating activities with the functional heads at the control location, that is, with officials who really don't understand the local conditions. The main argument for using a matrix operation is that functional heads will send good people to the remote location and will provide them with the supervision and guidance necessary to ensure satisfactory performance in their new role. In addition, a better check is thereby provided against errors by an inexperienced or overzealous project manager.

Interaction Between Control and Remote Locations. The less the interdependence between the activities of the central and remote locations, the stronger the arguments for projectization. On the other hand, if the remote location is heavily dependent on technical data, parts, temporary personnel augmentation, or other support from the central location, then there are strong reasons for using a matrix organization. This avoids situations where functional heads optimize their operation at the central location at the expense of providing adequate support to their remote counterparts. For instance, a manufacturing manager is not inclined to ship insufficient supplies of hardware to a remote location if he is responsible for completing the installation and ensuring the proper functioning of the equipment in the field.

Business and Commercial Considerations. Oftentimes a firm may have strong business or commercial reasons for wanting to establish a separate corporate identity. In this case, full projectization is automatically indicated. For instance, a project with considerable financial risk may require a subsidiary, or there may be advantages in assigning the project to a company incorporated in the jurisdiction where the activity is located. Also, a joint venture with one or more other companies may be prescribed as the best solution.

LOCATION OF THE PROJECT
IN THE ORGANIZATION

Projects should be located wherever in the organization they can function most effectively. Several reasons for having the project manager report directly to a high level in the organization may be mentioned:

- The project manager is charged with getting results from the coordinated efforts of many functions. He should therefore report to the man who directs all those functions.
- The project manager must have adequate organizational status to do his job effectively.
- To get adequate and timely assistance in solving problems that inevitably appear in any important project, the project manager needs direct and specific access to an upper echelon of management.
- The customer, particularly in a competitive environment, will be favorably impressed if his project manager reports to a high organizational echelon.

Good reasons may also exist for having the project manager report to a lower echelon:

- It is organizationally and operationally inefficient to have too many projects, especially small ones, diverting senior executives from more vital concerns.
- Although giving a small project a high place in the organization may create the illusion of executive attention, its real result is to foster executive neglect of the project.
- Placing a junior project manager too high in the organization will alienate senior functional executives on whom he must rely for support.

Both sets of reasons are well founded. Their relative importance must be evaluated to arrive at the proper decision for each project. A primary requirement is to maintain flexibility. At any given time, project managers may be reporting at three or four different levels in the organization, depending on the nature, size, and urgency of each project. Selecting the right level is an important general management decision.

Authority levels in project management

In determining where to place a project in the organization, it is useful to consider the various executive functions necessary to establishing and controlling a project. All functions above the level of the project manager may be carried out by the general manager or some other senior executive; however, they may be divided to achieve more effective results.

- The project manager is the executive directly responsible for the operational direction and success of the project.
- The directive authority is the line organization executive to whom the project manager reports.
- The chartering authority is the executive who establishes the project and delegates the necessary authority to the project manager.

The three positions are given in the order of their authority in the line organization, from lower to higher. In addition, a review authority may be created in a staff mode of operation with the responsibility for periodic review of the project, for evaluating its progress, and for providing guidance for its future activities. (The other ''authorities'' normally consist of one person, but this one may be a group.)

The advantage of splitting up these authorities derives from maintaining frequent and active upper management review and control while placing the project manager at a level in the organization where he will receive adequate executive supervision. Of course, all these functions can be combined in one executive. This is the simplest approach, and the best one if the other considerations do not apply.

The chartering authority

The chartering authority should have control over nearly all the organizational elements that must contribute to the success of the project. This is the best criterion for determining who the chartering authority should be. Normally this will lead to selecting the chief executive of the organization, his deputy, or the head of a large functional element. This is not a strange phenomenon, for the essence of establishing a project is the delegation of adequate authority to the project manager. Only a general manager has this authority to delegate.

It has been argued that the chief executive may not want to be bothered with signing a memo authorizing a project. This may indeed be the case, but if so, its symptomatic importance is great. If he is not inclined to sign such a memo, the chief executive is probably equally disinclined to delegate authority. The project manager will then be a coordinator on his way to inevitable mediocre performance.

The gains from having a senior general manager charter a project are great. Such a move provides evidence of authentic executive concern about the success of the project and is a specific delegation of authority. Many of the advantages of having the project manager report at that organizational level are assured without charging the general manager with all the administrative burdens of the directive authority.

Along with appointing the project manager and delegating the necessary authority to him, the chartering authority may designate both the directive authority and the review authority, provided that he does not wish to retain either of these functions for himself. By such actions, he both defines the authority of these persons over the project and assigns a responsibility to them that ensures their active interest in the project.

The directive authority

The directive authority is the project manager's immediate line superior. He performs the normal functions of such a position, for example, a review of budgets and schedules, personal performance review, approval of higher-level authorizations, and ratification of personnel decisions.

Selecting the directive authority is a crucial matter. If a project manager with the right decision-making qualities is compelled to report to a hack or perhaps to a conservatively inclined executive not attuned to progressive ideas, the whole concept of project management may be frustrated. It is tempting but unrealistic to assign an old hand to ''keep an eye on'' a promising project manager and expect all possible progress. That leads to the mistaken idea that a directive authority should have the complex combination of positive qualities prescribed further on for a project manager.

The chief job of the directive authority is to provide experienced guidance for the many more-or-less routine decisions of the project manager, to make the project run smoother by permitting only the tough project decisions to become project issues occupying managerial time and energy.

The review authority

In addition to the line direction given the project manager by the directive and chartering authorities, it may be appropriate to establish a review authority to evaluate the progress of the project and give it guidance. Normally this is a group of senior executives or specialists reporting to the chartering authority. The chief merits of having such a group, despite the slight increase in organizational complexity, are in bringing diverse viewpoints and experience to bear on the project and stimulating interest and a sense of involvement on the part of executives who may not otherwise be connected closely with project operations.

A quarterly review is often appropriate, although a monthly review may be better when a project is beset with problems or is going through a crucial decision-making phase. Some examples:

- A large hardware development project has several major subcontractors for the development of major subsystems. The review authority consists of the general manager of the prime contractor and the general manager of each of the subcontractors.
- A large project is being carried out in several divisions of a large corporation. The review authority consists of the corporate vice presidents of finance, manufacturing, engineering, and marketing, chaired by the corporate executive vice president.
- A data processing project is being developed for several users. The vice presidents of the user divisions are the review authority under the chairmanship of the division with the principal interest.

Examples of project location

Dozens of project organization arrangements come easily to mind. The point is to think through the matter and get the right solution for the project at hand rather than to follow a rigid set of rules. Several typical arrangements may be mentioned:

- The president of the organization charters the project; the project manager reports to the executive vice president.
- The president of the organization charters the project; the project manager reports directly to him.
- The vice president of engineering charters a research project; the project manager reports to the director of research.
- The executive vice president charters a data processing project; the project manager reports to the vice president—administration.
- The secretary of a military department charters a project; the project manager reports to the commander of the systems command.

INTERNAL PROJECT ORGANIZATION

The best internal project organization varies greatly in size, objectives, and end product throughout the life cycle of the project. It also varies according to the organizational forms that reflect the level of sophistication, capabilities, and attitudes of the parent organization. Therefore, great flexibility should be retained in setting up and modifying the internal organization of the project.

It is tempting to present examples of internal project organizations and comment on their workings. It is probably better to admit that the functional organization divisions of a project are determined by the nature of the end product and the parent organization scheme. However, a review of activities oriented toward project management and encompassing all functional departments will provide a basis for selecting the best internal organization for any particular project.

Is a deputy project manager needed?

In principle, a deputy project manager is not needed for project success, although a number of special situations make it advisable to appoint one. If a deputy is designated, he should have the full authority of the project manager in the latter's absence and in any project business he is assigned to look after. He should not be an "assistant to" with the title of "deputy."

Some projects require that the manager travel a great deal. In such cases it is a good idea to assign a deputy either to share traveling activities or to manage the project during the project manager's absence. Somewhat analogous is a contract project requiring that time be spent with the customer. Here again a deputy is justifiable. The project manager must not allow himself to become so involved with outside matters that he loses communication with and control over the project team.

Some projects require that their leader have a high degree of technical skill and broad-based management experience. It may be difficult to find a project manager with adequate skills in both areas. Appointing a deputy with experience complementing the project manager's is appropriate. He may be recruited from a major functional area, usually technologically oriented, as a means of inducing executives to adopt a project management concept. This is sometimes hazardous because of feuding executive camps. The ground rule must be clearly stated by general management: The project manager is the boss.

Management of project functional activities

Most of the work accomplished by a project will lie in the functional areas normal to the parent organization. For example, a project for developing prototype hardware will include engineering, manufacturing, purchasing, and inspection activities. A project for installing a major data processing system will involve systems analysis, programming, operations, procedures, and training.

Such project functional activities should be organized along the lines of the parent organization. Under this arrangement a single senior functional executive can be associated with each major functional activity. In a projectized environment, that executive can be held responsible for staffing the organization and providing staff surveillance of its work. In the matrix environment, he will also give policy and technical direction to the project functional manager. Thus it is easy to correlate the various responsibilities for functional support of the project.

Another reason for following the existing functional department division of responsibilities is the ease of applying existing procedures and systems. A project is often organized to facilitate the use of new practices, but such an action should be taken only when necessary. A large part of the project business occurs within the normal framework of the organization. If departmental responsibilities and interdepartmental interfaces remain unchanged, it is easier to get the new work under way without the definition of new systems and responsibilities. Special systems tailored for the project can be introduced where necessary, but the cost and effort of inventing them will be applied only where they will pay off.

Each major project function should be under the supervision of a manager who is responsible for all of that function's activities. This would principally include management of the efforts of project personnel who would report to the manager in a line role. But it would also include responsibility for work in effect subcontracted from time to time to departments of the functional organization not assigned to the project. For example, the project chief engineer would be responsible for all engineering work done for the project, the design work of engineers, the activities of specialists consulting from time to time on the project, and the work packages assigned to departments of the functional engineering organization.

The charter of the project functional managers must be clear. They must have the authority to make commitments to the project manager on behalf of their function, whether in the projectized or the matrix mode. In the matrix mode they should be delegated the authority of the senior functional executives, subject to appropriate limits of commitment. Strong functional managers are a key element in project success.

The project manager should deal directly with the functional managers as though they were direct line subordinates, although in a matrix environment he should avoid policy areas restricted to the senior functional executive. In some complex projects, noted below, the project manager may supervise senior managers or departments devoted to activities unique to the project and not directly relatable to a specific functional department. Such people or departments will normally have a projectized relationship with the project manager, even in a largely matrix project. The project manager should have the same relationship with the functional managers as with managers of his project departments. The latter should not be "more equal" than the former. In particular, he should not deal exclusively with project functional managers through managers on his direct staff.

Management of unique project functions

Certain important functions are unique to a project and not associated with any functional department. They cut across many or all of the functional departments and are an extension of the project manager's special authority. Examples are planning, systems engineering and analysis, control of changes, management of subcontracted effort, and project control in the sense of work authorization schedules and budgets.

These unique project functions may be performed by people who are assigned as staff to the project manager. When the functions are very important or complex, it is appropriate to set up departments to accomplish them. Usually they should be a projectized function, particularly in an environment where such an arrangement is new and a project manager needs responsive help in coping with sometimes hostile functional organizations.

Functions unique to a project must be staffed with people of high professional and managerial quality. The coordinator-expediter-negotiator type of factotum sometimes has his place in a project organization but not in a key managerial spot. Incidentally, this type of assignment provides excellent career development experience to a promising manager who has the potential to be a project manager.

The number of people assigned to functions unique to the project should be kept small. A project management staff that is large in proportion to the executing functional organizations is a symptom of unclear top management decisions, inept organizational arrangements, inefficient project management, or a combination of all of these. Department of Defense program management sometimes suffered from this malady during the sixties, both internally and in its dealings with its contractors.

Proliferation of unique program functions can be prevented by avoiding one-for-one surveillance of functional activities. For example, a design engineering organization usually is organized along technological lines, for example, aerodynamics, structures, propulsion, electronics. On a complex project, a systems engineering organization may be appropriate, but it should not be organized along the exact lines of the operative technologies, as a team of technical specialists to oversee each design activity.

On the other hand, a systems engineering function staffed with people specifically responsible for a flight vehicle, ground equipment, communications, facilities, the personnel subsystem, and overall systems analysis is very appropriate and may be the key to success in systems development. Personnel should be assigned to a project manager only when a task cannot be done in a project functional department, or when someone is needed to lead and coordinate all the project functional departments in doing it.

Although more than a dozen project functions are given special attention below, it must be emphasized that rarely will more than a few be required on any particular project. Each project will require its own set of managers. Often the functions can be combined under a single manager. Far from suggesting that a man representing each function be placed on the project manager's staff, the ideal project is organized with as few of such persons as are essential. The internal project structure should be kept as simple as possible while still providing adequate planning and control.

Administration. A project should use existing general administration support as much as possible. This can be provided on a matrix basis by the service organizations. A good secretary can do a lot.

On the other hand, a project of some size becomes intensely involved in administrative activity unique to the project. The amount of correspondence increases, meetings and visitors are frequent, security may be an issue, and data control becomes a problem. All this business must be transacted efficiently to avoid impeding project progress. As the tasks increase in size and complexity, responsibility can be assigned to the manager of project control or some other immediate subordinate of the project manager. However, these added administrative activities must not be permitted to divert him from his main tasks.

When the job becomes too large for someone to do as an adjunct to his normal duties, an administrative assistant or manager of administration may be appointed. He can be assigned on a matrix or projectized basis. The chief argument for the latter arrangement is that one man may be able to perform the tasks required of several functional organizations, which might be difficult if he were assigned to one of them.

Planning. Good planning is a key to successful project management. Its direction is a principal responsibility of the project manager.

Ordinarily the project manager does not need a manager responsible for planning. Most of the effort during the early phases of the project goes into planning; the project manager heads the planning team, which consists of all the key people on the project. Later on, as the project turns to execution of the accepted plans, the continued existence of a planning department may result in wasted effort, or even in actual interference in project execution because of excessive zeal in attempting to add unnecessary detail to the plan.

On the other hand, a development project or some other constantly changing effort must not only keep its plans current but must plan the next phase of its operations. When the initial planning phase is over and the team charges into execution, future planning tends to be neglected in favor of current operating problems. Under these conditions a planning manager should be assigned to the project manager. His personal staff should be small, since members of the functional departments will be aiding him in his planning activities.

Systems Engineering and Analysis. It was stated earlier that any activity that could be performed within the responsibilities of a functional department should be assigned to that department on the project. It can be argued that systems engineering is just such an activity and belongs in the project engineering department. Sometimes this arrangement will work. However, when the project involves hardware design and development, the project engineering manager is apt to be so concerned with the realities of making the hardware work properly that he has little time for the more abstract problems of systems engineering. This situation is even more likely to exist when some of the major subsystems are subcontracted. Then a systems engineer is required to balance and integrate the designs of in-house and procured subsystems.

When systems analysis is involved, the case for a separate project function is even stronger. Systems analysis implies significant consideration of factors that transcend technology: costs, sociological and human implications, and development of cost-benefit information. Such matters obviously go beyond engineering and should not be dominated by technology.

Because the continuing results of systems analysis may influence future project planning and may interact heavily with it, a single manager may be given the responsibility for both systems analysis and project planning. But it is not easy to find the man who can do both.

Contracts. Many projects require support from the contract department. A matrix organization approach is particularly applicable here since it ensures application of the best expertise available in negotiating and administering agreements the organization has with outside agencies.

A single senior contract administrator should be assigned to the project with other contract people under him. The project manager should not have to deal with a number of different contract administrators. The senior man need not work full-time on the project if the workload does not require it—often the case after initial negotiation—but he must be available to the project manager on a priority basis.

In government project organizations, the contracting officer is a particularly important member of the project team. Since the bulk of project funds is spent on work procured from one or more major contractors, the successful management of the contracting function is a key ingredient in project success.

Project Control. Project control is assumed to include budgeting, scheduling, reporting actual costs, and reporting progress in meeting scheduled events, or schedule status. It may also include responsibility for design of the work breakdown structure (WBS) and for operation of the work authorization systems. All these functions are done by persons serving in a staff role to the project manager who makes the final decisions on work authorizations, schedules, and budgets.

Almost any activity worth being managed as a project needs someone to do the project control job as a prime duty even if not on a full-time basis. On small projects, budgetary control may be exercised by counting heads, but several major tasks remain: preparing reports of schedule status, keeping track of action items, and managing the project baseline. As the project manager looks at the expanding range of problems that accompanies increasing project size, the first key person he turns to is the project control assistant, staffer, or manager.

The importance of the project control job becomes even more apparent in a later chapter.

Control of Project Changes. The project manager of a medium- to large-size project may require the assistance of a manager whose primary duty is to manage changes in the project. In the execution phase of a project, all the key project department managers are properly concerned with achieving project goals. Certainly they will respond to requirements for changes in project scope or direction. But someone is needed to pull the whole thing together from a project point of view. Changes in project specifications, costs, and schedules need the attention of many key people; a great deal of coordination is required. The project manager has the right credentials to do the job, and he must make the final decisions, but he too is busy with ongoing project work. Who then should pick up the task of managing changes to the project?

The project control manager or an equivalent administrator is naturally offended by changes. They disrupt schedules and upset budgets and create disorder in the control process. The systems engineer, on the other hand, likes changes. They represent necessary steps toward achieving a new optimal definition of the project and its end product, the system. Neither of these managers is the ideal person to entrust with the job of managing changes. Since changes affect all project functions, it is unwise to put change control under a functional manager who will probably see things from too parochial a view. Even if he doesn't, other functional managers will suspect that he does. Therefore, it is often best to assign a manager or senior project staff member to assist the project manager in control and management of changes.

If a manager or senior staff member has been assigned to manage project planning, it may be wise to make him the change manager as well. Because of his experience in planning the project, he knows the project baseline and understands the reason for the decisions that have been made. His obvious decision-making abilities may now be applied to updating the plan. Although his workload may have been heavy at the beginning of the project, it has tapered off. The work of managing changes will balance his load throughout the project.

If the project has a strong hardware content, a manager of configuration management may be appointed. Such an organizational arrangement is necessary for success in winning a DOD or NASA hardware or development contract. This manager will be responsible for controlling changes both in the program plans and in the configuration of the hardware. The subject will be discussed in a later chapter under the heading "Configuration Management."

Product Assurance. Some development projects with a complex end product, extensive test programs, and involvement with personal safety may require special attention to product assurance. This function should not be organized simply as an overlay on the inspection department. The service is required when there is a complex interaction between engineering and inspection—that is, between development tests and acceptance tests—or when an extra overview of safety is prudent. Under these unusual conditions a manager of product assurance may be appointed. However, his staff, if any, should be very small indeed to avoid duplication of the efforts of other functions.

Testing. If testing consists mainly of smaller component tests, the responsibility for managing the testing can be assigned to the chief engineer. If there are large complex tests conducted at different locations and needing extensive support from manufacturing, inspection, other departments, and major subcontracts, it may be appropriate to appoint a manager of testing to act for the project manager in coordinating these diverse activities.

When a project test must be conducted at a remote location, a manager on the site will be required. He should report to the project manager. In developing information systems, it may be well to have a separate manager of systems tests.

Construction, Deployment, and Delivery. Some major systems or construction projects involve design, development, and manufacture at the home plant; final construction, installation, testing, and delivery of the equipment are then accomplished at a remote site on a turn-key basis. When the project manager is located at the home facility, he will need a manager at the remote site reporting to him and responsible for the work there. If the project involves both testing and deployment at remote locations, the two functions can be assigned to a single manager.

Logistics Support. In an organization that supplies its customers with major systems or equipment needing continuing support, a major division called field engineering, service, logistics support, or something similar will normally do the job. Under these conditions a manager from that organization can be assigned to the project for planning, developing, and executing the necessary support, including training material, training, technical data, spare parts provisioning, and field engineering.

If an organization without such a function needs it for a particular project, it can assign a manager to the project manager to direct the required effort.

Management of Subcontracted Work. A substantial part of the total work of larger projects is usually done by one or more subcontractors. Even smaller study and research projects involve a subcontractor who has expertise in a technology outside the field of the prime contractor. The management of project work that is contracted out is very difficult.

In a government project office established to manage a major procurement, most of the project funds are spent by a prime contractor or several associates. The project office is oriented toward procuring and controlling that work along with support activities covered by smaller contracts and other government agencies.

Managing the project is even more difficult when part of the work is done in-house and part is subcontracted, or when there are several major subcontractors. The project manager must oversee every detail of these different but closely interrelated parts of the project and ensure proper coordination of their efforts—a nearly impossible task. His main responsibility is to make the tradeoff decisions that will optimize total project effectiveness.

Under these conditions it is well to establish a manager for each major subcontract or subsystem (which may include more than one subcontractor). The manager for that task reports to the project manager and is delegated some of his authority. His authority must be carefully coordinated with that of the contracting officer, who will play a key role in this area. The subsystem manager should not build up his own separate project office except in the largest projects. Although he may have a few technical, procurement, and project control people reporting to him, the project manager must see to it that the functional organizations provide adequate support. This involves creating a matrix organization within a project organization that may itself be a matrix.

The subject sounds complicated and it is, but the main point is the importance of appointing a manager responsible to the project manager for the successful direction of the subcontracted effort.

Internal organization of smaller projects

It is hoped that the array of possible organizational requirements discussed above primarily for their applicability to larger projects will not scare away anyone considering project management for small projects. Quite small projects will need a senior man from each department area of expertise involved in the study, but only the project manager and his assistant for project control will be required to perform project-type functions. In addition to the senior functional leaders, a somewhat larger project would require a project manager and two assistant managers—one for project control and the other for a combination of planning, systems analysis, and change control.

Thus it is seen that very effective project management employing all the useful principles will work on smaller projects with a small, uncomplicated, and efficient project staff.

Internal organization of larger projects

Larger projects are likely to encompass a wide range of activities—from systems engineering through deployment—and a large number of organizations both internal and external. Thus a larger and more complex project staff is needed.

The issue of span of control versus layers of organization must be considered when designing a project organization. Long communication lines extending through many layers of organization appear to be a much worse problem for a project than a fairly wide span of control. A project manager can comfortably handle ten or twelve people reporting directly to him. If he has fewer than five he probably has an unnecessary layer of managers.

A key requirement of successful project execution is that everyone get the same message fast, a goal best attained by reducing the levels of organization, and therefore widening the span of control. Since the project team is located together and has good lateral communication based on a common project baseline, coordinating the activities of ten people is not much more difficult than coordinating the activities of five.

A typical organization for a medium-size hardware development project might look something like this:

Project Manager
Administrative Assistant
Manager of Contracts
Manager of Plans and Systems Engineering
Manager of Project Control
Manager of Configuration Management
Manager of Tests and Deployment
Functional Managers (perhaps six)

For a very large and complex project with several major subcontractors, span of control begins to be a problem. One approach is to divide the project into a number of subprojects, one for each subcontractor and one for the functional work done internally. Functions required to coordinate the whole project are combined. Such a grouping could look like this:

Project Manager
Deputy Project Manager
  Manager of Plans and Systems Engineering
      Plans
      Systems Analysis
      Engineering Integration
  Manager of Project Control
      Contracts and Work Authorizations
      Budgets and Cost Control
      Schedules
      Data and Administration
  Manager of Product Assurance
  Manager of Field Activities
      Tests
      Deployment
      Logistics Support
  Manager of Configuration Management
  Manager of Internal Project
      Functional Departments

Manager of Subsystem A
Manager of Subsystem B, etc.

That is a formidable project organization, but it may be the best way to success. It should be remembered that only a small percentage of project funds for a large project is devoted to project management tasks as contrasted with functional organizations doing project tasks.

IMPLEMENTING THE ORGANIZATION

To establish the project, the chartering authority should sign an appropriate announcement. As a minimum it should designate the purpose of the project, establish the general organizational format for the project, appoint the project manager, and state general management's support for the project. It may also include other appointments on an organization chart and in policy statements. However, it is more important to get out the fundamental information early rather than delaying its release until all detailed organizational and staffing decisions have been made.

The announcement should be in whatever format is used for major communications to the organization. Although it may be addressed only to senior executives, it should have a wide distribution. The outline on the opposite page is a suggested format.

Organization charts

Preparing organization charts for projects can become an unnecessarily time-consuming exercise. However, the charts should be issued soon after the project is established, signed by the chartering authority.

It is easy enough to add the project manager to the basic organization chart and to show him reporting to the directive authority; this is preferably accomplished in the initial charter. A problem arises when the chart for the internal organization is to be prepared, particularly when a matrix form of organization is to be used. The old rules of chartsmanship do not easily apply here. Early solutions showed horizontal rows of project managers with various arrangements of lines

OUTLINE FOR A PROJECT CHARTER

Subject: Establishment of Project X
To: Key Executives
Copies to: Managers Affected

I. Charter for the project
   A. Project goals
   B. Name of the project
   C. Estimate of resources needed.
      (This may be omitted because it is sensitive; however, the estimate should be recorded somehow.)

II. Organization
   A. Management responsibility
      1. Establishment of a project manager
      2. Directive authority
      3. Review authority
      4. The executive responsible for completing the organization phase
      5. Chartering authority *(This is implicit in the signature of the charter and may be omitted.)*
   B. Organization affected *(division, departments, etc., that will participate in the project.)*

III. Schedule
   A. General time frame of the project
   B. Schedule for completing the organization phase
   C. Interim reviews (if desired)

IV. Resources allocation
   (This paragraph may be omitted if adequate resources are under control of the given responsibility for the organization phase.)
   A. Resources assigned to the organization phase
   B. Method of Cost Charging by Participating organizations.

V. Statement of management support for the project

Signed
Chartering Authority

leading from both a functional and a project box to each project functional manager. The results were impressive in their complexity.

A much better practice is to draw the organization chart of the project with all managers shown reporting in a conventional line to the project manager. Then a symbol added to each box containing a project functional manager will refer to a footnote that might say, for example, ''These managers report to the project manager for project direction and to the respective functional division heads for policy direction.'' Or the footnote may describe any other matrix approach desired by general management.

Although project functional managers appear on the project chart, they should also continue to appear on their respective functional division charts. Both project and functional charts should contain identical or essentially similar footnotes so that different stories will not be told to different people.

Unusual difficulty in getting project and functional executive approval of the charts should not be interpreted as a failure of chart graphics. The real problem is psychological: the executives concerned have not yet fully accepted the organizational arrangements made for project management.

Personnel appointments

Personnel appointments should be made according to the usual practices of the organization. However, appointments of project functional managers should be announced by an executive to whom both the project manager and the functional manager report. To permit functional executives to issue these appointments would suggest a weak project manager role—a clearly undesirable impression.

Even if the project management technique is used it is well not to let the project manager sign such appointments, for the impact of higher-level attention is lost and may be less acceptable to functional managers. Functional appointments below the level of project functional managers should probably be issued in the same way. However, for a large matrix project, it is often acceptable to have the project manager and the senior functional executive sign the appointment jointly.

If position guides are normally used in the organization, they should be issued for the project team. It is particularly useful to prepare one for the project manager. Any nonacceptance or misunderstanding of project management on the part of functional executives is likely to be detected early and can therefore be resolved before it causes problems. Most position guides for project functional managers present difficulties. However, the authority of these managers to assign their functional heads to project tasks should be spelled out, and the nature of the matrix relationship should be stated.

Managerial titles and levels should conform as much as possible to normal organizational practices. Usually the word ''project'' inserted in a title is adequately descriptive. However, when really new functions are being undertaken, they should not be disguised by assigning them conventional but misleading titles.

New and revised policy and procedural documents

If the organization's standard policy and procedural documents are to be followed, this should be stated. However, a project of any size or length will probably require some revisions, particularly if project management is new to the organization.

A project should not be permitted to operate contrary to existing policies and procedures except where this is specifically intended. For these cases, it is good practice to issue a single document stating that basic policies still apply, but that the project will develop its own procedures in certain areas; these exceptions should be specified clearly in the document.

Procedural revisions to accommodate project needs may be made in several ways. Applicable procedures may be revised in the normal way. Or the project manager may be delegated the authority to issue his own procedures, provided that they conform with existing policies. This is convenient, but it runs the risk of inefficient nonstandardization in systems, particularly when an organization has several projects. For a project of shorter duration, the administrative expense of procedure coordination may be avoided by giving the project manager authority to include procedures in his plans for project execution.

If possible, procedures for project management should be developed in advance of implementing a major project. However, under no conditions should lack of procedures delay establishing a project when that is what is really needed.

4

Integrated Quantitative Planning

ADVANTAGES OF PROJECT PLANNING

The discussion begins with the premise that planning is good, plans are useful, and planning and plans are necessary to project management. Without them, project management will lead to chaos and disaster for all concerned. With them, there is at least a hope for success and even glory.

Given that evaluation, the content of project plans will be described in some detail. A fairly wide gamut of possible useful plans will be touched on. Some very useful plans, such as schedules and budgets, will be covered even though they are often not thought of as "plans."

Communication develops within the project team

The early planning phases of a project provide an excellent vehicle for developing good communications within the project. It is assumed that the key functional managers and/or professionals will participate in project planning, and that every member of the team, even those in a peripheral or support role, will actively participate in developing each part of the total plan. Then all key players will have a chance to review and will be required to approve all plans issued for the project.

A project team is often composed of people from various departments who know each other only slightly or not at all. As they work together developing plans for their future interrelated activities, they develop a rapport that leads to a true project spirit. Differences are much more amicably resolved in a planning mode than in the heat of task execution.

During this planning phase, the capabilities of each department and the reasons for their preferences become known to all the team members. When future problems arise or changes in the plan become necessary, the special problems of each participating organization are already understood, thus facilitating constructive replanning and corrective action.

Integrated planning with full participation by the project team should lead to a common understanding of project objectives and how they are to be achieved. Common and enthusiastic acceptance of the plans is a major step toward project success.

Communication improves outside the team

Project plans are an extremely useful vehicle for communicating with the customer. The existence of a comprehensive project plan is itself a visible sign of progress, but more importantly a good plan will confirm that the customer's desires and objectives are really understood. Any misunderstanding can be highlighted early and resolved before the expenditure of extensive project resources.

Especially when a project has multiple objectives or many end products, joint examination of plans can be mutually profitable. For example, disproportionately large amounts of effort and resources are to be devoted to attaining objectives that the customer considers to be secondary, and this at the risk of not achieving primary objectives. A reordering of priorities will correct the fault.

Good planning uncovers areas of risk in the execution phase of the project. Careful evaluation of the risks and the implications of delay or failure may lead to modifying the project to reduce the uncertainties. Such advance recognition of high-risk areas creates an atmosphere of understanding and avoids that most uncomfortable feeling during critical periods of project development—surprise!

A project initiated under a commercial contract usually includes a carefully thought out statement defining the nature of the work, the accompanying constraints, and the resulting end products. Even in a well-conceived project, however, there are frequent misunderstandings about what is desired, particularly at levels of detail just below the contract work statement. An examination of initial project plans can often expose this misunderstanding.

This is not to say that every whim of the customer should be satisfied regardless of the contract language. On the other hand, if the true desires of the customer can be satisfied by a change that does not involve cost penalties or project disruption, it is certainly good business to use the project plans as a communications device for ensuring that the customer gets what he wants. In larger projects, sophisticated customers nowadays often require agreement on plans before new phases of the project are initiated.

When a project is chartered by general management or another component of the organization, project goals are less likely to be clearly thought out and precisely defined. Under these conditions, project plans are even more useful in bringing about an understanding of what is really required. If the project is substantially realigned or even canceled because a review of the plans reveals unexpected risks or side effects, the planning effort may be considered a success; it is far better to discern potential troubles early after small expenditures rather than real troubles later after massive expenditures.

Emphasis has been placed on the use of plans as a communications device early in the life of a project. Often, however, if a project is complex and extends through several phases, a review and approval of the plans for the next phase may be a required prelude to starting work on it.

Early identification of problems

Almost all projects start out with some sort of a planning base. It may consist of a broad objective, a time frame, a budgetary limitation, and some departmental plans for the immediate future. This sort of arrangement leads to situations in which it becomes apparent that the plans are not compatible with the unplanned activity that is proceeding. Controversy and inefficiency result. Some parts of the project may have to shut down and wait for another activity to catch up—a costly situation. It may become apparent that project goals and guidelines cannot be met.

Thorough planning reveals incompatibilities in the plans and assumptions of different departments early in the process. Detailed examination of the tasks required to complete the project exposes overly optimistic broad assumptions and leads to more realistic goals or schedules. Inconsistencies may be discovered between the desired performance of the product and the money and time available to develop it.

No amount of planning can ensure that no problems will occur during project execution. In fact, too much planning can delay and inhibit execution. But the right amount of thorough planning can prevent unnecessary difficulties from arising, leaving the project team to devote its efforts to solving the really unforeseeable problems.

Planning provides the basis for issuing project direction

Planning is carried out to provide a basis for action. While the planning process considers many alternatives, its goal is a specific definition of activities and techniques that can be, and are intended to be, carried out in the future. True, the definition will probably undergo some revisions, but it is the best current statement of the best way to get the job done. Planning not intended to serve as a basis for implementation is a waste of time.

The completed plan should provide a basis for issuing project direction. Ideally, it should be necessary only that the project manager prepare a directive saying "Do it," attach it to the plan, sign it, and issue it. In actuality it is not quite that easy, but most of the written direction should draw directly on plans, requiring little or no modification of them. The format desired for the written direction should be carried forward as closely as possible into the final format of the plans.

A STRUCTURE FOR DECISION MAKING
IN PROJECT PLANNING

It is a generally accepted management principle that planning is essential to success. Planning takes place at all levels of management and in all functional areas. As the planning process is carried out at successively lower management levels, the amount of detail increases. Planning is generally regard as beneficial because it leads to an optimal course of action; it generates efficiency because the efforts of all parts of the organization are synchronized to achieve a common set of objectives. All these concepts are applicable to project planning, which, however, has some features that require special emphasis.

Much of an organization's planning is quite properly associated with departments, divisions, and other organizational entities. Activities supporting a project are included, perhaps without special project identification. Project planning, on the other hand, is strongly oriented toward the project, and at lower levels toward project tasks, all of which may involve the activities of several organizations. In other words, the plan for a project does not subdivide immediately into plans for functional departments; it subdivides one or more times into plans for lower-level tasks, and eventually into plans for the subtasks assigned to each department. This does not prevent a department from consolidating all its tasks in its own plan, but the ideal project plan is primarily oriented to the project and its tasks rather than to organization.

Since project management is used for situations containing nonrepetitive tasks and elements of risk that require changes in the project baseline, flexibility in coping with the continuing changes in project plans is an absolute necessity.

Statement of basic project goals and guidelines

Project goals and guidelines are the basis for all project planning. They can be outlined as follows:

      Overall project goals
            Product performance requirements
            Project requirements
            Criteria for decision making

Overall project goals include a reason for the existence of the project, a brief discussion of its desired end product, and the philosophy for managing the project.

Product performance requirements define the end product of the project. If it is hardware construction or software, general or systems specifications may define it. If it is a study or research effort, a definition of the area to be examined and the subject matter of the final conclusions or recommendations will suffice. If it is a task that must be performed, such as completion of a move to a new facility, a description of the conditions to be attained and the broad objectives to be accomplished is needed.

Project requirements define any constraints on how the project is to be carried out. Completion schedules and budgetary limitations are in this category. Any requirements for doing the work in-house or by subcontract are stated, as are any management philosophies. The amount of verification of the project's end product performance may be defined.

Criteria for making decisions should be announced. The relative importance of project performance, costs, and schedules should be given. The relative importance of development cost, production cost, and ultimate operational cost may be defined. No effort should be made to foresee every possible contingency; general guidelines will suffice.

The information should all be written down. Ideally it may be given to the project manager as initial direction. If this is not done, the project manager should prepare the list of criteria, coordinate it with key functional executives, and have it approved by the chartering authority. It may be argued that such a course will provoke disagreements and cause needless difficulties. On the contrary, that is all the more reason for taking this action. Any basic disagreement about the fundamental goals of the project should be exposed early and not left to cause inevitable misunderstanding and trouble later.

Defining project end products

The definition of project end products serves as the basis for planning the execution of the project. In a hardware system, the system specification is expanded to a more detailed level and initial specifications are prepared for the major subsystems and/or hardware items. Enough description is provided so that plans to build and test the hardware can be developed.

During this activity, various designs may be considered to meet the top product performance requirements. The systems engineering process can be used to define and compare alternative approaches. The criteria used for making decisions should be followed in determining what is the "best" design for the project.

Developing project plans

As definitions of the products to be produced become available, plans for carrying out the project can be prepared. The required tasks should be organized in the form of a work breakdown structure, and the process of defining tasks can begin. Functional organizations can develop plans for carrying out the various required tasks, and schedules and budgets can be prepared.

Project plans should be made to comply with project requirements. Alternative plans should be compared and the "best" ones selected on the basis of the criteria used for making decisions.

Iterations

The preceding analysis implied a straightforward linear progression from examining requirements to designing a product to planning a program. The logic of such a process is sound. However, it is not followed just a single time; it is iterated within the various phases of the planning process.

After the initial product performance requirements and project requirements have been stated, a sequence of broad implicit tradeoffs results in a decision on how much is to be spent for how good a product. During the process of product definition, assumptions about one part of the design are found to place unreasonable requirements on some other part. Assumptions are changed, perhaps several times, in the effort to achieve the optimal design—an iterative process intrinsic to systems engineering.

Iterations again occur during project planning when an excessively high schedule estimate is changed, or when a dangerous schedule risk is reduced by spending extra money, say for a facility modification. Plans for accomplishing project tasks partly in parallel rather than totally in series are found to permit cost reductions large

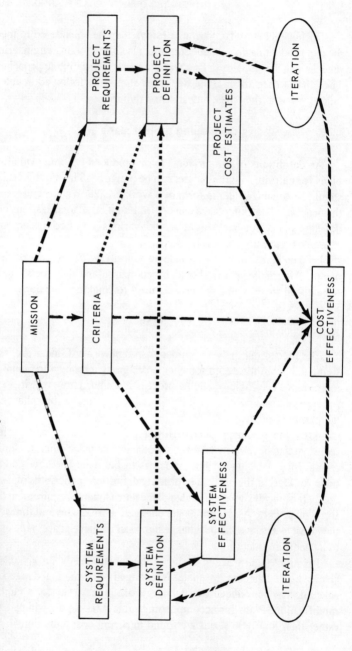

Figure 2. Cost effectiveness analyses.

enough to overcome the costs associated with the additional changes resulting from the overlap.

Even more significant are the iterations that occur between designing the end product and defining the project plans. It may be found that a certain design feature is the sole reason for a long schedule; modifying the design can result in a significant shortening of the schedule. Increasing project costs by a few percent to take advantage of an emerging technology may improve product performance, or installing a new operating system at some cost increase may considerably enhance the performance of an information system.

Dozens of these iterations are made during the planning phase; some are small and some compel major changes in the whole project concept. The integrated nature of the organization, the excellent communications procedures, and the fast decisions make these iterations possible on a project.

Finally, there are iterations between defining the product and planning the project on the one hand, and establishing project goals and guidelines on the other. It may be found that the desired product simply cannot be developed for the planned cost or within the specified time frame. A decision to relax either product or project requirements can then be made to permit a realistic set of project plans. Or perhaps the right decision is to terminate the project immediately rather than after a large expenditure in pursuit of unattainable goals.

The iteration process is a constantly active set of decision loops, indeed loops within loops, intended to produce increasingly better plans. Two critical problems arise in managing planning iteration. The first requires a continuing control of planning baselines so that everyone knows at all times which product performance goes with which plan, which budget, and which schedule. The second is the necessity to bring the planning process to a halt so that implementation can begin—before money is wasted on superfluous planning and unnecessarily detailed restrictions are placed on doing the job itself.

Figure 2 shows the planning process; here cost effectiveness is the prime criterion for success.

Products of project planning

The project planning process should result in specific end products that will serve as a basis for project direction and as a blueprint for project execution. These documents should be mutually consistent. Primarily because of the work breakdown structure, it should be easy to find the interrelationships between them. Although not all of them may be needed for all projects, the typical end products are:

Product specifications
Work breakdown structure
Definition of project tasks
Event networks
Functional project plans
Schedules
Cost estimates and budgets

Preparation of these planning documents will be discussed in some detail below.

SYSTEMS ENGINEERING AND PROJECT PLANNING

Systems engineering is a nearly indispensible discipline for the optimal execution of any large project concerned with hardware, facilities, communications, transportation, information processing, and so forth. It should be an integral part of project planning—indeed the driving part during the early phase of the process.

Small projects and some big ones do not require any systems engineering effort. The job may be done adequately in such an activity as systems analysis or preliminary design. If the end result of the project is clearly specified at the beginning, systems engineering will not be needed at all. However, if the project involves specifying an end product to meet a requirement, then its ideas are sound and will apply. Before discussing the use of systems engineering in project planning, its main concepts will be presented in a nontechnical manner.

The writer has coined a definition of systems engineering that he has found extremely useful in discussing this complex subject over a period of several years:

Systems engineering is a quantitative definition of a system and its components, designed to meet customer requirements and constraints and optimized in accordance with customer criteria.

Perhaps the key idea here is optimization. It is easy enough to put together a system that meets a customer's requirements, but difficult to put the "best" one together. In a competitive world, this is obviously of critical importance. Also, "best" is measured in terms of the customer's requirements and criteria, and this may be different from the organization's ordinary ideas of what is best.

It is appropriate here to note that a system is the entire combination of hardware, information, and people necessary to accomplish the specified mission. Optimizing the most conspicuous element of a system and hoping for good system performance will no longer do; all components must be considered.

For example, in earlier days of flying from uncrowded airports, the basic requirement to move people rapidly from the entrance of one airport to the exit of the next could pretty well be met by concentrating on the design of an airplane that would fly rapidly and reliably between the airports. With today's mammoth airports, the problem is not so simple. There is little point in flying faster to save a few minutes if one must wait an hour to buy a ticket and another hour to reclaim one's baggage at the end of the flight. So the whole system of rapid air transportation is being optimized by the use of sophisticated computer-based reservation systems, fast and efficient jets, and mechanized baggage handling, each an important component of a complex modern system.

An objection is often raised that there is nothing new about systems engineering: "Our engineers have always designed the best product they could." The statement is usually true, but does nothing to refute the claim that systems engineering has contributed significantly to progress in recent years. Earlier engineering efforts were concerned mainly with getting the job done. The nation was delighted that railroads could be built to the west coast; no one worried about their optimal number or their construction patterns.

Second, systems have become larger and more complex and their components more interrelated. Earlier, it was sufficient to optimize the components separately and in isolation; now all the subsystems must be optimized in the context of total system performance. Many of the woes of BART, the forward-looking transportation system in the San Francisco area, are attributable to a failure to recognize that one simply cannot buy a number of complex subsystems, hook them together, and have an optimal system.

This brings us to this further refinement:

Systems engineering is a design process that synthesizes a system by combining subsystems in an optimal manner. To do this, it uses analysis. Its end products are specifications.

The point here is that systems engineering is a utilitarian process fundamental to project execution, and it is the first step in the design of the end product of the project. It may and usually should use some sophisticated analytic techniques to get the job done, but its fundamental purpose is to turn out a set of specifications that, if met, will provide a total integrated system that works well and meets requirements.

In sum, systems engineering designs systems that are effective and efficient. Effective implies that all performance requirements are met within the desired time frame. Efficient implies optimal application of technology, economic allocation of new resources, and maximum utilization of old resources, all within existing fiscal constraints. These are laudable objectives for any design effort, but systems engineering can do it best for complex projects.

Systems engineering and project management

If systems engineering is a useful discipline for project management, then it should fit into the model of the project management process already described. It does, indeed, readily fit into that model.

Customer liaison is concerned with finding out the requirements of the customer. Systems engineers carry out a crucial part of this activity. They must ascertain not only the desired specific end-product performance, but also the customer's reasons for desiring the various specified attributes. If the reason for a requirement is understood, it is much easier to find the best way to meet it. The criteria for evaluating total performance should also be understood. Sometimes a significant gain in one parameter can be made with minimal reduction in another; one must know their relative importance.

Systems engineering plays its largest role during the planning phase of the project management process. In a project concerned with designing a complex end product, systems engineering defines the end product. It also establishes the requirements that dominate most other parts of the planning process.

Direction to implement the project includes release of specifications that prescribe what the end products of the project are to be. Systems engineering produces these specifications as its principal end product. In some cases it may also produce test plans that can be issued as project directives.

During project evaluation, controls should be established to ensure that the parameters prescribed in the specifications are being met or are likely to be met. Failure to meet any specified parameters, or the cost of corrective action to achieve them, should be evaluated in the same systems engineering framework and according to the same criteria that were used to establish the optimal system and specify the parameters in the first place.

Reprogramming should take place in the context of the initial design optimization. However, initial specifications should not be followed slavishly. Often the right decision is to alter a specification parameter rather than to spend a great deal of time and money achieving it.

Reporting should include comparing end-product test results against specifications. Variations in lower-level performance should be interpreted in terms of their effect on system parameters. Opportunities to achieve better overall project performance by changing system requirements should also be pointed out.

Thus it is seen that systems engineering fits neatly and constructively into project management. Not all projects need systems engineering, and those that do not should not add any practices just to comply with the name. Those that do need it will find that it falls naturally into the management cycle. And the central idea of systems engineering always applies—to give the customer an end product that meets his requirements in an optimal way.

Design-to-cost in systems engineering

In projects for the development of both commercial products and military systems, there may be a basic initial requirement that the unit cost of an end product not exceed a fixed amount. In systems engineering this is regarded as a design parameter.

As the system is further defined in terms of subsystems and end items, the unit cost is subdivided appropriately among them, with new cost numbers included in specifications below the system level. When hardware design begins, costs may be further divided and allocated to hardware components.

Life cycle cost optimization

For major systems development projects, cost should be estimated for development, production, and operating and maintenance. In many Department of Defense systems, the latter costs may be by far the largest. Therefore, it may be economical to spend more money in development and production to save money later.

Tradeoffs between these costs should be made as part of the systems engineering process. An analysis of the total integrated logistic support system is required to support this effort. Studies of this type now assume considerable importance in DOD.

Systems engineering and project technology

It is important to recognize that systems engineering does not include all the engineering that goes into producing a system that is an end product of a project. Except in its early phases, the major part of engineering on a project (say 90 to 99 percent) is devoted to designing individual components of the system and not to systems engineering design. Some aspects of managing these efforts and their interfaces are discussed below; however, the matter is brought up here to avoid misunderstanding in intervening sections.

Systems engineering concerns itself with a systems performance as seen by users of the system, not by technologists concerned with the mechanisms that make it work. These performance parameters are of major interest to the project manager. Some typical systems engineering parameters (expressed as questions) are:

- How often will the user have to wait more than five seconds for a reply to an inquiry fed into a computer-based information system?
- What percentage of the time will the system be inoperable?

- How much will the cost of operating the system increase if the volume of work is doubled?
- How many elevators should be put in a building so that no one waits more than 30 seconds more than once a day?
- How large an airplane should an airline buy to maximize profits, considering losses because of low-load factors and failure to provide for peak capacity?
- How many check stations should a supermarket have to avoid keeping a customer waiting more than three minutes, except at rush hours?

Answers to each of these questions may involve inputs from several technologies. It is the job of the systems engineer to create an analytic framework that accepts quantitative data from different technologies, processes them in a single model, and produces answers in a format useful for project decision making.

Systems engineering has some technologies of its own. Queuing theory addresses the problem of how long it takes to service the needs of a system's users when they arrive at different times. Linear programming shows how best to use a combination of scarce resources. Dynamic programming defines the sequence of decisions that will best move a system from one condition to the next. Computer simulation programs reproduce the behavior of a system under thousands of different input conditions. All these techniques are independent of the technologies they analyze.

Mechanical, aeronautical, electrical, civil, and structural engineering—all these technologies provide inputs to systems engineering. Systems engineering can be highly useful in solving problems involving only one of these technologies, but it is indispensable to providing the optimal answer when two or more technologies are involved.

Systems engineering, then, is directed toward optimizing the performance of the total system being designed. Its philosophical approach is general in nature, but this very generality permits its useful application to any of a wide variety of technologies and particularly to a combination of them. It may often select the better technology; for example, should people be moved to an airport by helicopter or monorail?

The systems engineering process and project planning

To repeat: Systems engineering tries to design a system that best meets all the requirements of a project. It translates broad system requirements into specifications for hardware or software components. Several fairly obvious but often forgotten deductions should be mentioned.

- Every system requirement must be met.
- It should be possible to trace how each system requirement is being met.
- No requirement for the performance of a component should be specified unless it is necessary to meet a system requirement.
- Every component requirement should be traceable to one or more system requirements.
- Every component requirement should contribute to optimal system performance, not just to optimal subsystem performance.

It is appropriate here to say a word about the importance of maintaining traceability of requirements from the system level to the component level. First of all, engineers responsible for component design are motivated to provide the most modern technology; this may result in their selecting components that are much more elaborate and expensive than needed. Evaluating the contribution of each component performance feature in terms of system performance will help to eliminate "gold plating" and the unnecessary introduction of new, less reliable technical features.

Second, a system requirement may unintentionally result in the unavoidable use of a high-cost or high-risk component. When an overall review of the system discloses this fact, it is possible to find out why the component was specified and often to relax the requirement so that the system is cheaper, simpler, or less risky.

The systems engineering process thus begins with a statement of the requirements for producing the end product of the project—the desired system. Frequently, this is given at the beginning of the project as a system specification. If it is not provided, then the known requirements should be assembled into a form of system specification that defines all the desired system performance parameters.

The next phase is concerned with translating system requirements into detailed component requirements. As an example, if there is a reliability requirement for the system, then reliability performance measures can be assigned to each of the system components. Computer running times or storage requirements can be assigned to each of several programs in an information system.

One tool that is sometimes useful is functional flow analysis. In this approach the function of the end product in its operational mode is shown as a series of block diagrams. A diagram can show the top-level functions; then each block—that is, each function—can be analyzed in greater detail to show the lower-level functions necessary to complete it. This can be repeated several times, although creating more than three or four levels of diagrams becomes unwieldy and time-consuming—if not a futile exercise in proving the obvious. During the sixties, engineers forced to use this technique to unreasonable limits on airplane design expressed dubious and colorful delight when their calculations showed that the airplane needed a landing gear!

On the other hand, the technique,.particularly in projects pushing the state of the art, can keep legitimate requirements from being forgotten. As an example, in a program involving special construction, the technique can reveal the previously unrecognized need for several special tools. The standard method of designing data processing systems is very similar to this approach.

After all the necessary functions have been identified, similar functions can be combined to establish the requirement for a particular piece of hardware. For example, many of the functions will require a power supply. All these requirements can be combined to establish a profile of the power to be supplied during different modes of the total operation, thereby contributing an input to a specification for a power supply.

The same procedure can be followed for specifying other pieces of hardware. Thus all system requirements are now satisfied by some combination of the component specifications. Conversely, any additional requirements that creep into component specifications can be immediately recognized as superfluous to project success. It is at this time that information can be supplied to cost estimating and scheduling groups for their work in project planning.

Obviously, different combinations of components may be synthesized to meet system requirements. The most reasonable looking combinations can then be fed into the system model and tested for optimal performance in meeting total system requirements. This is often referred to as a tradeoff study. Comparisons can also take place earlier at a lower level to determine which of several solutions will best meet one of the lower-level combinations of functional requirements. For example, several different power supplies may be examined to determine which will perform best regardless of the system configuration selected. However, care must be taken, for in some cases different system approaches require different components for best performance.

Now that the best system has been defined, the system specification is updated. Specifications are prepared for all the components and/or subsystems comprising the system; these contain the requirements generated by the functional flows. The systems engineers may go on to generate test plans to ensure that all specified parameters are met. All this information is a necessary and useful base for planning all other aspects of the program. And so the system is created and its development is under way!

The above sounds marvelously neat, but it doesn't work quite that way in actuality. All the ideas are sound; they fit into a useful, logical structure; and they should be complied with. However, any detailed implementation should be initiated only when it is productive. Functional flows are great—sometimes. A good systems engineer knows how to use all these techniques; an excellent one knows when not to use them. Whatever will ensure meeting the customer's needs in an optimal way should be used. Figure 3 shows the interaction of systems engineering and project planning.

Pitfalls in systems engineering

Systems engineering can be a most useful tool in project management, but if misused it can result in a waste of money and even in seriously impeding project progress.

Many problems in systems engineering stem from faulty input data. Much stress has already been placed on the importance of using realistic criteria to determine which of several courses of action is preferable. This is particularly true in systems engineering, a process

Figure 3.   Systems engineering and project planning.

● MISSION REQUIREMENTS

▼

● PARAMETRIC SYSTEM SYNTHESIS
● SYSTEM-PROJECT TRADEOFFS
● SYSTEM OPTIMIZATION

CONCEPT
FORMULATION
(ADVANCED
STUDIES)

▼

● SYSTEM SPECIFICATION
● PRELIMINARY DEVELOPMENT PLAN

▼

● FUNCTIONAL ANALYSIS
● SUBSYSTEM OPTIMIZATION
● HARDWARE FUNCTIONAL REQUIREMENTS

▼

CONTRACT
DEFINITION
(PROJECT
DEFINITION)

● HARDWARE PERFORMANCE SPECIFICATIONS

▼

● PROJECT PLANNING AND OPTIMIZATION
● SCHEDULING AND COST ESTIMATING

▼

● PROJECT PLANS, COSTS, AND SCHEDULES

DEVELOPMENT
AND ACQUISITION
(OR DESIGN AND
DEVELOPMENT)

that uses analytical methods and is therefore dependent on precisely specified quantitative measures of merit. Perfectly rational systems engineering efforts have often produced results that have looked silly merely because of unrealistic input criteria.

Another such failure results from inaccurate performance data about subsystems. As noted earlier, systems engineering operates on data from other technologies; it is important that these data be accurate, and that they be the same data as were used by subsystem designers for their own design optimization.

Systems engineering often fails because it uses models that are too complicated. It might be well here to explain why the word *optimal* is used throughout the book instead of *optimum*. Optimum implies *the* best solution; optimal implies a solution that is very good, near the best, but not demonstrably *the* best. A great deal of useless effort can be wasted searching for an optimum solution when a good enough solution can be found more cheaply and much sooner. Usually the accuracy of input data and the assumptions of the model depart from reality enough that the apparent optimum is not exactly the ideal solution. Therefore, systems engineering models should be kept as simple as possible while giving adequate treatment to all the major issues in system design.

A frequent fault in systems engineering is failure to use its results in subsystem and component design or selection. This may occur because the results are not available in time to be useful, often a reflection of excessive complexity, or because the output of systems analysis may not be in a form that is useful to people faced with real-life hardware decisions. One sometimes sees the woeful systems engineer limping along behind the rest of the project team crying out his unpopular message, "You could have done it better."

ORGANIZING PROJECT WORK

It is important that the work to be accomplished by a project be subdivided to provide a means for adequate management controls. Ordinarily, in the absence of a project approach, existing organizations, using standard management systems, will subdivide the work for their specific purposes.

The examples at the top of the next page show how different organizations subdivide the work of a project to provide the structure, information, and controls they regard as necessary to successful project management. Of course, on any given project, only two or three of these departments may be concerned.

The fact that each department organizes and subdivides in a way that best suits its management needs is not intrinsically bad; rather, it is good in that it produces useful information and controls in a flexible manner.

However, project management in essence requires an integration of all project efforts and a penetrating view of the interaction between the activities of various departments. Without that integration it is difficult to obtain the desired insight into related tasks and departmental interfaces. Thus it is highly desirable to use a common projectwide framework for subdividing project effort.

Organization	Basis for Subdividing Work
Engineering	Standard drawing system
	Technical process
	Technology responsible for design
Manufacturing	Assemblies, subassemblies, and parts
	Locations
	Departments
	Processes
Marketing	Region
	Class of customers
	Customer
Management systems	Benefiting organizations
	Computer programs
Accounting	Departmental accounts
	Classes of labor and material
	Cost accounting classifications
	Customers
Scheduling	Milestones to be tracked
Construction	Type of labor doing work
	Physical subdivision of building
	Type of system installation

Work Breakdown Structure (WBS)

The term *work breakdown structure* is used here to describe the subdivision of project effort. The various other terms used in various companies or industries to describe this approach are all conceptually similar, if not identical.

Basically, the idea of the work breakdown structure is to divide the total work of the project into major groups, then to subdivide these groups into tasks, then to subdivide these tasks into subtasks, and so on. The work may be subdivided through as many stages as necessary to provide final units of the desired size. The lowest level of sub-divided work should be small enough to permit adequate control and visibility without creating an unwieldy administrative burden.

The work breakdown structure can then be used as a common framework for several activities:

Describing the total effort of the project

Issuing work authorizations

Budgeting

Scheduling

Status reporting

Tracking technical performance (sometimes, and with some limitations on the general WBS rules)

It is an extremely useful tool for integrating these important aspects of project management and for providing a common basis for planning and control by all departments and organizations participating in the project.

The work breakdown structure should be organized according to some orderly identification scheme; each WBS box is given a unique identifier. One way, basically a decimal system, is to set up a first subdivision of numbers, for example, 1.0, 2.0, 3.0, and so on. Then 1.0 is divided into 1.1, 1.2, 1.3, and so on. 1.1, in turn, is divided into 1.1.1, 1.1.2, 1.1.3, and so on. The process is continued as many times as desired.

The term decimal is not meant to limit the subdivision of any particular work element to no more than ten subelements. The work may be subdivided into as many immediate subordinate packages as desired; for example, 2.1.18.7 is an acceptable number. The level of subdivided work will be numerically greater by one than the number of decimal points in the identifier; for example, 3.6.12.4.3.10 is the sixth level of work subdivision.

Normally it is desirable to give a title as well as an identifier to each division of work in the WBS. This makes it much easier for line managers to use the device in their normal work. The names need not be long and complicated. In no case should the title of a level repeat words used in the subdivision; the numerical designation provides the traceability to larger groupings of work at higher levels. The main idea is to give the piece of work a usable, understandable name.

There is nothing essential about the numerical decimal scheme just described. Letters may be interspersed with numbers if this is mnemonically helpful. Also, the decimals may be omitted, although this restricts the number of next-level work subdivisions to ten in a numerical representation and to 26 in an alphabetical representation (not a great practical limitation in the latter case).

Another question that arises in numbering WBS boxes concerns the significance of individual elements of the number. That is, does a number or other WBS identifier mean anything other than its inclusion in the immediately superior identifier? For example, 2.3.11.4 is a subdivision of 2.3.11, but does the 4 also specify work that is being done in a department with code No. 4, or does it specify an operation No. 4?

It is easiest to develop a WBS if the elements of the identifier are purely random, which makes it easier to tell when a subordinate box is missing. Also, summation logic is simpler if computer systems are used in project control. On the other hand, if using the WBS can be made easier by assigning significance to one or more elements of the designator, it is desirable to do so.

Graphic representation of the WBS is often helpful in conceptualizing the project. The simplest way is to use a numerical listing with progressive indention for successively lower levels:

```
1.0 _____
   1.1 _____
      1.1.1 _____
          1.1.1.1 _____
          1.1.1.2 _____
          1.1.1.3 _____
      1.1.2 _____
      etc.
```

A graphic display similar in layout to an organization chart is a highly effective way to represent project work planning. It can be displayed on a wall to give team members a total view of the project and the interrelatedness of the various project tasks. Typically, each box contains the task identifier and the name of the task. Subtasks are shown in the same way in lower-tier boxes.

It is now appropriate to summarize some characteristics of a WBS that are implicit in the above discussion:

• The work specified in each WBS element is the sum of all the work specified in the elements immediately below it. When a work element is subdivided, all the work in that element is put into one of the immediately subordinate subdivisions.

• The work specified in each WBS element is the sum of the work specified in all the lower-level elements into which it is subdivided.

This is true even though the various lower-level elements may be subdivided a different number of times, for example, into a different number of levels.

- No work is described in more than one element at a specific level of subdivision.

- To maintain clarity in and to promote a common understanding of the WBS, it is usually desirable to provide a supporting verbal description of the work in each WBS element. The description need not be highly detailed, and redundancy should be eliminated in the various subdivision descriptions. Statements that exclude work from a specific element are often the most succinct way to describe the scope of the included work. The basic idea is to describe the work so that the people doing it and affected by it understand what is in each WBS element. This implies that jargon is unacceptable. One must not permit the growth of a select cult whose members are the only fortunates privy to the true meaning of the work description.

- On large projects, the total work description is sometimes called the "WBS Dictionary." This title has the advantage of implying authority—the tome is to be consulted when information is needed; it is not meant to be read. However, these advantages may be offset by an inclination to verbosity and esoteric language on the part of its authors, and by its intimidation of line managers, supervisors, and workers, the intended beneficiaries of the work.

- Properly done, the WBS description can be used as a basis for preparing any or all of the following: pricing work statements, contract work statements, work authorizations (at various levels), subcontract work statements, and progress reporting. Careful initial preparation of the WBS description may eliminate much redundant and often inconsistent effort in the areas listed above.

A key issue in constructing a WBS for a project is the depth to which the WBS should be extended. Two principles are particularly important:

- Each part of the WBS should be subdivided to the number of levels useful for managing the project.
- No effort should be made to extend the WBS to the same number of levels for all project tasks.

A large percentage of the unhappy experiences with the WBS device have occurred because of excessive zeal in pushing the WBS into too many subdivisions, thus creating an unproductive administrative burden; or because of insistence on a uniform number of subdivisions for all tasks, resulting in final subdivisions that are too small in some cases and too large in others.

A key issue in subdividing the WBS has to do with dividing the work according to organizational lines. It is possible to make the first subdivision according to organizational lines, for example, 1.0 is Project Management, 2.0 is Engineering, 3.0 is Tooling, 4.0 is Manufacturing, and so on. This approach, however, defeats one of the main objectives of a WBS: to highlight the interfaces between different departments in the many tasks where their efforts are interrelated. Dividing the work organizationally at a high level nullifies the usefulness of the WBS; any schedule below the first level will reflect what is required only of one department and will not reflect that department's dependencies on or obligations to other departments.

In some cases, functional divisions are hostile to project management and are properly suspicious that the WBS will give the outside world, and the project manager in particular, an insight into their internal workings and progress. When confronted with possible use of a WBS, they seek to avoid exposure by enthusiastically embracing the WBS while insisting that the first division be by major organizational function, the second by department, and so on. The project manager then has no better insight into project task interrelationships than he would have had under previously existing management practices.

Thus one can suggest two principles:

- Tasks should be subdivided into smaller tasks according to the interrelatedness.
- Dividing tasks according to organizational responsibilities should be deferred to a low level in the WBS.

The reasons for these principles will become even clearer in follow-up discussions of work authorization, budgeting, and, in particular, scheduling.

Some criteria generally applicable to subdividing tasks may be suggested:

- It should not be difficult to understand what the WBS task is.
- Lowest-level WBS tasks should not involve ridiculously small costs.
- It should be possible to construct a schedule or a network for a WBS task, if that is desired.
- Routine, repetitive work should not be excessively subdivided.

As already noted, if a task is to be subdivided at all, the entire content of the task must be assigned to one of the subtasks at the next lower level. Confusion sometimes occurs when there is a logical division of most of the work, but some of it is associated with integrating the other parts, or is not readily divisible according to the logic used for the other parts.

As an example, suppose that the design and manufacture of an airplane are divided into separate work on the wing, the fuselage, the tail, and the engines, but some work is associated with the entire airplane. The WBS could be structured as follows:

2.0 Aircraft
    2.1 Final assembly
    2.2 Wing
    2.3 Fuselage
    2.4 Tail
    2.5 Engines

The problem is easily handled by dividing the work as thoroughly as possible into subtasks that represent divisible components of the task, and then setting up one additional subtask to describe the nondivisible subtasks.

While it is undesirable to encumber the management of a project with too many work packages, the project manager should not be constrained from subdividing work in areas that are complex, high-risk, or otherwise critical to project success. On the other hand, a project manager should not subdivide work to usurp controls that are the proper responsibilities of the functional supervisors.

Since a good WBS is designed to serve many project purposes, it should not be necessary to manage all project activities to the same level of WBS breakdown. For example, work authorization may be done at a rather high WBS level, budgeting may take place at an intermediate level, while scheduling may be done at the lowest level. The summation aspects of the WBS make this option available while preserving logical consistency among the different tasks and different aspects of project management.

The WBS structure is flexible in that it can be expanded over time, in both depth and scope. The WBS need not be held for issuance until it is expanded to the desired depth in all areas. In fact, an early issue containing only two or three levels of task subdivisions provides a necessary and sound basis for project planning. Then as the time approaches for initiating certain parts of the project, tasks can be subdivided two or three more levels as appropriate for cost and schedule control. As noted above, tasks at any level of the WBS need not be subdivided into the same number of lower subdivisions or subdivided at the same time.

Flexibility can and should be maintained as the WBS develops throughout the life of the project, but it should not be achieved on a piecemeal basis. The entire structure should be thought out early in the project in such a way that it can accommodate all aspects and phases of the project. The detailed implementation can be done later.

Another virtue of the WBS approach is its capacity to provide an appropriate level of detail to all management levels. Thus managers at different levels and with different responsibilities can look at large or small segments of the project presented in varying degrees of detail. Yet all information is logically consistent. Without the WBS approach, different systems may be used to disseminate planning information and to collect data at different levels or within different departments. The WBS is the framework for managing from a common set of information.

Use of the WBS in work authorization

The work breakdown structure is the basis for work authorization. It can be used with whatever type of work authorization system is ordinarily adopted by the organization or is established for the project.

All work authorizations should include the identifier and the title of the work that is released. When a particular task is authorized at a specific level in the WBS, all subtasks at all lower levels are thereby implicitly authorized, for by definition the tasks released are simply the sum of the lower-level tasks. In the release, only the reference to the highest-level task need be made.

It is frequently convenient to use the work authorization system to release the WBS description as a reference document. Then, when specific tasks are to be authorized, they can be released by identifier and title, with a reference to the WBS description for specific definitions of the tasks to be performed.

Use of the WBS in budgeting

The WBS is the basis of the budgeting and cost collection structures for the project. Accounts may be established at whatever WBS level is desired for project control. Actually, accounts may be subdivided into a level lower than appears in the WBS; in this case, however, the rationale for dividing the WBS tasks into lower-level accounts should be fairly obvious; for example, different departments or cost elements.

At the time the budgets are released, a table should be issued to show the relations between accounts and WBS identifiers. As actual costs are collected during execution of the program, they will naturally be collected by account number, but provisions should be made for summing the accounts according to the logic of the WBS, so that the costs incurred for any task at any level in the WBS can be examined if desired.

One can now easily derive the following rules regarding budgeting and the WBS.

- The budgeted value for each WBS task is the sum of the budgets for all the subtasks at the level just below.
- The budgeted value for each WBS task is the sum of the budgets of all the lowest-level subtasks (that is, only the tasks that are not divided into further subtasks).

- The budget associated with a WBS identifier contains the entire budget for that task.
- The budget for any given WBS task is in one and only one WBS-identified budget element.
- There is no released budget element (that is, budget available for expenditure) that is not assigned to some WBS task. An example illustrates the first two rules:

Task			*Budget*	
2.2.1				$100,000
2.2.1.1			$30,000	
2.2.1.2			40,000	
	2.2.1.2.1	$20,000		
	2.2.1.2.2	15,000		
	2.2.1.2.3	5,000		
2.2.1.3			20,000	
2.2.1.4			10,000	
	2.2.1.4.1	5,000		
	2.2.1.4.2	5,000		

The first rule is illustrated by

$100,000	= $30,000	+ $40,000	+ $20,000	+ $10,000
(2.2.1)	= (2.2.1.1)	+ (2.2.1.2)	+ (2.2.1.3)	+ (2.2.1.4)
$40,000	= $20,000	+ $15,000	+ $5,000	
(2.2.1.2)	= (2.2.1.2.1)	+ (2.2.1.2.2)	+ (2.2.1.2.3)	

The second rule is illustrated by

$100,000	= $30,000	+ $20,000	+ $15,000	+ $5,000
(2.2.1)	= (2.2.1.1)	+ (2.2.1.2.1)	+ (2.2.1.2.2)	+ (2.2.1.2.3)
		+ $20,000	+ $5,000	+ $5,000
		+ (2.2.1.3)	+ (2.2.1.4.1)	+ (2.2.1.4.2)

The preceding rules apply for actual costs as well, for they are collected according to the same logic, WBS structures, and account numbers that were used for release of the budget.

Use of the WBS in scheduling

The WBS is the basis for top-level scheduling. It is usually desirable to issue schedules for each of the first-level tasks, also showing one or two levels of subtasks with their WBS identifiers and titles. It is not necessary that a schedule be issued for each WBS element; in fact, this would usually be redundant. However, as many WBS-element schedules should be issued as are necessary to provide project control. It is often desirable to issue schedules at a lower level than the lowest WBS level. However, reference should be made on them to the appropriate WBS task identifier.

Three fairly obvious but sometimes misunderstood principles follow from the preceding statements:

- A WBS task is started whenever one of its subtasks is started.
- A WBS task is completed only when all its subtasks are completed.
- If all the subtasks of a WBS task are completed, the task is completed.

DEFINING PROJECT WORK

The first reason for having a project work statement is its usefulness in developing schedules and budgets. These can be prepared accurately only if there is a common and fairly detailed understanding of what is to be done. For instance, the cost of tooling or testing can vary by a factor of ten, depending on what policy is employed.

If work is to be done under contract, the definition of work serves as a basis for the contract work statement and provides additional information for accurate cost estimating and pricing. A pitfall on many contracted projects is expansion of the scope of the work beyond what was intended and agreed to at the beginning of the project, thus leading to cost overruns. A good work definition helps prevent this. If work is not described in the work statement, a contract change with additional funding is required.

A project work statement is a valuable communications device. The project manager can issue specifications and provide general direction to the functional organizations assigned to the project. They can respond with a work statement for his approval. This highlights any misunderstanding about what is desired from each department.

When agreement is reached about its contents, the statement forms a basis for agreements on future action. It also facilitates communication among departments. When a project functional manager reads the work statement of an interfacing department, he may find that he is expected to provide something he had not planned to provide, or that his colleague's plan does not specify supplying him with something he expected and needs. These issues can be resolved and the plans brought into synchronization.

Finally, project work definition serves as a primary basis for direction. The work statements provide most of the textual material used in work authorization documentation.

Form of work statements

The fundamental requirement of a project work statement is that it follow the organization of the work breakdown structure. In fact, sometimes a WBS dictionary is prepared to define the work in each WBS box and to designate the organization(s) responsible for performing it. This may suffice as the work statement.

It is important that there be only one project work statement. That statement should refer to specifications rather than repeat data found in them. If two or more work statements are available, for example, one for planning and one for pricing, wasted duplicate effort and confusion will result because the two statements will almost certainly not be the same. If a contract work statement exists, it is good practice to put it at the beginning of the description of the appropriate WBS level, identify it as such, and then add supplemental material for planning and pricing purposes.

The requirement for a single project work statement does not preclude functional departments from issuing more detailed work instructions for accomplishing their tasks. Such internal documentation should be merely supplemental—subdividing the work further, giving instructions on how to do it—not a rewrite of the work description. It is often good practice to require that the appropriate part of the project work statement be included verbatim in any lower-level work instructions.

Responsibility for defining project work

The project manager is ultimately responsible for project work definition. All the key managers play a part in it. One of the project manager's principal subordinates should be charged with the responsibility of preparing and maintaining the project work statement. However, there is no universal agreement about who this person should be; it depends on the nature of the project and the project organization.

On a smaller project where few people other than the project functional managers report to the project manager, the manager of project control is the obvious choice. The WBS work statement, schedules, and budgets can be prepared efficiently by a small group. This is the best solution in the majority of situations for large projects as well.

If a project is oriented toward research or a study in matters of high technology, the work statement may simply be outside the capability of anyone but a technical manager, such as the chief systems engineer, the chief of systems analysis, or the chief engineer. Even here, however, the technical manager may be charged with preparing the initial draft of the work statement and the manager of project control may then be given the responsibility for putting the statement into a form suitable for pricing and work authorization and may further be responsible for keeping it up to date. The technical manager should be required to review the final draft to see that business-oriented additions or revisions have not altered the technical intent.

If there is a manager of plans the solution is not so easy, for the project work statement is fundamentally a planning document. The manager of plans may be charged with preparing the top planning documentation and schedules jointly with the manager of project control who was responsible for the work statement. This can lead to an uncertain division of responsibility, which is why creating a manager of plans is not always a good idea except on very large projects. A typical planning sequence might be the one shown at the top of the next page.

The work statement should of course be kept up to date, and changes should be incorporated in it by the same procedures.

Project Manager:	Issues planning guidance.
Chief Systems Engineer:	Issues specifications and technical plans.
Manager of Project Control:	Issues the WBS.
Functional Managers:	Prepare a detailed work statement for their particular activity.
Manager of Project Control:	Integrates the work statement: prepares final draft.
Project Team Managers:	Review and concur in the draft.
Project Manager:	Approves the work statement.

PROJECT SCHEDULE

Any project, however small, needs a written set of schedules. The process of scheduling forces determination, first, of the order in which events must occur, and second, of the time it will take to do them all. These are fundamental planning decisions.

Schedules are also a fundamental basis for control. Schedules coming out of the planning process should be in a form suitable for immediate issue and use in tracking status.

Throughout the entire spectrum from very small projects to very large ones, scheduling is perhaps the first project management tool to be applied after the fundamental one of setting up a project and appointing a project manager. Even in a small project, good and fairly detailed schedules are a necessity.

Event networks in scheduling and planning

Event networks are an extremely powerful tool in project management. They are useful in a number of activities:

Planning

Identification of key events

> Defining work sequence
> Validating project time constraints
> Resource identification
> Scheduling

Control

> Status of project schedule compliance
> Identifying problem areas

Event networks are also an essential part of PERT, CPM, and other similar project management tools. It is important to note, however, that event networks can be applied very productively *without* using these tools.

An event network is a graphic means of portraying the sequential relations between key events in a project. Specifically, an event network shows, for each event, (1) all the events that must take place *before* that event can occur, and (2) all the events that cannot take place *until* that event occurs.

Graphic conventions for drawing event networks abound; however, they all come down to this:

- A box is drawn around the name of the event E under consideration.
- All the events that must occur in immediate sequence before event E can occur have their names in boxes to the left of E's box.
- A line is drawn connecting the right side of each of these boxes to the left side of E's box.
- All events that occur in immediate sequence after E, and that cannot occur until E does, have their names in boxes to the right of E.
- A line is drawn from the left side of E's box to the right side of each of these other boxes.

Some further event network rules that follow from the above are:

- An event can occur in only one box in a network.
- Two events in a network may be unrelated to or independent of each other; their boxes will then not be sequentially connected.
- A box cannot have lines connected both to the left and to the right

of another specific box. (This avoids the logical problem: "When two trains meet at a crossing, neither shall cross until the other has done so.")

- An event E cannot occur until after the occurrence of all events in boxes connected in a leftward sequence of lines and boxes.
- An event E can occur without the previous occurrence of an event in a box to its left if its box is not connected to E's box by a leftward sequence of lines and boxes.
- An event E must occur before the occurrence of any event in a box to its right that is connected to E's box by a rightward sequence of lines and boxes.
- An event E need not occur before the occurrence of any event in a box to its right that is not connected to E's box by a rightward sequence of lines and boxes.

Note the words "leftward" and "rightward." In a network, all the boxes are eventually connected to each other by lines and other boxes, but only the left-to-right and right-to-left sequences are logically significant. Zigzagging is not significant or permissible.

The question may be asked, "Isn't an event network just a flow chart?" In a sense the answer is "yes." Perhaps a better answer is that it is a combination of a large group of flow charts, each of which has events that are interdependent with events appearing on some of the other flow charts. Nothing about flow chart logic is incompatible with event networks. However, the emphasis in networks is on the many complex interrelations between events, rather than on the single-path string of events normally conceived of when a flow chart is used.

It is possible to include various items of information in each box of an event network. Normally, the title will be shown in the box. Relation to the work breakdown structure is given by including the number of the lowest-level WBS task that contains the event. An arbitrary identifier may be used for simplicity in tabulating data about the events. An organization or individual holding responsibility for the event may be added; this is most appropriate in detailed, lower-level networks, for in the higher-level network the responsibility for many events involving several organizations could logically be assigned only to the project manager or one of his immediate subordinates in the project organization.

It is possible to construct networks that show the start and finish of fairly major tasks without depicting the numerous significant events that occur during the accomplishment of the task. Then a subordinate network can be developed for the task itself. This can be extended downward to more than one lower tier.

How many event boxes to employ on a single event network is a question of convenience and workability. Some comparative characteristics are:

Large Networks	*Small Networks*
Tell the whole story	Lose the big picture
Show all interrelationships	Drop out significant interrelationships
Are too complicated to use	Tell the story clearly
Are unwieldy to handle	Are convenient to handle
Are constantly under revision	Require that only pertinent networks be changed
Require only one display	Create too many pieces of paper.

Obviously the idea is to get the right-size networks. Some rules of thumb are:

- A network usually should have at least 20 events; 10 events is a practical minimum.
- A network usually should not have more than 100 events; 300 events is a practical upper limit.
- There should normally not be more than two tiers of networks—certainly not more than three.
- The more dynamic the project, the fewer the number of events on a network and the more tiers.
- The more complicated the project, the larger the networks and the fewer the tiers.

It is important to note that not all aspects of a project need be described in comparable detail. Some may be defined by relatively few events, reflecting only major subtasks, while others may be subdivided into a large number of events. Characteristics of project tasks that justify the use of a large number of descriptive events are criticality, high risk, involvement of many organizations, technical complexity, and activity in diverse locations.

The capability of showing network logic in different levels of summarization has several advantages in project planning. In the development phase of a project, work can first be planned in large subdivisions, then planned to greater detail within the same planning framework. Parts of the project that need immediate implementation can be given early detailed attention while a view of their impact on downstream activities is retained. If part of a project becomes critical, it can be examined in greater detail to ensure proper management attention.

In a large or complicated project, planning and status reviews by different management echelons are facilitated by the use of detailed and summary networks. Higher levels of management can view the entire project and the interrelationships of major tasks without looking into the details of individual subtasks. Lower levels of management and supervision can examine their parts of the project in fine detail without being distracted by those parts of the project with which they have no interface.

The event network is an extremely useful tool in the planning phase of a project. The network can be the graphic focus of the combined efforts of the entire project team. It provides a communications vehicle that is direct, logical, and easily understood. It does not readily accommodate hazy, imprecisely stated requirements, nor does it respond to verbose or emotional generalities.

Each project team member is stimulated to define the activities and products he requires from the rest of the team. A good rule that injects sober and thorough consideration into planning is, ''If it isn't on the network, you won't get it.''

The event network also clarifies the obligations each team member has to his fellows. Project problems too often occur because each department concerns itself with only those tasks it must accomplish to complete its main contribution, rather than giving equal attention and priority to tasks required of it by others for their end product.

The existence of a project event network eliminates the confusion that results when each department has its own view of the project and its particular place in it. The overview enhances the cooperative feeling, "We're all in this together."

Format of schedules

Schedules should be issued in the format normally used by the parent organization. In the unlikely event that the parent organization does not have one, many workable formats can be found in good texts or purchased on the open market.

The principal innovation that project management may bring to schedules is a requirement to show the WBS identifier on each schedule or schedule line item. This is extremely important in maintaining control of the work statement-schedules-budgets baseline. It ensures that all events get scheduled. It also makes it easier to control schedule changes when the scope of the work is changed, and easier to examine the effect on cost when schedule changes are made.

When event networks are used in project planning, it is usually a good idea to use them as a basis for making schedules as well. Events on networks should coincide with events on schedules—always a good practice, but essential if PERT or CPM is used.

Project schedules may exist in several tiers—the larger the project the more the tiers. In a major hardware development project, the following layers of schedules may exist:

Project master schedule

Development and test schedule

Hardware end-item production schedule

Assembly schedule

Parts fabrication schedule

A similar hierarchy of schedules would exist for test and analysis activities. Incidentally, it is a good idea to insist on schedules for systems analysis and study work. People in those fields do not like to be controlled and pretend that their work cannot be scheduled, but this is not true.

It is usually a good practice to require that all pertinent dates from higher-level schedules be included on lower-level schedules with a particular identification. An exception may be made when scheduling policy calls for some work to be completed earlier than the project requires in order to provide a hedge against possible difficulties.

Not all work need be scheduled in comparable detail. Schedules should be prepared to the extent that they validate planning and provide a basis for direction and control.

Responsibility for developing schedules

The project manager is responsible for developing project schedules. Responsibility for managing this effort should be delegated to the manager of project control.

As noted above, project schedules will be issued in a hierarchy of several tiers, the number depending on the size and complexity of the project. The project manager will lead the effort in developing the top level or two. He will want to approve schedules at one or two tiers further down. He should not attempt to approve detailed schedules, but should review or have the manager of project control review them to ensure that they are consistent with higher-level schedules. Project functional managers develop detailed schedules for carrying out their tasks consistent with higher-level project schedules. A sequence for preparing project schedules might look like this:

Project Manager:	Issues an overall schedule encompassing targets and guidelines.
Manager of Project Control:	Prepares and coordinates a schedule draft primarily of end dates.
Project Functional Managers:	Provide intermediate dates and validations.
Manager of Project Control:	Prepares a final schedule draft adjusting inconsistencies.
Project Manager:	Approves concept.
Project Functional Managers:	Concur in schedule.
Project Manager:	Approves and issues schedule.

This process can be repeated for a lower level of schedules that the project manager may desire to issue. The process for developing such a schedule might look like this:

Manager of Project Control:	Issues a requirement for lower-level schedules for functional departments.
Project Functional Manager:	Prepares draft of functional schedule.
Manager of Project Control:	Ensure that the shedule conforms with higher-level schedules and coordinates elsewhere in the project as required.
Project Functional Manager:	Approves revised schedule.
Project Manager:	Approves schedule.

For certain highly technical schedules, the chief systems engineer or his equivalent may have the leading role in putting the draft of a schedule together. He and the manager of project control should work closely together throughout the scheduling process.

Perhaps more than any other part of project management, scheduling depends on and highlights the interdependence of all tasks and all departments of the project. Thus, effective schedule management is one of the most important responsibilities of the project manager.

PROJECT BUDGETS

Top-down budgetary estimates

Top-down budgets are based on past experience in doing similar tasks. They are also based on the judgments of experienced executives. The analysis is applied to the project as a whole and to major subdivisions of it, but not to detailed tasks. Estimates of relative complexity and cost are obtained from the organization's cost data bank and are shaped by executive experience. The following hypothetical and simplified example illustrates the principles better than a lengthy discussion.

A previous project developed a hardware device somewhat similar to the one being planned. Its costs are shown in Exhibit 1.

EXHIBIT 1
(K = 1,000)

Project management	$ 200K
Mechanical hardware	
Design	1,000K
Manufacture	700K
Test	400K
Electronic hardware	
Design	1,500K
Manufacture	2,300K
Test	800K
Ground equipment hardware	
Design	600K
Manufacture	1,100K
Test	400K
Integrated test	2,000K
Direct expenses	400K
	$11,400K

As a result of systems engineering and project planning, the new system is designed and a comparative analysis can now be made for the new project:

• The new device will weigh twice as much as its predecessor. This is expected to increase design cost by 20 percent and double the manufacturing cost. No change is expected in testing.

• The electronics design can rely on existing technology; this will cause a 20 percent reduction in design cost. Manufacturing will cost about the same. However, the previous product was not fully debugged when it left development; a 100 percent increase in test costs will be expected to do it right this time.

• Ground equipment is expected to use twice as many consoles as in the previous model. Design and manufacturing costs will be increased proportionately and test costs increased by half.

- The integrated test will cost about 30 percent more because of increased complexity.
- Direct expenses are expected to increase by $600,000 because of increased travel to a remote test location.
- The previous project experienced a substantial overrun because of questionable project management and an unplanned schedule delay. The relative cost of the next project is conservatively expected to decrease by 25 percent because of better management. However, this will increase the cost of project management by 50 percent.
- Costs have increased by 10 percent a year in the two years since the previous project started.

The cost estimate for the new project is shown in Exhibit 2.

Exhibit 2

Project management	1.5 × 200K	$ 300K
Mechanical hardware		
Design	1.2 × 1,000K	1,200K
Manufacture	2 × 700K	1,400K
Test		400K
Electronic hardware		
Design	0.8 × 1,500K	1,200K
Manufacture		2,300K
Test	2 × 800K	1,600K
Ground equipment		
Design	2 × 600K	1,200K
Manufacture	2 × 1,100K	2,200K
Test	1.5 × 400K	600K
Integrated test	1.3 × 2,000K	2,600K
Direct expenses	400 + 600K	1,000K
		$16,000K
Estimated project cost		$16,000K
25% reduction for better management		4,000K
		$12,000K
20% increase for inflation		2,400K
Estimated project cost		$14,400K

This type of parametric cost estimating is a very useful device. Subsequent detailed budgets may be more accurate, but sometimes they are not. Difficulties are sometimes not foreseen, and some necessary tasks are forgotten in the detailed estimates. Any major discrepancies between top-down and bottom-up estimates should be understood and resolved before embarking on a project.

Bottom-up budgetary estimates

After a project work statement and project schedules have been developed, budgets can be prepared. Budgets should be developed in complete conformity with the work breakdown structure, down to its lowest levels.

Project functional managers should base their budgets on the schedules and the work statement and should use techniques normally employed. For production items, learning curve analysis may be applied. The organization's statistical methods and industrial engineering standards should be used. Frequently it is a good idea to make estimates in terms of man-hours and materials and then convert them to dollars. The best available techniques should be used.

After the departmental budgets are prepared, they are reviewed by the manager of project control and the project functional manager. Differences of opinion are resolved by the project manager. Finally, the manager of project control prepares final budgetary estimates organized by the WBS, and a separate set is organized by department.

A project budgetary philosophy

A common philosophy of budgeting should be established early in the planning phase. Ideally it can be stated with the project requirements at the time when the order establishing the project is issued. A clearly understood set of ground rules about cost estimating and budgeting will prevent much unproductive bickering between the project manager and functional executives.

The first items of budgetary philosophy that should be agreed upon are the degree of conservatism in the estimates and the amount of the allowance for contingencies. One approach follows the industrial engineering standard cost methodology and provides an essentially minimum cost budget under the implied assumptions that everything will be done as efficiently as possible and there will be no unforeseen adverse developments. Another approach looks at past performance and gives the best estimate of what the present job will cost. In still another approach, an allowance for contingencies is added to the best estimate so that the job will almost certainly be completed with actual costs less than budgets.

It does not matter too much which method is used provided that it is applied uniformly in all parts of the project. It is inconsistent, unfair, and conducive to hard feelings to give one department a tight "standard cost" budget while giving another a budget replete with contingency allowances. Whatever the approach, it should be fully understood and uniformly enforced throughout the project.

Another fundamental issue in budgetary philosophy is the treatment of reserves. If a budget is made at a lower organizational level, reserves for contingencies added subsequently at each higher organizational level will result in cost estimates that are unreasonably high. If accepted as budgets, they will permit, if not actually encourage, inefficient performance. If used for pricing, they will result in uncompetitively high prices. On the other hand, problems do occur in projects that require funds beyond those originally planned.

The best approach is to estimate all costs as realistically as possible; these can then be summed for a total project budget. Departmental budgets can be issued at some percentage of the estimated cost—say 90 percent. The remaining 10 percent can be held in a combined project reserve under the control of the project manager.

The existence of the reserve should be known to all the managers on the project. Such a practice encourages good cost performance and retains a fund for unexpected difficulties. However, this must not be permitted to serve as a scheme for rewarding inefficiency.

A similar approach is to prepare functional budgets in the amount of the estimates and to add a percentage to the total project cost for contingencies. For contract work, it may be appropriate to issue budgets at less than contract cost to help ensure profitable performance. But in the long run it may be just as effective to issue budgets at contract cost levels and to encourage underruns. In any case, the important thing is to establish a consistent policy that is understood by everyone.

Responsibility for developing budgets

The project manager is responsible for project budgets. The manager of project control should be assigned the responsibility for their preparation and administration. Each project department head participates in developing them for his own activities. A typical sequence in budget preparation would look like this:

Project Manager: Issues the WBS project work statements, schedules, and budgetary guidelines.

Manager of Project Control: Issues detailed requirements for budget preparation and formats. Develops top-down budgetary estimates.

Project Functional Managers: Develop bottom-up budgets for their tasks.

Manager of Project Control: Reviews bottom-up estimates and compares them with top-down estimates.

Manager of Project Control and each Project Functional Manager: Jointly review departmental budgets.

Project Manager and the Project Team: Have a full-scale review of all project budgets.

Project Manager: Issues budgets as direction when project execution begins.

PROJECT PLANS

Project plans are communications devices, and so should be easy to read and should convey their message in a simple, straightforward manner. Maximum use should be made of charts and graphs, but no significant effort should be expended on elaborate and fancy artwork.

Plans do not have to be long to justify their existence. A one-page plan can be highly effective in reflecting project decisions. For instance, a very useful one-page tooling plan might state, "No new tooling will be developed for the project. The following tools are available for minor modification and use: . . . ." Plans should be as short as possible while still conveying the message.

Plans should be geared to the work breakdown structure. They do not necessarily have to follow the numerical sequence of the WBS, but each section and even each paragraph should have a reference to the appropriate WBS item number. This is of particular help when changes are being planned.

And, as noted earlier, plans should be written as a basis for action.

Plans involving several departments

The project manager must take the lead in planning activities that involve a number of departments. An example would be the plan for occupancy of a new facility.

Such planning is usually initiated with a kick-off meeting in which key issues are identified and discussed. A schedule for completion of the plan can be worked out. The scope of the planning activity should be defined. Action items may be assigned.

Early in the planning phase, an event network can be started. Subsequent meetings should review the logic of the network. After agreement is reached on it, scheduling can begin. Periodic meetings should be held to discuss problem areas and to review presentations by key managers involved in their part of the plan.

It is a mistake to start writing the plan too soon. The event network and the planning concepts, expressed in summary chart form, should be fairly well shaken down before any detailed text is prepared.

Plans for functional activities

The need for planning by functional departments participating in a project is indisputable. That they should prepare formal planning documents is less clear.

A small project has little need for a formal plan from each functional department, for their inputs can be provided by and integrated into the project schedules and plans. A large project gains much by having a plan from each functional department. For projects of intermediate size, the answer is not obvious. Each project manager must make his own decision about what is needed.

In many projects, the input to the project work statement suffices as documentation for all project planning. Justification for further documentation in the form of functional plans occurs primarily in complex projects. The work statement tells what is to be done; the functional plan elaborates on how it is to be done.

The functional plan as an informal contract

The matrix form of project organization is always confronted by an incipient problem: ''Will the functional departments do exactly and only what the project manager desires that they do with project funds?'' The functional plan is a good way to eliminate this problem. If it is based on general direction from the project manager, is prepared by the functional department, and is approved by the project manager, it provides a good basis for mutual understanding. It becomes an informal contract between the project and the functional department and works to eliminate misunderstandings and consequent disputes.

Responsibility for project plans

The project manager is responsible for the creation and maintenance of project plans. He is assisted in this by all the key managers on the project team.

A first step in planning is to recognize the need for defining what plans will be prepared. A plan for planning is in order. The project manager, assisted by all the managers on the team, should develop it and issue it at the beginning of the planning phase.

In laying the groundwork for the planning phase, it is a good idea to assign prime responsibility for each plan. A matrix chart can be prepared enumerating specific plans across the top and showing organizational or managerial responsibilities on the left side of the chart. Then, responsibilities for prime preparation inputs and their review can be shown by code letters in the appropriate intersections of the chart.

Each manager responsible for a plan should prepare it and develop a summary of the plan in transparencies for overhead projection. It should be presented to the entire project team for review. After appropriate revisions, the project manager should approve and issue the plan.

A selection of project plans

A project should do enough planning to provide a basis for project direction and to validate the entire project concept. It should not do planning for its own sake. The number and size of the plans are matters of judgment.

In a small project, a specification and a single plan containing a WBS, schedules, and budgets may suffice. On a medium-size project, fewer than a dozen plans may be appropriate. A large project may require two or three dozen.

Only a large project would need all, or nearly all, the plans discussed below. On smaller projects, the subject matter of some of the plans would have to be addressed, but that could be done as a page or paragraph of another plan; for example, security and correspondence control can be discussed in the management plan. The following fairly comprehensive list should not frighten anyone away from project management. The important thing is to plan how the project can be done most efficiently and then to issue the fewest documents necessary to firm up the story and communicate this clearly to all concerned.

Specifications define the performance and characteristics of the end product.

The work breakdown structure is an outline of tasks to be performed by the project. It may be a single chart.

The project work statement is a description of the work to be performed by the project, organized according to the WBS.

Project schedules are top-level schedules for the project.

Project budgets are top-level budgets for the project.

The management plan describes how the project will be organized and administered. It may contain charts, position guides, and delegations of authority. It may designate the manager responsible for each of several plans or control actions. It may contain administrative data that would otherwise be contained in the next few plans discussed below. It may describe information and control systems to be used.

The data and correspondence control plan describes who has the authority to sign various types of correspondence and what degree of coordination is required. It describes the files to be kept and specifies by whom. It may list contractual data items to be furnished.

The security plan describes any special security measures to be undertaken and the classification of various aspects of the project.

The configuration management plan describes the procedures to be used in maintaining product configuration and in controlling changes. This is particularly necessary if procedures not ordinarily used in the organization are to be followed.

The schedule plan describes the levels of schedules that will be used by the project, who has the responsibility to prepare them, and who has the authority to issue them.

The budgetary plan describes the levels of budgets that will be issued, and the attendant responsibilities and authorities. It states the practices to be used for reserves.

The development plan gives the overall approach for carrying out the design, integrating the activities, and testing the work of the project.

The test plan may be a part of the development plan. It describes the simulations, laboratory tests, special tests, environmental tests, and systems tests. It shows the sequence for testing the hardware required and specifies the facilities to be used.

The production plan tells how development and production articles will be produced. For smaller projects, it may contain the information discussed separately in the next few paragraphs.

The make-or-buy plan describes which major articles will be produced in house and which will be produced outside. It gives the policy for making decisions regarding lower-level hardware.

The procurement plan states the policy on competitive procurement and any requirement for, or restriction on, multiple sources. It specifies the procedures to be used in managing the work at the major subcontractors, and designates the number and the roles of contractor people at his facility.

The tooling plan states the policy on tooling type and rate capability. It indicates the major tools that will be required.

The manufacturing plan gives a description of the flow that will be used during the manufacturing process. Positions will be described.

The quality assurance plan describes the inspection activities that will take place during manufacturing. Policies on acceptance testing and sampling will be stated. Any special procedures for handling rejected material will be described.

The facilities plan describes the buildings and related facilities to be used in the project.

The training plan describes any special training that must be provided, either to project personnel or to the ultimate user of the end product, for example, a plant or an information system.

The logistics support plan describes a procedure for providing technical data, spare parts, and other services to the customer after delivery.

The transportation plan provides for shipping hardware from the point of manufacture to the ultimate installation.

The personnel administration plan is particularly necessary when a large number of people are to be moved to and supported at a remote location. It describes all special administrative policies and procedures.

Other plans could be described, but this list conveys the idea that project planning is a complex business to be taken seriously. It should be reiterated that any plan on the above list should be prepared *only* when it will help manage the project better or is required by a customer. Whenever planning information in the above areas can be combined, it is advantageous to do so.

5

Project Direction and Control of Changes

PRINCIPLES OF PROJECT DIRECTION

As pointed out at some length in the preceding chapter, planning is a fundamental prerequisite to successful project execution. For efficiency, the results of the planning phase must be fully utilized in the project direction phase that launches project execution. It should not be necessary to expend much effort to convert plans to direction. Ideally it should be sufficient to take a project plan and issue it with the standard work authorization statement, ''Execute this plan!'' In practice it is not always that simple, for it is often desirable to subdivide work authorizations for control purposes. However, the idea of using plans as a direct basis for project direction should be followed in principle.

Major project inefficiencies will result if the planning process becomes separated from the mainstream of project direction and activity. This will happen if the plans are voluminous or if the planning process is too slow and cumbersome. During the sixties the Department of Defense required that its contractors maintain excessively detailed plans and systems engineering documentation, a specific form of technical planning, with the result that a number of talented people wasted their time in detailed planning exercises that

151

never had a significant effect on the actual decision-making process and work of the project. Things are better now.

Just as planning should assume a form that is suitable for the issuance of direction, direction should appear in a form that is consistent with the collection of information that will be used for project control. The corollary of this is obvious: Plans should be presented in a form readily adaptable for control. Efficient execution of the project management cycle *Planning—Direction—Evaluation—Report* depends on a common structure of information.

Authority of the project manager

The project manager must have the authority to issue direction to initiate all work required for accomplishing project tasks. Conversely, no one should be able to initiate a project task, or do work using project funds, without the express positive direction of the project manager. He must also have the authority to issue associated technical specifications, budgets, and schedules.

Now holding this strong directive authority, the project manager must use it judiciously. First of all, he should avoid the temptation to issue direction in excessive detail. He should follow the normal management principles regarding flexible delegation of executive authority to subordinates. He should also avoid giving specialized direction on how to do a job. Selecting specific techniques and the appropriate professional approach is best left to the manager of the individual functional department of the project.

Standard systems for issuing project direction

Whenever possible, the standard systems of the organization should be used for issuing project direction, primarily to economize. First of all, it costs money to develop new systems. Secondly, people will be more efficient operating familiar systems. Finally, the introduction of new systems may lead to delay in getting the project under way, and this also adds to project costs.

If existing systems do not exactly fit project needs, the first choice should be to modify an existing system rather than design an entirely new one. Changes can often readily be made either by deleting or adding approvals in the direction cycle without altering the format of the information in any major way.

A permissive attitude by general management is appropriate regarding modifications to systems that are fundamental to project business, for example, scheduling and budgeting. However, a skeptical attitude is in order toward changes in general administrative systems, for example, travel and facilities requests.

Special project direction systems

Project needs for special direction systems can be met in many cases by simply adding a requirement that a document be approved by the project manager or his designee in addition to or in place of being given the normal managerial approval. Issuing a single directive requiring project approval is the simplest way to implement project direction in a hurry.

Simplification is a good reason for making changes in systems for project use. A fundamental idea of project management is the delegation of general management authority to the project manager so that he can make project decisions rapidly. Therefore, it is reasonable and efficient to dispense with a number of the functional concurrences often required in an authorization cycle, particularly when a consensus approach to management is used.

In a stable, routine environment, an approval cycle of days or even weeks may be acceptable. However, in a rapidly changing project environment, rapid direction must be achieved, requiring streamlining of the authorization system so that it can react rapidly, perhaps in hours. Grouping all project personnel in the same area is a key factor in attaining this rapid response.

Functional divisions may oppose such simplification, but this can be overcome by general management supervision. One way to assuage their discontent is to ensure that they receive copies of all authorization documents and are given an opportunity to appeal what they regard as unacceptable direction. Of course the simplification of direction systems should not be used by the project manager as the occasion for issuing directions precipitately without first consulting project functional managers. The flexibility of project organization and the mutual proximity of the key managers on the program should permit a rapid direction system while maintaining all needed coordination.

Special management systems may be demanded by customers for contracted projects. The Department of Defense requires that work authorization systems meet certain criteria, often Department of Defense Instruction 7000.2. Any major DOD request for proposal calls for submittal of a management volume as a part of the proposal. Failure to demonstrate strong project management procedures, which would include a project manager with strong authority, is tantamount to losing the competition. Lower-level subcontractor competitions frequently require the same approach. Other government agencies stipulate specific contract requirements for work authorization.

Ad hoc direction by the project manager

Work authorization systems and their related specification, budgetary, and schedule systems are a useful and necessary part of project management. Nevertheless, the most effective direction is achieved through the personal contacts of the project manager with the managers of his project team.

Documentation is necessary to maintain an orderly planning structure and to establish a quantitative directive baseline against which actual performance may be measured, but the real driving direction of the project must come about through personal direction from the project manager to his key subordinates, and so on down through the project team.

PROJECT DIRECTION

Work authorization

All work authorized for the project should be specifically authorized by the project manager. Conversely, no project work should be done without his specific authorization.

A single type of document should be used for authorizing all project work. Such documents are known by such titles as work authorization, work order, work release order, project direction memo, and technical direction memo. Work authorization (WA) will be used here as a generic term for such documents.

Work should not be authorized in a variety of documents, for it is then difficult to keep track of the total project baseline. However, this does not preclude functional departments from using a subordinate internal work authorization document for subdividing and adding details to the work direction. Any subordinate work authorization should refer to the WA that is the basis for its issue. The project manager may elect to see copies of all lower-level departmental work authorizations to ensure that they do not initiate more work than is authorized by WAs; he should not slow things down by approving them in advance, however.

A departmental work authorization should not cover work described in more than one WA, for this makes it difficult to trace the baseline; however, a WA may be implemented by one or more subordinate departmental authorizations.

Each WA should have a serial number, preferably arbitrary. If a subsequent change is made, the revised WA should be issued with the same serial number and a revision number. The WA should include a date. It should be signed by the project manager or his designee.

The fundamental framework for all project direction is the work breakdown structure. It should be released at the beginning of project execution and kept up to date by adding tasks as work is added to the project or by expanding it to include lower levels as a particular task is defined more precisely.

The WA document should begin with a designation of the WBS identifier covering the work described in the WA. There should be no arbitrary rules tying the work authorization to a particular level of the WBS. Some WBS tasks may be covered by a number of WAs at low WBS levels. Other WBS tasks may be covered by a single WA; in this case, each subdivision of the task should be identified by its lower-level WBS number.

The WA may include specific budgets, schedules, and specifications for the work to be done. However, on larger projects it is usually less cumbersome to release this information in separate documents, for these are subject to rapid change and may also be released through a simpler system requiring fewer or a different set of approvals.

The set of WAs should be kept meticulously up to date. Even though more paper will be used, it is a good idea to issue revised WAs in toto with notations of the revised sections rather than issue only the changes. Then the complete set of WAs will represent the complete project work baseline.

Technical direction

Specifications are the most suitable vehicle for the project manager to use in controlling the technical content of a project concerned with construction, hardware, software, or processes. This does not imply that he must control all detailed specifications, but only those at the higher level. For instance, in hardware this would include the system specification, the subsystems specifications, and the performance specifications for individual items of hardware.

Specifications should follow the good engineering or technical practices of the technology concerned, and should contain only as much detail as required to achieve the performance necessary for fulfilling project goals. They should contain the broad test requirements necessary to verify the desired performance but not a detailed test plan. They should be relatable to the WBS. It is usually a needless complication to require preference to the WBS in the specifications; it is better to have the WBS refer to the specifications. Additional information should be shown in drawings, code, or subordinate specifications. The project manager should approve the specifications. If there is a project systems engineer, he should also do so.

As noted above, specifications describe the desired characteristics of the project and its product. In a development project, it may also be appropriate to issue project direction on how the development effort should be carried out. One way is to issue a set of special technical direction memoranda (or whatever seems appropriate) to prescribe the desired action. These should be dated, should be identified as to revision number, and should include references to relevant upper-level specifications.

Another approach is to issue a WA as a cover for a development plan, a test plan, or a similar requirements document and for subsequent changes. This may have the disadvantage of requiring a more cumbersome approval cycle including the signatures of people who do not really contribute to the technical decision-making process.

Drawings, process specifications, and software code are the ultimate definition of project end products. They should be released through the normal technical channels. The project manager may elect to approve this documentation and changes to it. However, he should normally confine his review to ensuring that the documentation meets the requirements of the specifications, and not participate in second-guessing the design approach. Of course, any apparently deficient design solution may be questioned.

Schedules direction

The project manager should issue schedules for all significant events of the project. All events should be specifically related to the WBS.

The top project schedule is often called a master program schedule or a master phasing chart. It contains required dates for completing all major project events. Below this, and consistent with it, are more detailed schedules that add requirements for reaching intermediate milestones. The project manager should issue these schedules; lower-level schedules may be issued by the project scheduling manager or by functional departments. However, the project manager should retain the right to approve any lower-level schedule when it becomes critical to project performance.

Project schedules should certainly include delivery dates of all major hardware items. They may also include dates for significant preceding events such as engineering release, procurement of material, availability of tooling, and completion of fabrication.

In the development and test phase of a project, the project manager may wish to issue schedules to a greater level of detail. This phase presents numerous opportunities to make tradeoffs among schedules, budgets, and technical performance. Therefore, the project manager may wish to retain detailed control over all three factors in order to effect rapid response to tradeoff decisions.

Budgetary direction

Budgets for project work should be issued by the project manager. This is an area where he should be delegated authority by general management to allocate funds to functional organizations, even if the matrix form of project management is employed.

Project management, with its emphasis on planning, assigns budgets to a lower level than usual in functional organizations. Budgetary values are associated with WBS subdivisions of work. In major Department of Defense contracts, dollars are assigned all the way down to the lowest boxes in the WBS, and then divided there into cost accounts, one for each function doing work on that task. Provision must be made to collect actual costs in the same framework as applied to the budgets.

If there are no external requirements, the level of detail that will be employed in issuing budgets is a matter of management judgment. Here again it is desirable to use the existing practices of the organization to the maximum extent. If budgets are issued in terms of man-hours rather than dollars, then that practice should be continued. The only changes made for the project should be an extension of detail as necessary to ensure adequate project control. However, using a WBS and assigning dollars to its subdivisions is a good practice that should be followed in any project management. The discretion comes in determining how far the funds should be subdivided.

Budgets should be coordinated thoroughly with the project department heads before being issued. They should be prepared by the manager of project control for the project and issued over the signature of the project manager.

It is important that changes in the scope of the project be accompanied by corresponding budget changes. Respect for the whole budgetary process will decay in the operating departments if the budgetary figures bear no real relation to the current scope of the program. The necessity to keep scope and budget in synchronization is the best argument for issuing budgets on work authorizations; however, good discipline can accomplish this through separate release systems.

A common issue in project budgeting is whether or not it is

desirable to keep a reserve of project funds. Certainly the uncertainties that in part explain the very existence of projects suggest the desirability of maintaining such a reserve. Prudence demands the retention of some funds to cope with unforeseen project difficulties.

Another issue is whether or not these reserves should be kept a secret from or should be made known to the team of project managers. It is almost always the best policy to let all the key people on the project know of the reserve funds. If they cannot be trusted with this knowledge, then the project is probably poorly staffed.

On the other hand, discipline must be used in distributing project reserves; they cannot be considered a cookie jar filled with funds to be grabbed by the greediest, the most charming, or the least competent. Reserve funds should be used to finance unforeseen new tasks necessary to complete the project, not to cover unnecessary overruns or work unnecessary for project success. The project manager should approve the transfer of any funds from the reserve to departmental budgets. The Department of Defense encourages its contractors to keep a ''management reserve'' in their funds for execution of major cost-type contracts.

Procedural direction

Project activities should be executed in accordance with the policies, directives, and procedures of parent organizations. Since a project is often established to permit departure from and improvement on existing practices, it is consistent to issue new or revised procedures to describe the new practices authorized for the project. It is unwise to permit the project to deviate informally from standard procedures without proper authorization. This invites constant bickering between functional managers and the project team. If changes are constructive, they should be authorized formally.

One approach to prescribing new procedures for the project is to revise existing directives. For a project of long duration, this is the best method of exercising management control. Functional executives should be included in the coordination of such directive changes.

An alternative approach is to give the project manager authority to issue directives for his project. It is prudent to specify the directives that may be superseded by the project manager's directives. An open-ended delegation of procedural authority will invite the project manager and his team to "reinvent the wheel" in areas unimportant to project performance.

General operating direction

It may be necessary to issue project direction beyond that contained in the system for work authorization, technical direction, scheduling, and budgeting. However, paperwork that goes beyond defining realistic project baselines inhibits good project management. Project management is devoted to the simplification and elimination of paperwork, not to its proliferation. Project managers usually understand this but their staffs sometimes do not.

Releasing project plans under the cover of a work authorization may be a useful communications and directive device. However, this should not merely repeat what is already in the work authorization system. Also it should not create a situation where a considerable amount of effort is expended on keeping excessively detailed plans up to date.

A great deal of lower-level project direction can be transacted in project review meetings. When written direction seems necessary, memoranda can be used. In some situations a special serialized type of project direction can be used. However, it is well to avoid the proliferation of special formats for communicating project direction.

Necessity for a clearly documented project baseline

It is necessary to have a well-defined, clearly understood, and readily accessible baseline at all times during project execution. The baseline should include clearly related documentation of:

1. A work breakdown structure
2. Descriptions of all work authorized
3. Schedules for all work
4. Budgets broken down by subordinate organizations and associated with specific tasks
5. Specifications for the end product of the project

All these elements of the baseline must be in synchronization with each other; for example, budgets should not be issued for work not yet defined, or schedules prepared for a hardware configuration that has been changed, or tasks authorized without budgets.

The need for such a baseline is fairly obvious: It is necessary to keep the project under control. The problem is to do it. It is important to recognize that attaching a package of change sheets randomly to the original baseline is not a good way to form a baseline. It does not meet the criteria of being clearly understood and readily accessible. Periodically, the various elements of the baseline must be updated so that it is as easy to use as the original one.

However, in the process of updating, the reasons for making the changes and departing from the original baseline should be recorded. Traceability back to the original baseline elements must be maintained. Subsequent discussions of change management expand on the need for this requirement.

ADMINISTRATIVE DIRECTION

Personnel

The administration of personnel is an extremely important issue in project management. The project manager should have adequate directive authority in this area, the exact amount depending on the organizational form selected for the project. This subject is discussed in detail in Chapter 7.

Security

The project manager should be held responsible for defining adequate security requirements for the project, and in doing so must comply with all applicable security regulations of the organization. He may determine to some extent how to implement them, and he may add security requirements to the standard ones. In all this he should work through the existing security organization.

Government security regulations are well defined and are a subject of the contract for government work. For a firm new to government contracting, compliance may require a special effort. The security checklist should be issued through project direction channels. When general regulations do not meet government standards, special project regulations that do so should be issued.

Similarly, work on a development confidential to the organization because of a competitive situation should be subject to company security. If no general rules are forthcoming, the project manager should be delegated the authority to publish his own.

Once adequate systems are installed, security usually ceases to be a problem. The only touchy issue involves "need to know"; who has access to the secrets? The project manager should have the authority to determine who is included in the access list, but he ought to make his selection judiciously. It is usually impolitic to exclude his immediate superior from the list.

Facilities

Facilities, communications, and related support required for the project should be identified and authorized in the initial charter of the project. If a project passes through several phases of increasing size, new facilities should be authorized as the charter for each new phase is approved. Actual processing of the additional paperwork should proceed through normal channels. Approvals should be given automatically, however, for presumably the chartering agency has authority to allocate required facilities.

As discussed earlier, it is most important that the people assigned to the project be located together. Particularly when a matrix organization is used, the physical proximity of offices is a key factor in creating productive teamwork and effective communication.

It is desirable that project office space compare in quality with that occupied by people doing similar work. The temptation should be resisted to use that old shed on the remote inaccessible corner of the property. Also, the offices and related status symbols furnished to managers should compare in prestige with those of their counterparts in other parts of the organization. While particularly lush quarters for the project will arouse needless resentment in the other departments with whom the project must work, a squalid set of offices suggests that top management really doesn't care much about the project. It is true that good project leadership can overcome such situations and even use them to foster esprit de corps, but there is no good reason to build in handicaps to the project in advance.

Among certain people, an erroneous mystique exists about the bullpen—a large, open office area for everyone on the project with enclosed offices for practically no one except the project manager. The rationale for its superiority is that everyone gets acquainted rapidly and communications are improved. This is perhaps true, but it is also true that efficiency is lost, particularly during the planning phase of the project when team members should be spending a large part of their time in concentrated uninterrupted thought rather than in lengthy conversations about plans not yet clearly visualized.

If the project is located at a remote site, or involves construction of a new facility, the project manager may be given certain well-defined lines of authority for regulating the facility's activities. If the task is large enough, a member of the facility organization should be assigned to the project team.

In summary, all the new facilities activity on the project should be subject to the same careful higher-level controls that are ordinarily exercised in the organization. General management should give the project adequate facilities, but these should be implemented and administered in accordance with standard procedures. This is not an area in which it is appropriate to give an undue delegation of authority to the project manager.

Authorization of entertainment expense accounts

The project manager should have authority over entertainment expenses charged to the project or incurred by personnel in the course of their assignment to the project. If the project is largely oriented to the marketing of a new product, entertainment expenses are a significant resource that should be used effectively and in accordance with a customer contact plan.

If the project has high public relations visibility, as in the activation of a new facility in a community, expenditures for entertainment should be carefully controlled. Indiscreet entertainment of the wrong people can have a poor influence on a newly forming image. Also, it is desirable that entertainment be administered so as to give more or less consistent treatment to people in equivalent ranks in the local power structure.

If entertaining is not really vital to project success, the project manager may as well control it anyway, since any significant expenditure would probably be inappropriate.

Authorization of travel

The project manager should have the authority to approve all travel necessitated by project work. This is a key tool in giving him adequate control over contacts with customers or other organizations having an interface with the project. Also, he should be able to direct travel using project funds without a string of approvals; this may require revisions to existing procedures. However, travel expense reimbursement should follow standard procedures.

If a project involves one or more remote locations, travel can represent a significant cost element that should be under project control. Also, too many people seem inclined to attend remote-site meetings. This often signifies failure to map out possible solutions to the problems before the meeting and to establish a project position in advance.

Even though travel may not ordinarily be required on the project, it is still advisable to put it under project control, following the policy of giving the project manager authority over exceptional items.

With the exception of the entertainment expenses discussed above, there is ordinarily no point in having the project manager approve travel expense reports. Any gross discrepancies should be caught by the normal fiscal approval cycle.

General administration

The discussion has covered some areas where the project manager must be given special consideration or special directive authority. A few dozen other areas could be discussed individually, but more will probably be gained by suggesting principles for their management.

First, the project manager should be authorized to make decisions or approve actions in the maximum possible number of areas within existing administration systems, provided that no unusual indirect costs are thereby incurred by other departments. For example, he should be on the list of those who can authorize overtime, or outside printing, or any of a host of things that traditionally can be approved only by functional division heads. He must not be compelled to waste project time by sending staff members humbly back to a functional department for a routine approval whose only justification is understood by the project team. Bureaucracy must not be allowed to slow down the project.

On the other hand, questions concerning supportive activities not directly involved with project work should be resolved through the normal channels of the organization. The project manager should not be allowed to issue unilateral direction about things that are of common concern to all managers—for example, office amenities. If he makes a good case for an exception, his request should be granted after normal appeals if these are necessary.

The trick is to make it easy for the project manager to operate rapidly within existing administrative systems and policies without giving him license to depart completely from them on peripheral issues not really germane to the business of managing the project.

CONTROL OF CHANGES

It is a truism in Department of Defense circles that ''Project management is change management.'' As a project unfolds, the initial planning may seem to have been child's play compared with the problems of replanning and redirecting the project while it is in the midst of full execution in the original direction.

Changes originate from within and without. During the execution of a complex development or construction project, the customer usually changes his mind a few times about what he really wants or really can afford. These desires must be accommodated—with appropriate changes in specifications, funding, and schedules, of course. Then there are changes generated internally because the project is not going exactly according to the original plan. These circumstances are not necessarily an indictment of the project management effort, but more likely serve as evidence of why project management was properly selected in the first place. When internal and external changes interact and occur at the same time, the game is particularly sporty.

Direction on costs, schedules, and performance

Earlier discussions on planning have stressed the importance of achieving a balance of costs, schedules, and product performance, optimized in accordance with project goals. Similar considerations apply when implementing changes to the project, whether internal or external.

A good department reacts well to changes. A technical problem or an external change in specifications elicits prompt and constructive action by the engineering departments. The problem is twofold. First, the effect of the resultant changes on all the other departments must be determined. Then the technical change creates changes in schedules and budgets. For example, the material requirements may change, manufacturing schedules may change, the requirements for use of a test facility may change, and so on. All this must be coordinated by the project manager.

Efficient management of changes demands that all aspects of the project affected by a change be modified simultaneously to reflect its impact. Specifications, work authorization, budgets, schedules, and plans must all be modified together to reflect a common and accurate understanding of the change; time lags between different implementations should be insignificant; and all departments must recognize the internal effects of the change at the same time. The principal reason for the temporary disaster or ultimate failure of more than a few major projects may be attributed to their inept management of changes.

Since changes to different project baselines utilize different administrative release systems, it is a prime task of the project manager to see that all systems are activated in synchronization. A useful technique for managing both internally and externally generated changes is to assign a change number to each change. Then the changes made in the specifications, schedules, budgets, and plans can all refer to this change identification, and traceability of the project baseline is maintained more easily. This change identification is in addition to but not a substitute for continuing to identify all project work in the WBS.

Issuing change direction

Project direction to implement changes must be issued through the same systems that authorized the work in the first place. Changes to WBS task descriptions must be issued through the work authorization system by a revision of the appropriate WA. Specification changes must be issued through the specification release system. And so on for all changes in project documentation: they should require the same approval as their initial authorizations. Provisions should be made for a fast reaction to properly authorized changes, with a further requirement for following up to ensure compliance with all normal procedures.

Nearly everyone on a project would agree with the preceding statements. But project people are aggressive and oriented to results rather than procedures, and therefore to effect changes by informal activity and conversation rather than by formalized direction. The fact that people from different departments can work together on a project team to effect immediate required changes is a sign that the project is a good one rather than a bad one. However, zeal for immediate corrective execution to solve problems must be accompanied by an orderly change in the definition of the project baselines through established systems.

If required project changes cannot be accommodated by the administrative systems, the answer is not to abandon the principle of baselines and systems but rather to change the systems to meet project needs. Good systems will respond to frenetic demands and frequent changes. They may be momentarily untidy, but they must be responsive to their users and must have the capacity to stabilize themselves after hectic episodes.

Care must be taken to see that change direction is issued promptly to all major subcontractors and suppliers—and through the same channels that were initially used in negotiating the subcontracts, which would certainly have provisions for changes.

When a subcontractor's hardware interacts closely with the prime contractor's hardware, it may be desirable to have one of the subcontractor's representatives participate in meetings of the change control board. Certainly his input and advice should be sought before effecting major changes in his hardware. Informal contacts between the project personnel and engineers of both the prime contractor and the subcontractor are highly desirable. However they should not serve as a means of authorizing changes that bypass the formal contractual direction cycle.

Responses to customer-directed changes

Contracted work is of course defined by the work statement of the contract. Typically the customer will desire changes in a project as it progresses. Some changes will be bilaterally recognized as significant enough to require a contract revision; others may not alter any part of the contract but may still require a significant revision of the internal project plans. Judicious handling of these requests for changes is a major responsibility of the project manager. In relation to the project management concept defined earlier, the process begins with customer liaison and proceeds through planning into direction.

Changes large enough to warrant revising a contract will have an impact on work authorization, cost, schedule, or performance specifications—probably on all four, but at least on more than one. To keep track of all the subordinate changes that flow down from the principal change, it is important to give an arbitrary identification to the change. Some kind of log should be kept to determine what boxes of the WBS are affected by the change. Reference to the change identifier should be made in all direction documents that implement the change.

Some mechanism should be established to ensure that at the scheduled end of the change, all necessary included activities have been completed.

It is often easy enough to tell when a change has been started, but difficult to determine when it is completed. Failure to keep track of the full ramifications of changes is one of the biggest contributors to confusion and poor performance during the middle stages of a project. This discipline is important in any type of project, large or small, hardware or not.

CONFIGURATION MANAGEMENT

The evolution of configuration management

Good engineering organizations have always maintained a baseline definition of their product through specifications, drawings, and software or process specifications. They have also maintained control of changes to these definition documents.

However, as projects came to be larger, more complex, and executed on a more collapsed time scale, control of product definition and product changes became more difficult for several reasons. Systems became more complex, consisting of many interrelated subsystems and hardware components developed by people in different organizations and at different locations. A seemingly minor improvement in one of the components would create havoc in the performance of another component or even of the overall system. Even when the interaction of changes was recognized, there existed the problem of getting the changes incorporated in hardware items of comparable serial numbers.

Project as well as technical considerations became important. As systems were developed on a rapid time scale, a small change that created a delay in one component would cause costly delays in most of the rest of the project effort. Also, since the project manager was held responsible for overall project success, he needed to compare anticipated benefits from proposed technical improvements against probable adverse cost growth and schedule delay.

In an effort to gain control over product definition and project changes, Department of Defense and NASA agencies developed a set of operating procedures called "configuration management." The intent and ideas behind it were sound and constructive, but the constrictive procedures and resulting paperwork gained for the system a dubious reputation. Nevertheless, the technique was a success in that complex projects delivered products in workable condition, even though at considerable cost.

Subsequently, the government agencies reexamined their detailed requirements, revising them as necessary while retaining the underlying good ideas. Good but reasonable configuration management is a requirement today on major government development projects. Its techniques, applied selectively and intelligently, are useful in any complex project. Contractors use it as a matter of course on commercial products.

Problems in maintaining the product configuration baseline

The topics addressed in the remainder of this chapter are related in that they have a common objective: to ensure that the end product of the project will meet its specification requirements. Some of the activities serve other ends; for example, design reviews are a key event in the development cycle. In fact, most of the material could have been placed in Chapter 7 as an aspect of controls. However, they are discussed here because of their importance in controlling the product configuration baseline.

One might adopt the philosophy that if you want to find out whether a product meets its specifications, simply build one and test it. While that is certainly a good idea, it is not the whole answer. The right idea is to take every sensible precaution during its development to ensure that the end product will meet its specifications.

Suppose one has a good set of specifications with careful control over changes, a good set of drawings also under adequate change control, and a good set of inspection documentation. Change controls and inspection prevent changes from creeping into each set of product definition documentation. Should there now be any uncertainty about whether or not a produced article will meet the specifications? The answer is a resounding "yes!"

The problems arise when the product definition passes from one set of documents to the next. How can one be sure that the drawings will meet the specifications? How does one know that the tooling or the process builds a product that conforms with the drawings? How can one be sure that the right parameters and dimensions are measured during inspection? The various processes described below address these problems.

Specifications and product identification

Specifications form the fundamental baseline for product identification. In hardware and construction projects, drawings and detailed specifications also become part of the baseline. In software projects, programming specifications and code become part of it.

Management of product identification also includes policy decisions on several issues: lot numbers, serial numbers, part numbers, change letter control, physical part identification, substitution practices, use of vendor identifiers, and the like. These issues are closely related to the nature of the product and the internal practices of the organization. No attempt will be made to discuss them in detail here. The point is that they are part of configuration management and should receive the attention of the project manager.

Flexibility in making changes should be permitted in the early development of each part of a project baseline. After a management review of the results, the baseline should be placed under change control; that is, changes must be approved through a formal process including review by the change control board. For instance, a system specification assigned as part of project goals would be under control from the beginning. After passing through systems engineering, the end-item specifications become part of the baseline under control. Top-level drawings are put under control after the first design review, and detail drawings after the second.

Thus there is always a firm product baseline around which project plans are made. Changes can be made only after proper coordination and review. As the project progresses, the baseline becomes more detailed to ensure that decisions made during development are carried out.

Design reviews

Design reviews are a most useful control on the design process, both for hardware and for software. They are essential to good engineering practice and form a part of the internal engineering management system. They can also be used by the project manager in verifying the product configuration baseline.

Design reviews are often done in two or more phases. The first uses rough layout drawings, sketches, flow charts, supporting analysis, and test results. Trade studies showing why the selected design approach is superior to others are considered. Reliability, producibility, and maintainability are discussed.

The intent of the review is twofold: to demonstrate as thoroughly as possible that the design approach will meet the specifications and to prove that it is a good design, hopefully the best one available. Attendees are invited to ask pertinent questions about whether the design is feasible and to offer suggestions for improvement. While innovative thinking should not be stifled, amateur inventors should not be encouraged to make design recommendations outside their sphere of competence.

The second review uses drawings and accompanying detailed specifications that are nearly ready for release. The drawings are compared with the previously approved design approach. Recommendations may be made to change details not apparent in the previous review. The purpose is to confirm that the design meets the specifications and to approve the quality of the design at a more detailed level.

Design reviews should be scheduled by the chief engineer with the approval of the project manager. They should be chaired by the chief engineer. Those attending should include the project manager (at least during the presentation on meeting requirements) and managers from procurement, tooling, manufacturing, inspection, logistics, and all other affected engineering technologies such as structures and specialties such as reliability. A great deal of time will be saved if attendees are given advance copies of relevant technical data. The meetings should start with a presentation justifying the approach and demonstrating that the design will meet specifications. Questions are then encouraged.

Minutes of the review should reflect all decisions and record the rationale for not accepting serious requests for design change. Completion of the second design review clears the way for releasing drawings to production unless there is to be substantial redesign. The two reviews may be combined into one, but this runs the risk of wasting the effort required to complete drawings for a design concept that is rejected.

At the end of the design reviews, the resulting corrective action should provide reasonable confidence that the design will meet the specification. Subsequent changes to the design can be controlled by the change control board.

Control of changes

All changes to product definition documents should be implemented by being processed through the same formal system that was used for their initial release.

Nearly all design changes should be coordinated in advance with all elements of the project likely to be affected by them. For instance, manufacturing is likely to suffer a schedule impact, procurement can expect a cost impact, and subcontractors may experience design, cost, and schedule impacts. As already noted, all the related changes should be related through a common change identifier. A useful means of accomplishing control of changes is described in the next section.

Development of a complex product may require many design changes that have no impact on product performance, costs, or schedules. If the project engineering management is responsibly managed and has a good understanding of what its design changes will do to other organizations, it may be delegated the authority to issue design changes directly rather than having to coordinate its efforts in advance. However, these changes are subject to review or appeal if an unpredictable outcome results from them. These are sometimes called class II changes; class I changes have a project impact on cost schedule, performance, or interchangeability.

The change control board

The change control board is at the heart of good configuration practice. It is a means whereby the project manager leads his team in planning all the changes that affect the building of his project and the creation of its hardware or software end product.

The project manager is the chairman of the change control board. The executive secretary of the board is the manager of configuration management or whoever is assigned responsibility for assisting the project manager in managing changes. Other members are the chief engineer and the managers of production, procurement, major subcontracts, quality assurance, and logistics support, or whatever the equivalent titles are.

The project manager must serve as chairman of the board to ensure quick, incisive decision making, and he must have a good attendance record at its meetings. If the manager of configuration management is permitted to run the board, either formally or informally, it will decline in effectiveness. Its decisions will be ignored or a constant stream of appeals will swamp the project manager. Also, the project functional managers must be required to attend meetings regularly in order to participate in making important project decisions.

Basically, the board meets to approve any change in the project that affects the technical performance specifications of the product or alters project costs, schedules, or contract provisions. Board meetings should not retrogress into design reviews. These reviews are a very useful tool for achieving technical control of the project, but they should have been completed before changes are presented to the board.

In general, changes should be reviewed twice by the board. The first review should be made when the idea of the change is first conceived or when direction to make the change is received from the customer. A rough estimate of its impact on the project should be available. The board then decides whether or not to consider the change at all.

The project manager should not permit expensive design changes to proceed without approval when an early review would have stopped them at the beginning. The board's approval authorizes sufficiently detailed design work and planning to define the effects of the change on performance, costs, and schedules. The time for a final review of the change is established. Changes must not be permitted to coast along unmanaged.

The manager of configuration management is responsible for keeping track of the status records of all changes being considered by the board. He should not duplicate records of the functional departments. After the board has conditionally approved a change, he will see that it is coordinated with all departments concerned, and that information flows freely back and forth. If the project is large, he will need several people to help him do this.

When the board meets for final consideration of the change, all the members should have a thorough understanding of the impact it will make on their departments. Board meetings should be used not for passing out information, but for making decisions. The manager of configuration management presents the final change package with the estimate of the impact on each department, and each manager is asked to confirm or reject the estimate and to recommend approval or disapproval of the change. It is well to obtain a consensus. However, the board is not a voting organization; the project manager makes all decisions. That is why he must be an active participant.

If the change is approved, it is implemented through normal channels. The only further responsibility of the configuration manager is to ensure that the change is verified and that accountability records are closed. It is not his job to expedite and oversee the implementation of all changes.

It was noted that the board should meet twice to consider each change. For changes expected to have only a minor impact on the project, full approval may be given after the first consideration of the change, with a requirement that the board reconvene only if problems develop. It may also be desirable to permit all minor (class II) changes to be made without board approval. A good control procedure is to have the manager of configuration management screen all such changes. He can do this without being in the approval loop and thus avoid causing delay; however, he should bring up any questionable releases to the board for review.

The board should meet on a regular schedule at a standard time. It should meet at least once a week with more frequent meetings as required. In the peak of a development, it may need to meet daily. Nothing will encourage bypassing the system more than failure to get prompt board action on proposed changes.

The board should not hold the philosophical view that its mission is to prevent changes. Board members are there to prevent changes that are not in the best interests of the project. However, equally important is their obligation to plan, coordinate, and expedite changes that are good or necessary for the project. Project changes are not necessarily bad; uncontrolled changes are.

Review of tests

Well-designed development tests give a good indication of whether or not the product will meet its specifications. Qualification tests prove the product at extreme conditions and lend statistical weight to performance estimates. Such tests not only verify that the product meets specifications, but also tend to confirm that the inspection requirements ensure conformance of the hardware with drawings. Tests finally close the verification loop.

An organized review of test results should verify the product configuration baseline. A way to do this effectively is described in Chapter 6 under the heading "Measurement of Product Performance."

First article inspection

First article inspections provide assurance that the hardware has been built to conform with the drawings. They verify a successful transition from drawings to hardware just as design reviews verify the transition from specifications to drawings.

The "first" article inspection is done on an article taken early off the line. It need not be done on the very first article if that one is needed for other purposes or does not have all the changes built into it. The article is made available for inspection along with all the drawings and other product definition documentation. It may be subject either to test or to disassembly as required.

People conducting the inspection are mostly the same persons as those who attended the design reviews. However, this time the designers are the key figures. It is up to them to verify that the product indeed conforms with their drawings and their design intent. It is to be hoped that this is not the first time that they have seen the article, since close liaison between engineers and manufacturing personnel is the best way to conduct a development.

Discrepancies are noted and a record is kept. The first article inspection gives assurance that the product meets the design intent, and it is another step in verifying that the product will meet specifications.

Configuration verification and accountability

Records should be maintained to describe the exact configuration of an end product. Initial engineering release documentation should reflect the effectivity of all changes, that is, the serial numbered item or the lot in which each change is introduced. This describes what the product is supposed to be.

Manufacturing and inspection records describe and verify what was actually built. They should be compared with the initial drawing requirements to ensure that the product conforms to them in all respects, particularly in the effectivity of changes. Good internal systems will meet most of the requirements of configuration accountability. For complicated products with frequent changes or many variations to meet customer requirements, computer-based systems greatly promote efficiency.

Effective configuration management

Configuration management relies heavily on the product configuration system. Its successful implementation requires thorough coordination of all departments of the project to ensure that everyone is working according to a common baseline and a common plan for incorporating changes.

Another requirement for successful configuration management is integration of product configuration control with budget schedules and work authorizations. When one is changed, all should change together in a coordinated and traceable manner.

As noted in the discussion on the change control board, the right idea is not to prevent changes but to approve only those that should be made and to implement them in a coordinated, efficient manner. This task requires the coordinated efforts of the project team under the leadership of the project manager.

6

Project-Oriented Controls

FUNDAMENTALS OF PROJECT CONTROL SYSTEMS

Planning and direction—baseline for controls

It was pointed out earlier that project direction should be based on project planning. Similarly, project controls should be based on the direction issued for the project. This should be done first of all in the interests of efficiency. There is no justification for incurring the extra cost of developing a separate set of standards for project controls that differs from the set issued in the project direction. For this reason the desired controls should be studied and decided on during the planning process.

If project requirements, plans, direction, and controls are bound closely together, it will be easy to measure performance to ensure that all project requirements will be met as the project is completed.

Standard systems and data for project controls

Project efficiency demands that a single set of information systems be used throughout. This does not mean that a single monolithic data system must be developed, but that there should be no duplication of systems. No single set of management operations should have the same characteristics of its performance described by redundant systems. There should be a single system that produces data for all users, not separate project and departmental cost control systems.

The requirement for a single set of systems does not mean that a functional department cannot have detailed control systems for use only in managing its own internal affairs. It does mean that the data in the system are the same as those summarized to a higher level, or sorted differently for project control analyses.

When functional and project systems are based on different data with diverse conventions about time periods, adjustment procedures, editing standards, conversion factors, and accounting practices, considerable effort is likely to be wasted in arguing about which of the systems is telling the true story, and in attempting to rationalize the numbers.

In the 1960s the Department of Defense imposed PERT-COST on several of its larger contracts. It was a laudable attempt to relate costs and schedules in project status control and reporting. The PERT-COST requirements for data organization and processing were so detailed and far-reaching that the system could not be used compatibly with contractors' internal accounting systems without expensive modifications that departed from the existing systems. The result was that most contractors in effect kept two sets of books: one to manage by and one to report on. This was done at considerable cost and effort. Nothing was dishonest, but it was inefficient.

Later DOD removed its detailed requirement and substituted a set of Cost Schedule Control System criteria that can be met, after some modification, by an internal contractor project control system. Projects now tend to be run from a single set of books. Overzealous application of the criteria can still require the generation of too much data not required to manage a project. There is a continuing constructive dialog on the subject between DOD and industry associations.

The message for project procurement activities is clear. Ask for needed control data from contractors or subcontractors, and make every effort to accept the information in the form generated for internal project management. Intelligent use of the WBS is a flexible but effective way to ensure that the data are organized acceptably, but without rigid requirements.

General administrative controls

The project should start with the assumption that it will use the same administrative controls as the rest of the organization. It has enough problems in optimizing project-oriented systems without getting involved in its own special administration. One attractive feature of the matrix form of organization is that it permits administrative support and control to be provided by functional departments, thus leaving the project manager and his team free for project problems.

A project conducted at a remote location may need special administrative controls. Standard controls should be applied as a basis for planning, simplified where possible. New controls may be developed to meet the special or additional needs.

In a projectized organization, the functional executives should take a large part in developing and implementing these special controls.

STATUS OF SCHEDULED EVENTS

Schedule status review

Schedule status should be discussed at each project review meeting. The review should include the top two or three levels of project schedules and lower-level schedules where problems exist. Reasons for missing any schedule dates since the last review are examined. It is a good technique to highlight all the events scheduled for completion in the immediate future, say the next month.

Project functional managers should know about their own problems as they occur and not hear of them first at review meetings. Each attendee should come prepared with a knowledge of his own schedule status and problems. The purpose is not to acquaint managers of the schedule status of their departments but to get a common perspective on overall project status and the interaction of different departmental problems. The objective is to arrive at a common recognition of problems and prepare a common set of activities and schedules for their resolution.

The project control manager should have the responsibility for obtaining data and presenting a report on overall project status. Two modes of operation are suitable. In one, his people may collect all project status information. He supplies information about departmental status to each department head, who then is responsible for analyzing causes and impacts. The project control manager analyzes the overall status of the project based on the basic data and on judgments given him by the department heads. This method of operation is suitable for small to medium-size projects, and for those using the project management form of organization.

In the second mode, the functional departments collect the source data and supply them, with analysis, to the project control manager. From these inputs he prepares the overall project status report and assessment. This method is more suitable for large projects using the matrix form of organization.

Either method will work. It is important that the project control manager and the project functional managers avoid duplicating their efforts in examining and assessing schedule status. Such exertions are wasteful and lead to strained personal relationships. An exception may occur when the project manager has reason to doubt the quality of inputs from a department. He may elect to have the project control manager audit the status data of that department. Even then it should be done jointly with the project functional manager.

PERT-CPM

PERT and CPM are systems that describe the sequential relationship of project events in a network; the network reflects the project plans and is based on inputs from all departments of the project team. Schedule dates are assigned to all the events on the network. Lower-level supervisors or working task leaders are asked to give their estimates of how long it will take to deliver the work after all events necessary to start it have been completed. By comparing schedules with elapsed time estimates, a projection is made. A six-week negative slack means the event is estimated to be six weeks late. The estimates are repeated periodically. Changes to project plans are reflected in revised networks and new schedule dates.

The above is indeed PERT and CPM in a nutshell. Nothing would be accomplished here by describing the details of how these systems work, but there is a point in duscussing how the project manager and his team should use them. Many meetings on project management address little else.

The first question is whether or not to use PERT or CPM at all. Construction, study, software, and research-and-development project managers find it to be useful in the majority of cases. It is not as well suited to repetitive production, although it may be used to manage the production of the first article. Use of the technique should be considered in any complex project. There is no doubt that the output information would be of value, if the procedure is carried through properly. Two principal questions should be answered: "Can it be carried through properly in the organizational form and time frame of the project?" and "Are the results worth the cost?"

A key to successful operation is the attitude of the team members. If enough people in the line organizations are hostile to the idea, the system is not likely to provide useful outputs. Success depends on the subjective opinions of workers, not on measurable events. It also depends on sympathetic departmental managers. If a manager's attitude is, "We are going to meet the schedule and no one is going to suggest that we will not," then the grassroots estimate of the time required to do jobs will never be provided by his subordinates to the PERT computations.

Another factor influencing the decision is the organization's sophistication in using the tool. Although a number of PERT and CPM packages may be easy to install, there is still almost always a period of initial installation difficulty: the system should therefore be checked out on a pilot basis. Only in a crisis should it be introduced in the middle of an ongoing project. On introducing it to an organization, every effort must be made to sell the idea. Users must understand that it is their estimates that make the system work.

Another requirement for successful use of the system is a prompt updating of the networks and schedules to reflect the changes in project plans. If the system is putting out data based on old schedules, project personnel will quickly lose confidence in and respect for it. (Incidentally, this writer has been particularly curious about why PERT-CPM is so much more popular in the construction industry than in hardware development. A tentative conclusion, unverified, is that networks are much more stable in construction projects. There are only a few sequences in building a building. Schedules and time estimates change frequently, but the networks do not. In other hardware development projects sequences can be altered and events can be added or deleted at will. The problem of keeping the networks up to date is far more difficult and time-consuming than in construction projects.)

An issue that must be settled is how often to run the system to get new slack estimates. Weekly runs are appropriate in very fast changing projects. It is well to allow enough time between runs for the effect of replanning or of applying additional resources to the critical path to become visible to the time estimators. The interval may be increased as the project stabilizes. It is not necessary to exercise all the networks every time. Only those in trouble or with high activity need be run every period.

A useful way of looking at the output is to plot the three or four most critical path estimates against time. A ten-week critical path that has been increasing in value one week every two weeks is much more cause for concern than a twenty-week critical path that has been decreasing by two weeks with every passing week. An unchanging critical path value indicates that more vigorous corrective action is needed.

Criticisms of system outputs by operating managers should be respected. While they may reflect hostility to an unwanted system, they more often show a failure to make the system's procedures understandable. Perhaps the project team is not all working according to the same plan, or perhaps the event dependencies are wrongly portrayed. If PERT-CPM is to be used, it should be an active part of project communication.

Line of balance

Line of balance is a technique well suited for measuring the progress of a project that involves repetitive production or other repetitive activities. It tracks how many articles of a production lot should have achieved completion in each of a number of steps in the production process. It then compares that figure with the amount of articles actually completed. The results are presented in easy-to-understand bar-chart form. Several informative elaborations can be made to the basic line-of-balance system which can be operated without computer support. Line of balance is a well-documented technique.

Many organizations have sophisticated systems that produce and display the same information as line of balance. Use of the line-of-balance technique should be considered by a production project manager as a convenient way of visualizing the results of a myriad of Gantt charts.

Event completion count

A relatively unsophisticated but low-cost and highly effective control on project progress is the event completion count. It is a method for summarizing data from a number of Gantt charts along with schedules and status information.

When schedules are complete, the cumulative number of all project events is plotted against time. The events are not evaluated as to importance or sequential relationship. The resultant plot looks like a cumulative budget chart.

As the project progresses, the number of events actually completed is also plotted against time on the same chart. No distinction is made as to whether or not the events were completed according to schedule. Events completed early, on schedule, or behind schedule are counted and plotted together. The plot looks like an actual cumulative cost curve plotted against a budget.

The whole thing sounds oversimplified and unsuited to detecting really subtle schedule problems. So it is. Nevertheless, it is a useful indicator of general project progress. Its greatest applicability is for short, fast-moving projects involving a number of people. In such cases there is no point in trying to run a PERT network, for it cannot be kept up to date or recycled often enough to be useful. The data described can easily be updated daily, and the results are more obvious than the bewildering data of a host of Gantt charts. It is a good, easy technique for getting a quick look at project progress and schedule trends.

Policy on rescheduling late events

The project manager should establish a standard policy about when to reschedule events that have fallen or are likely to fall behind schedule. On any set of events that affect several parts of the project, the same policy should be followed for all departments concerned.

At one end of the spectrum, it is unwise to reschedule a whole series of related events because of one late intermediate event. That would lessen the incentive to correct problem areas and might permit related departments to relax their efforts unnecessarily. Some scheduling systems give higher priority to events that are behind schedule. As soon as events are rescheduled to a later date, they lose their higher priority. The same lack of priority that caused the problem in the first place may cause it to be repeated.

It may be wasteful to hold some departments to the original schedule if it is likely that the total effort will be delayed because of schedule problems in other departments. Some departments may be applying overtime or other special resources to get on schedule. That will involve them in wasteful waiting until the late department finally completes its work. This sort of situation particularly occurs in projects where several design technologies are involved or where several departments are producing hardware, data, or software for a test. Another consideration is that the on-time departments may be able to do a better job because they have been given the extra time made possible by the behind-schedule departments.

If any part of a project gets behind schedule, the scheduled date may be useless in day-to-day coordination of work. No department will know when its products or services will be needed. Under these circumstances, a recovery schedule is issued to provide for temporary actions to meet requirements. The end dates of the issued schedules remain as requirements, but the immediate dates are altered. This is an effective technique for dealing with spot problems. Its use should not be widespread, for the project will then find itself operating according to "two sets of books."

Whenever schedule changes are made, they should be issued through the standard system used for release of the individual schedules.

CONTROL OF PROJECT COSTS

Project and WBS costs

The fundamental tool in controlling project costs is the calculation of budgeted costs versus actual costs. This is done at the project level and down through selected levels of the WBS. Budgets are subdivided to as low a level of the WBS as adequate control demands. Budgets and actuals may be tracked to different levels in different parts of the WBS. Similarly, a given part of the WBS may be tracked to different levels during different phases of the project.

Actual costs are usually available on a weekly basis. In some project activities such as subcontracted work, actuals are available only on a monthly basis. The actual costs should be given to the various departments and to the project control manager as soon as practicable following the week that they are incurred. It is usual to present the costs as weekly increments. Cumulative costs are also presented, perhaps on a less frequent basis, say monthly.

Weekly costs are compared with weekly budgets and variances are analyzed to determine their cause. These costs are a good indicator of how the project is going right now. However, schedule variations of only a week or two may create major variances that are not good indicators of eventual overrun or underrun. A major change in the weekly expenditure is usually an indication of a problem, or at least a situation that needs examination and explanation.

Comparisons of budgetary cumulative costs to date give variances that are less sensitive to short-term problems. However, they give a better indication of the overall status of the project and the trends toward final expenditures.

In periodic reviews, the budgets and costs for each WBS task are examined down to the selected level. It is frequently a good idea to examine each functional division's cost performance for that WBS, for this may turn up problems not obvious on the surface.

For instance, the WBS cost variances for a console may be very small. However, closer examination of the functional cost performances may show that engineering is overrunning considerably while manufacturing and quality assurance are underrunning significantly. It is also ascertained that engineering is having trouble making some key circuitry work, so that they will probably remain in an overrun situation. The other two departments are underrunning because the engineering package is late and the hardware is late going into production. When they do start, they will probably exhaust their budgets. Thus an examination of total WBS costs indicated there were no problems, while a detailed look showed there was a problem and likelihood of an overrun.

As another example, the cost variance for a WBS box describing a test hydraulic module was small; however, examination of departmental costs for the WBS item disclosed that engineering had underrun and manufacturing and quality assurance were beginning to overrun. Investigation showed that engineering had considered the job to be an easy one and had merely modified an older module. In fact, the module is very hard to build, and this results in a high rejection rate. The obvious answer is for engineering to spend some hours improving the design to prevent future overruns in manufacturing and quality assurance. Quite possibly the question was first raised in a different discussion, but examination of the cost records threw further light on the subject.

On a government project, the WBS depth of cost accumulation may be determined by contractual requirements. If it is discretionary, the project manager has a decision to make. Costs at lower levels give earlier indications of problems and sometimes make the solution easier. But lower-level data cost more to obtain and, more importantly, cost more to analyze. Costly detailed analysis to uncover a few minor problems is inefficient.

Functional department costs

The project manager will want to review the cost performance of each functional department working on the project. This gives an indication of how each department is being managed. Overruns may be the first hint of development problems, or they may show that the functional division is assigning too many people to the project because of lack of work elsewhere.

Underruns, although superficially less painful, should be scrutinized just as carefully. They may indicate that some other department has failed to provide the input necessary to do the tasks as planned. They may have come about because the department is not following its work plan. Or they may show that the department is having trouble getting all the people it needs to do the job.

It is often easier to track fundamental budgets in terms of man-hours rather than dollars. The data may then be available earlier. Also, line managers and supervisors may refer more readily to man-hours, which they can control directly, than to costs, many of whose components are outside their control. Some organizations use man-months or analogous time units as a figure of measure.

Major subcontractor costs

The project manager will want to review the cost performance of major subcontractors, particularly on cost-type contracts. Their work should be integrated into the WBS, and the subcontract should include provisions for reporting costs against the WBS. Monthly reporting may be more practical than weekly reporting. However, when reporting costs, the same time frame should be used as applies to the rest of the project.

Estimates at completion

Periodically the project manager should require an estimate at completion (EAC). This is the sum of the costs incurred to date plus an estimate of all costs assumed to be required to complete the project. The manager of project control should take the lead in this effort.

A clear set of assumptions should be given to all departments. The work authorizations, schedules, and specifications already issued form the basis for the estimate. If the project is behind schedule, planning assumptions may be provided to indicate when certain key events will be completed.

The functional departments should prepare their estimates based on a thorough bottom-up analysis. Their EACs should be divided according to the WBS. The manager of project control should review the estimates with each department head. If there are disagreements or discrepancies, the project manager can intervene to resolve them. Then the departmental EACs can be assembled to form an EAC for WBS elements and the whole project. EACs should usually be prepared to the same WBS depth as applied to project budgetary control, although sometimes a higher-level summation may be appropriate in the interests of speed or in parts of a project where no difficulty is anticipated.

A quarterly frequency often works out well in many projects. Monthly changes can be made only for those WBS elements in which a major problem or change has occurred.

After the final EAC has been prepared, the project manager can decide whether or not to establish new budgets. These should not be issued too rapidly, for that would reduce the pressure to meet budgets. Although redistribution of funds among departments is sometimes appropriate, it should be done infrequently, for it is seen by the team as rewarding the inefficient at the expense of the competent. A good practice is to leave the existing budgets intact, but to show the results on the plot of cumulative budget versus cumulative actuals.

MEASUREMENT OF PRODUCT PERFORMANCE

The purpose of product performance measurement is to give a continuing estimate during the execution of a research or development program as to whether the performance goals of the project end product will be met. It is like making EACs to predict whether the project will overrun or underrun.

It could be assumed that this would happen as a matter of course. First of all, many development projects depend on a major test program toward the end of the project. The engineers, their management often included, regard this as their demonstration to the project team and the rest of the world that their product meets its requirements. Until then they regard the analytical results and the component test data as their own affair.

Second, engineers are always worried about fiscal personnel who meddle mindlessly in technical business; it is objectionable enough to be called to account for cost and schedule performance, but it is nearly intolerable to have to account for technical performance.

And finally, most engineers and scientists are dedicated professionals who are convinced that they can make their product work. Any interference in their endeavor is seen not as a helpful control but as an obstruction that will delay completion of their work and perhaps lessen the chances of achieving ultimate success. Even chief engineers have some difficulty in getting status information from technological departments.

However, experience has shown that the chances of achieving project success are much higher if intermediate estimates of performance and test results are examined on the same continuing basis as applies for other project controls. Such reviews are necessary for properly balancing the project manager's cost-schedule-performance tradeoffs. Also, the reviews may more readily spot the need to reallocate resources among technologies. If conducted intelligently, reviews consume very little time and require the generation of no data beyond those needed by the chief engineer and his technology chiefs to manage their work properly.

Establishing technical performance requirements

The fundamental performance requirements the project's end product must fulfill are contained in the systems specifications and in subordinate process, software, and hardware end-item specifications. To help in meeting these requirements, more precise characteristics are defined in detailed process specifications, program specifications, programs, and drawings.

Only the upper levels of performance parameters should be put under project control; those at a lower level should be tracked by the technical people responsible for design. This is analogous to budgeting, where the funds are subdivided through several levels down to individual accounts but only the top two or three levels are ordinarily tracked by the project management.

As a first step in deciding what parameters should be tracked, a performance tree should be constructed for each major system parameter down through several levels. For example, range of transmission may be an important consideration in designing a communications device. This depends on, among other things, the transmitted power and the antenna efficiency. These can be subdivided into other parameters.

As another example, the range of an aircraft depends on its empty weight, its fuel capacity, its propulsive efficiency, and its aerodynamic characteristics. The empty weight is the sum of structure, engines, equipment, and so on. All the values defined on the tree should be obtained from the specifications. The analytical relationship between successive levels of parameters should be identified. In the case of weight, this can be done simply, for each parameter is the sum of the next-lower-weight parameters. Most of the time the relationship is more complex and must be expressed by an equation, a set of equations, or even a computer program. No new technical work should be necessary, for the desired information should be readily available from the analytical work already done to validate the specification values in the first place.

After the parameter tree is constructed, the decision should be made as to how many parameters should be tracked. Although top-level parameters sometimes cannot be physically verified until well into the development program after months or years of work, a considerable confidence may be obtained much earlier by combining physical verification of lower-level parameters and then substituting these values in the equations describing how higher-level parameters depend on lower-level parameters.

There are many good reasons for tracking quite a number of parameters down through several levels in the technical definition:

- Technical problems will be detected earlier in the project.
- It is easy to assign responsibility for a specific performance to a particular technical organization; at higher-parameter levels, the responsibility is diffused.
- A lower-level specification value can be relaxed when higher levels of performance can be met with a less stringent requirement; this saves money.
- It is easier to relate technical progress to schedule performance on the project.
- It does not track anything that should not be tracked anyway in proper technical management.

On the other hand, there are good reasons for limiting the number of parameters that are tracked at the project level:

- Project attention is focused on major technical issues rather than diffused on secondary specialized design problems.
- It is easier to keep the technical assessments current.
- Costs are not wasted in excessive tracking.

The right number of parameters to be tracked varies in different phases of the project. Performance measurement should begin as a control device early in the project, in the planning phase before hardware or software design ever begins. Design at that time is largely parametric, and therefore only two or three levels need to be tracked.

Later, when detailed design begins, it is desirable to increase the tracked parameters almost by an order of magnitude, pushing down a level or two in the parameter tree. Then, as hardware becomes available for testing, tracking of lower levels can be discontinued since actual test measurements can be made at intermediate levels, thus eliminating the usefulness of subordinate measurements. Finally, production measurement should be based on a cost-effective inspection plan. Control of product performance should follow the best practice for the product or in the industry.

Selection of technical parameters is not as inappropriate for study projects as it might at first appear. Findings may be evaluated on the number of data points examined, the correlation coefficients between causes and effects, the variance of the data around the expected value, and a probabilistic calculation of the correctness of the results. Study teams, and particularly their individual members, usually do not like to subject themselves to this sort of analysis, but it is healthy for them if it is not carried to unrealistic extremes.

When the product performance parameters to be placed under control are determined, the information should be released through a formal direction system. When parameters are added to or deleted from project control, the changes should be released through the same system.

As a rough guide to the size of the effort, ten parameters are usually worth tracking in any technically oriented project. The number can go as high as two hundred during the development of a complicated product with several subsystems.

Tracking the verification of technical performance

After the parameters to be tracked have been selected, the plans for verifying each parameter should be obtained from the development plan, from the test plan, or directly from the technical group responsible for that parameter's success. As development proceeds from initial analysis to test of a production article, confidence that it will meet the requirements either increases or decreases. As an example, an electronic black box might pass through the following stages of verification:

Parametric analysis	January 1976
Detailed circuit analysis	April 1976
Breadboard of key circuit	June 1976
Brassboard performance test	November 1976
Components environmental tests	February 1977
Prototype performance test	March 1977
Prototype environmental test	June 1977
First production unit test	December 1977

Nothing is to be learned from the dates selected; they merely serve as steps along a hypothetical progression of increasing confidence in product performance.

The verification dates should be assembled along with the specification values and their tolerances. If a contract value for the tolerance differs from the internal specification, this should be shown too. It is not unusual to issue internal specifications that are tighter than the contract value in order to leave a margin for minor nonconformances that will not violate the contract.

An 8-1/2 × 11 inch chart should be constructed to keep track of performance estimates and verification. If necessary, it should be made into a transparency for projection in the project control room. The vertical scale should show the parameter being measured and the horizontal scale should show the calendar time. The specification and contract values should be shown as horizontal lines. A symbol should be shown for each verification milestone at the value that is expected to be measured there; for example, a calculated weight of 37.4 pounds at the weighing of the first prototype article in June 1977.

Figure 4. Performance weight.

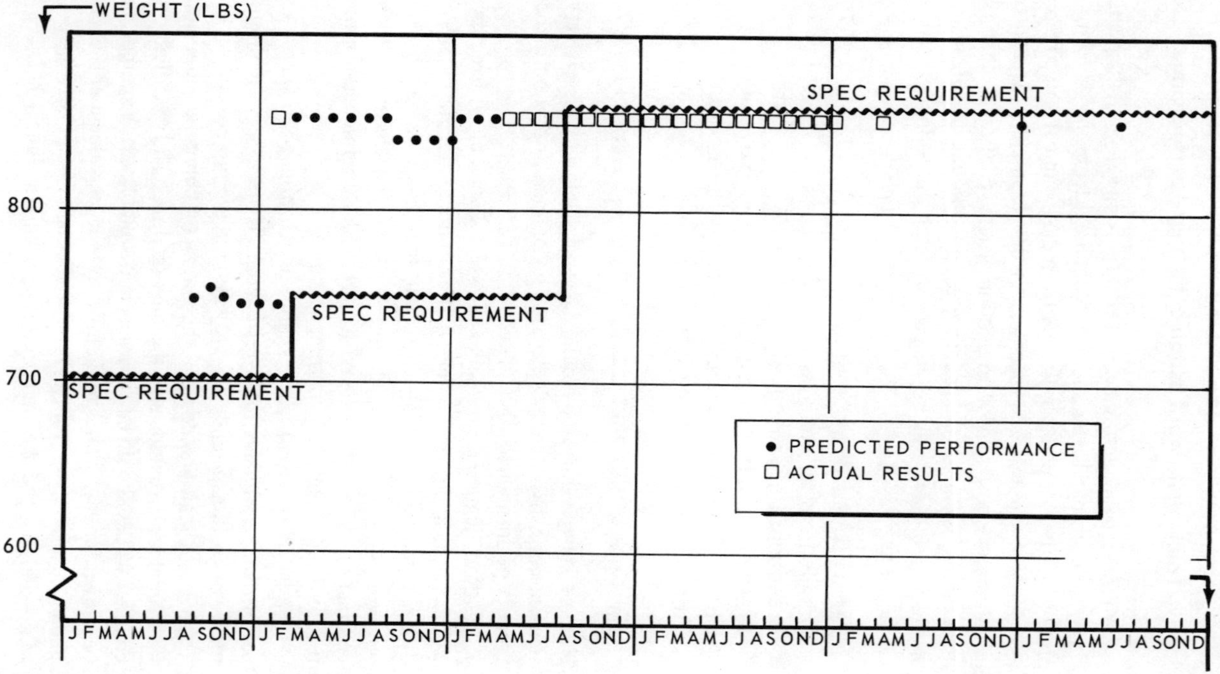

Then, each month, the best performance estimate should be plotted on the chart. If actual test values are obtained, they should be plotted along with revised estimates. After the initial preparation of the chart, the cost of keeping it up to date is negligible. A typical format is shown in Figure 4.

Review and evaluation of actual results

The estimates of technical performance should be reviewed periodically. The project manager, the chief engineer, and the chief systems engineer should conduct the review. The technical estimates should be made by the lowest technical group directly responsible for the design with the support of any intervening levels of technical management.

It is important that the designers be given the responsibility for presenting the estimate so that they may feel they are a part of the performance review process. If estimates are made by people outside the design team, the designers will regard the process as an extraneous intervention in their professional work.

The estimates should be supported by the results of analysis and testing. It is proper for the project manager and his review team to challenge the estimates. They may even change them, but this should be done only in unusual cases.

In large research or development projects, many technical performance estimates change every few months rather than monthly. A useful procedure may call for a monthly review of only the parameters that have changed. Then every three months a review may be made of all parameters.

Adjustments to plans and performance parameters

The technical review process described above should not be made a part of the normal project review meetings. Most of the project team cannot make a useful contribution to the assessment of technical performance. However, when certain parameters depart from performance specifications or show a trend that suggests they will do so, the matter can be brought into the total project review process to determine the effect on costs and schedules and to develop a plan for corrective action.

If it is decided that a significant change in project activities is required, appropriate changes should be directed by changes in work authorizations. Budgets and schedules should be revised to meet the revised work plan.

Careful examination and adjustment of internally prescribed specification values can save money for the project. Consider a component that has a contractually specified upper weight limit. The technical performance review indicates that its weight is remaining within specifications. However, a review of the three assemblies that make up the component shows that one is much lighter than the specified value and another is heavier. A significant amount of money would be required to redesign the overweight component to meet its specification.

A logical solution is to increase the specified weight of the heavier component so that no redesign is necessary. But it is also necessary to reduce the specified weight for the underweight component so that its designers will not at a future time believe they have a weight margin available to them for possible improvements.

Another type of change can be made when a component gives much better performance than is required. A change of design can often result in producing a cheaper article with relaxed tolerances that will meet the true needs of the end product perfectly well.

It can be seen that product performance measurement comprises an important feedback loop in the systems engineering process.

A major guideline for change control

When a change in the project plans is proposed, the change control board should ask how that would affect the capability of the end product to meet contractual specifications. The ramifications of changes made in lower levels of hardware are more readily evaluated by tracing their effects up through the technical performance tree.

Product performance measurement can also be a most valuable tool in preventing unnecessary design changes. Engineers are constantly, and properly, looking for better technical solutions to problems. Particularly after an initial design for a prototype is released, second thoughts appear on a design solution apparently better but not really needed to meet product performance. When such a change is presented to the change control board, an analysis of its impact on the upper-level performance parameters may be required, using the product performance analytical framework.

Often it turns out that the proposed change is "better" at the lower levels of the end product but creates no real improvement in the important top-level performance parameters. Thus a means is provided for rejecting unneeded changes.

On the other side of the coin, design change may obviously make the end product more suitable for its intended use even though it does not affect any of the top-level performance parameters. This suggests that the top-level specifications are incomplete or inadequate. Objective analysis of such changes may lead to additions to or changes in specifications.

EARNED VALUE MEASUREMENTS

The concepts of earned value are discussed at length in the industrial engineering literature under that name and several others, and for that reason they will be covered here only briefly. The basic ideas are simple. At the completion of a package of work it is easy to determine whether the budget for doing it was overrun, underrun, or met exactly. But when half the money in the budget for the task is spent, is the job really half done? What is the best forecast of whether it is apt to finish over or under the budget?

The conventional approach subdivides the task into a number of subtasks, and the portion of the task budget that should be spent on each subtask is estimated. For example, a task of 1,000 hours may be subdivided as shown at the top of the next page.

When task A is completed, credit is allowed for 100 hours. When tasks A, B, and C are completed, credit for 600 hours is allowed. If 500 hours actually have been spent, then the task is underrunning. Performance in that case is sometimes estimated at $(600/500) \times 100$, or 120 percent. If 750 hours actually have been spent, then performance is $(600/750) \times 100$, or 80 percent, and an overrun is occurring. This does not give a strong statistical inference that the ultimate re-

Subtask	Hours
A	100
B	300
C	200
D	250
E	150
Total task	1,000 hours

sults are going to turn out at the same percentage, but it does give a fairly good idea of whether the ultimate actual expenditure will be over or under the budget.

If materials and other cost-generating items are considered, similar results may be obtained if all values are converted to cost dollars. A slight variation of the preceding calculations gives credits for milestone dates rather than for completions of subtasks. Thus, when the first milestone is passed, 100 hours are credited; when the second is passed, 200 hours are credited; and so forth. In practice it is almost the same thing.

When a large job is broken into many small tasks, it may not be worth the effort to break each of the small tasks into subtasks and estimate their values. A simplified approach assigns an arbitrary percentage of the value when the task is started and the rest when it is completed. If the greater percentage of effort is expended near the end of the task, a higher value is credited at its completion than at its start, and vice versa. Say a task requires 200 hours and most of the effort is expended soon after it is started. A ratio of 70 percent to 30 percent is estimated as appropriate. When the task is started, credit for 140 hours is given. When it is finished, 60 hours is earned.

Obviously this gives a very crude estimate about the status of any given task. However, when the job consists of many tasks, the summation of the hours earned by this method gives an acceptable estimate. An even simpler method arbitrarily assigns 50 percent of the value to the start of the task and 50 percent to the completion. This eliminates the work of estimating how the effort is to be divided without losing very much accuracy.

Some tasks are concerned with maintaining a capability to do a certain class of work. The exact nature of the tasks or their order of execution is almost impossible to estimate, but the total effort can be determined fairly well by past statistics. Under this scheme, called "level of effort," credit for work is given as hours of work are expended. For instance, it may be estimated that two people will be required to do a job for a total of 4,000 hours a year. After six months only 1,800 hours have been expended; thus 1,800 hours will have been earned. The theory is that half of the work (2,000 hours) has not been done and therefore a backlog of 200 hours remains to be done in addition to the 2,000 for the next six months.

A task related to a larger task may be given credit for earned value at the same percentage rate as the larger task. This is an "allocated value" scheme. For example, a manufacturing task may be estimated as requiring 2,000 hours to complete. Inspection, whose completion is very closely dependent on manufacturing completion, is estimated as requiring 400 hours. Thus when credit of 600 hours, or 30 percent of the manufacturing task, is earned, the credit for 30 percent of the 400 hours, or 120 hours, is earned by inspection.

"Tasks" can be set up to describe the consumption of material. As material is utilized in production, credit can be given for its use.

Developing a project earned value baseline

To develop a project baseline, the work authorized in the WBS is further subdivided into tasks. The value of each task is estimated along with its start and completion dates. These dates should be consistent with project schedules. A method for assigning earned value is determined for each task, and an analysis is made to determine how much value should be earned each week. For example, if during one week a 50 percent to 50 percent task of 600 hours is started and a 40 percent to 60 percent task of 1,000 hours is completed, then 300 + 600 = 900 hours should be earned that week. This can be added to the value expected to be earned at the end of the previous week to find the new cumulative value.

The questions may be asked, "How long should a task last?" and "What is the maximum number of hours or dollars that should be permitted in a task?" The answers depend on the size of the project and the amount of money available for time controls. It may be said that one to three months is a good median value for task duration.

The hours can be converted to dollars to give a cumulative cost curve. Ordinarily this will be identical with the cumulative budget curve, for presumably budgets are issued to cover the cost of work at the rate that is planned for its performance. It may be necessary to make some arbitrary force-fitting of task values, for budgets are not always derived by going as low as tasks.

There may be reasons for temporarily letting planned earned value depart from budgetary values, thereby making a more flexible system. The reasons for such variances must be understood and steps must be taken to bring them ultimately back into synchronization.

A cumulative planned earned value curve can be developed for each level of the WBS that is under project budgetary control. The values can be summed to get the project value. It is also possible to use the technique only on selected WBS elements.

At the end of each week the amount of value earned that week can be summed for each WBS element. A curve can be made of actual earned value versus time. It can be compared with the plot of planned earned value versus time.

In its criteria for cost schedule control systems, DOD refers to planned earned value as budgeted cost of work scheduled (BCWS) and actual earned value as budgeted cost of work performed (BCWP).

Variance analysis

When an earned value system is used, periodic data will be available for controls. Four parameters can be used in the comparison:

Cumulative budget
Cumulative planned earned value
Cumulative actual expenditures
Cumulative actual earned value

For brevity, these will be referred to respectively as budget, planned EV, actuals, and actual EV. It should also be noted that in the majority of earned value systems, cumulative budget is always equal to cumulative planned earned value. This assumption is used in the analysis that follows.

When actuals are greater than budget, there is a current overrun. When they are less, there is an underrun. This variance primarily tracks whether the money is being spent faster or slower than planned. A current overrun may indicate that there will be an eventual overrun, but not necessarily, for the work may be getting done faster than planned. Conversely with underruns.

When actuals are greater than actual EV, it is a sign that tasks are costing more than planned. When they are less, the work is costing less. These conditions suggest respectively that there will be an eventual overrun or underrun.

When actual EV is less than planned EV, it is a sign that the work is behind schedule. When it is greater, the work is ahead. The amount of the variance gives an indication of how much will have to be spent to get back on schedule. (Without other data, this does not necessarily indicate an overrun. It merely shows a behind-schedule condition.)

It will be seen that the last two variances give more insight into what is happening than the first variance gives by itself. This explains the popularity in some circles of earned value systems.

Six possible cases can occur, depending on the relative magnitude of the parameters. These will be discussed using the following hypothetical values, given in no particular order:

Case	Budget and Planned EV	Actuals	Actual EV
I	1,000	800	600
II	1,000	600	800
III	1,000	1,200	800
IV	1,000	800	1,200
V	1,000	1,400	1,200
VI	1,000	1,200	1,400

Case I: There is a current underrun (actuals are less than budget), but things are not really rosy. Since the work is being done at less than 100 percent performance (actuals are greater than actual EV), an eventual overrun can be expected. The schedule situation is even worse (actual EV is much less than planned EV). The behind-schedule position obscures the poor performance. This is one of the worst cases, spelling trouble ahead.

Case II: There is a present large underrun (actuals are much less than budget), but some of the news is good and some is bad. The work is being done efficiently, with a predicted eventual underrun (actuals are less than actual EV). However, the work is behind schedule (actual EV is less than planned EV).

Case III: There is a current overrun (actuals are greater than budget). But things will probably get worse, with a larger overrun in the future, for the work is being done very inefficiently (actuals are much greater than actual EV). The work is behind schedule, too (actual EV is less than planned EV). This situation is very bad; disaster looms ahead!

Case IV: There is a current underrun (actuals are less than budget). The work is being done very efficiently (actuals are much less than actual EV). The work is also ahead of schedule (actual EV is greater than planned EV). Things should look even better in the future. This is a project manager's delight!

Case V: There is a large current underrun (actuals are much larger than budget). The work is being done inefficiently, and the project will probably have an eventual overrun (actuals are greater than actual EV). However, things are not quite as bad as they seem: the work is being done ahead of schedule (actual EV is greater than planned EV) and this makes the current overrun look worse than it probably will be.

Case VI: There is a current overrun (actuals are greater than budget), but things are really going very well. The work is being done efficiently (actuals are less than actual EV), which predicts an eventual underrun. The work is well ahead of schedule (actual EV much greater than planned EV) and is the real cause for the current overrun, to the point of obscuring the efficient work performance. This is a happy situation for the project manager, probably the second best he can hope for.

There are actually six other cases when the figures for each of the three pairs of variables are equal and the figure for the remaining variable is either higher or lower, and a seventh case when all figures are equal. These cases will not be discussed here since they occur less often, and are easily analyzed following the logic used above.

An important caution: The conclusions derived here are only as good as the data in the earned value system. Also, the predictions about outcome are the best available but apply only to the extent that the trends continue and no one takes corrective action. The purpose of these controls is to find out early about incipient trouble so that something can be done about it.

Suitability of earned value concepts for project management

The usefulness of earned value measurements in project management is controversial. The most enthusiastic managers regard it as the best way to prevent surprises and as a most workable tool. Others consider the information helpful in managing the project but not worth the cost of obtaining it. Still others say the information becomes available too late or there are better ways to obtain it. The most critical managers view it is a complete waste of time.

To compete successfully on most major DOD programs, a contractor must offer among other systems a BCWS/BCWP system. There are few signs that the government will relax this requirement in the near future.

If an organization has an earned value system built into its existing engineering and manufacturing systems, it will be relatively easy to apply the system to project management. If it has no such system, its introduction may be difficult.

If the system is selectively applied, perhaps in terms of man-hours rather than costs, it will be much easier to install it and gain acceptance of it. Availability of good computer programs will make its use easier.

For projects other than major DOD developments, whether or not to use the system is a decision for the project manager. He must make it on the basis of estimated costs, the organizational attitude and capabilities, and the needs of his particular project. It is important to note that the technique may be applied selectively to appropriate parts of the WBS rather than to all project tasks. This eliminates many of the criticisms described above.

COMPUTER-BASED SYSTEMS FOR PROJECT CONTROL

When computer systems are being considered or designed for project systems, the first step should be an examination of existing systems. Consideration should be given to modifying them to meet project requirements. When this is not possible, the next step is to look for commercially available software packages that will do the job. Their cost should be compared with the cost of developing new systems for project use.

When it is not possible to modify existing systems and new ones are required, every effort should be made to have the new systems operate on data driven from the existing systems rather than on data collected independently. It is a disadvantage of procured systems that they are often somewhat more difficult to interface with existing systems.

Computer systems for project management should be used to produce the necessary data at minimum cost, not to produce more data sliced more ways. In specifying a system, it is tempting for the project manager to ask for reports slicing the data every possible way that he might need them. A better solution is to specify a system with a versatile report generator that can generate the special kind of report that may be needed to cope with a particular problem at a particular time.

Large projects generate a great deal of paper even when the output is controlled. Use of computer-output microfilm packaged in a microfiche format can save money on paper, handling, and storage costs. In addition, the convenience and transportability of microfiche speeds up data transmission.

Work authorization system

Keeping track of the baseline of authorized work can be a formidable task on a large project. A computer program can be used to relate the issued work authorization to the WBS and to maintain the revision status of all work authorizations. Even a very limited computer capability for listing and sorting can be a big help in keeping this information straight.

A problem in major development contracts involves keeping track of all the changes to the contract. On-line systems exist to track the changes through their cycle involving rough order-of-magnitude estimate, firm quote, and negotiated and internally budgeted and authorized work.

Schedule-oriented systems

Many organizations use automation in their scheduling systems. The principal change required to accommodate project management is usually the capability to provide an identifier indicating what WBS boxes are associated with particular schedules. Sometimes cross-referencing of the cost accounts or shop orders can accomplish this.

If PERT is used, it may be necessary to provide an identifier for schedule dates that become events on the PERT networks. This requires initial coordination between operating schedules and PERT schedules, for it is confusing and inefficient to have two sets of dates. Ideally, schedule dates should be driven into the PERT system directly from the schedules system.

It is usually wise to buy a PERT or CPM system that is available on the market rather than develop one's own. One of the most time-consuming and costly aspects of PERT and CPM was the actual drafting of the networks. Now there are software packages that in conjunction with the high-speed printers accomplish the job much more quickly and economically.

Cost-oriented systems

The maximum use possible should be made of existing accounting systems. Many of these have no capability for accepting budgetary data. Packages have been developed to enter budgetary data into the system efficiently either in the batch or in the on-line mode. Capabilities exist to describe a wide number of budgetary load shapes with a minimum amount of effort. It is desirable to have the system compute variances between budgeted values and actuals.

One major change may involve restructuring accounts to provide compatibility with a WBS. Tables can be used to provide information about the cost accounts or their equivalent that comprise WBS elements. It should also be possible to extract budgets and actuals reports from the system for WBS elements rather than for departments. As noted above, a flexible report generator capability is a big help in project fiscal systems.

Many outputs of fiscal systems wind up as graphs. A great deal of money may be saved by using computer graphics, sometimes in conjunction with microfilm to save manual plotting work. Software packages are available.

Projectwide earned value systems require so much data processing that a computer-based system is a necessity for a project of any size. Data from the cost and schedule systems should be used to the maximum extent.

Technically oriented systems

Of course, computers are used extensively in research, design, development, and study work. The application of project management should have no effect on this major computer usage other than perhaps to give more visibility to the costs incurred.

For hardware projects, computer-based systems can be of considerable help in controlling the initial release of and subsequent changes to the engineering configuration and in generating parts lists. They can also be used in manufacturing and quality assurance to verify that the product built and inspected matches the requirements of the drawings. Basically they are oriented to the product itself and not to program management in general. Systems for controlling logistics support are also important to the success of some projects. Software that does this effectively is now on the market.

The computer can be of help in developing information systems. Complicated data bases may be stored, controlled, and retrieved in various combinations of data elements.

There has been very little successful direct coupling between scientific programs and project management. Attempts have been made to combine costs, schedules, and technical performance in a three-dimensional set of parameters to predict the effects of various project actions. However, the job seems too big to do on a generalized basis going to a low level. Of course, this does not preclude using the computer to store technical performance data, which can be used with cost and schedule data from other computer-based systems to arrive at judgments of cost-schedule-performance status of the project.

Computer support is highly effective in systems and project analysis. Parametric cost methods, statistical analysis, risk analysis, and simulation are valuable aids to development. They are best carried out at a high level rather than on a detailed level.

Administrative systems

A number of general administrative tasks call for computer support if it exists in the organization, or can profitably be developed or procured. Control of documents lends itself to computer-based control. Particularly when documents are classified, or extensive document deliveries are involved, savings are possible. Correspondence control is a related case. Action items and their status can be stored, sorted, and retrieved to simplify control of project action.

Where projects operate at remote locations, teleprocessing systems can greatly speed up the transmission of data between the home plant and the field. Costs are often saved in addition.

THE PROJECT CONTROL ROOM

All projects, regardless of size, can benefit from a project control room. This is a room assigned to the exclusive use of the project or, as a minimum, assigned to the team project on a priority basis with exclusive control over the data displays in it. It should be a conference room suitable for project review meetings, project working sessions, and display of project data. The principal value of the room is administrative convenience for the management and key personnel of the project. Many projects refer to this as a chart room, or some other similar name, but the idea is the same. "Control room" has the advantage of connoting dynamic action as well as the static display of data.

The project control room can also be used effectively in building esprit de corps and promoting communications on the project. When team members are accustomed to meeting regularly and frequently in the same place, their sense of being in familiar surroundings contributes to easier communication. Team members who wish to have a meeting but hesitate to do so because of reticence about creating too large an issue over something routine, or because of mere administrative inconveniences, will be more likely to use meetings as a useful communications device if the project control room is an available and accepted place for such discussions.

In the initial stages of a project, particularly one organized on a matrix basis, the control room can be used to create a sense of project identity and to heighten the feeling of belonging to a new team. It is also a useful symbol of the project, visible to higher management and to the customer. As the project progresses, the control room is likely to be the spot where crises are confronted by the team and successes are announced and celebrated. This can contribute to the feeling of project teamwork.

Use of a control room may seem a fairly mundane subject, but it is worth examining in some detail. When improperly used, a control room can be a futile exercise, wasting project money and even exposing the project to the ridicule of the rest of the organization. When properly used, it is a highly efficient tool for promoting good communications in the project.

Physical design of a project control room

A project control room is basically a conference room with provisions for projecting and displaying data. It should be a functional and comfortable room, but it should not be showy or ostentatious.

The room itself should accommodate a project review meeting. In most climates, this implies adequate air conditioning. The room should have adequate insulation to prevent any outside noise from disrupting a conference. It should have a centrally located conference table large enough to seat the key managers of the project team and a few senior visitors—a seating capacity of one to two dozen people.

The chairs need not be elegant, but they should be comfortable, for project meetings on occasion will last half a day or more. It is convenient to have an additional row of chairs along each side of the conference room. If the project is a large one, additional rows of seats may be provided at the end of the room facing the projection screen. The room should not take on the look of an auditorium, with resulting impediments to conversation. A large room can always be obtained temporarily, if required. If the size of the project review meetings requires a hall, this is a symptom that the meetings are too large anyway.

The room should be secure enough that project data can be left in it unattended. Normally, it is enough to provide a lock on the door with keys available to senior team members. Additional security, if required, can be provided by an electronic or mechanical combination lock. If new documents or sets of transparencies of a more sensitive nature are required frequently, a locked file for their storage can be provided.

It is often convenient to install some communications devices in the room. A speaker attached to a telephone may be useful for conference calls. The telephone number should be restricted, or other means provided, to prevent incoming calls from disrupting project meetings. If the project uses a computer-based management information system with teleprocessing capabilities, a terminal for inquiry into the system can be very useful. Where communications with remote locations are a major factor, it is better to have a communications center near the project control room rather than incorporated in the room itself.

Since the control room is primarily for project meetings, means should be immediately available for projecting data in whatever physical form is commonly used in the organization. This implies assigning projection equipment to the room to avoid constant delays. The convenience of producing overhead projection transparencies on an immediate basis from printed copy makes their use very attractive. Many organizations have a ready capability for producing 35-mm slides, which are attractive because of their portability.

Some projects frequently use motion-picture clips, so this projection capability is required. The old standby, the blackboard, may be conveniently placed at one end of the room, with a projection screen that can be pulled down over it on demand. At one side one can have a lectern, and at the other a stand for 3 ft × 4 ft charts.

In addition to its function as a meeting place for reviews, the project control room should be a place for displaying project data, either for convenient quick inspection by key team members or for small informal working sessions. The side and back walls of the room are ideal for this purpose. It is advisable to cover one or more walls with corkboard on which to pin charts and other graphic material such as schedules and event networks. Magnetic boards with readily movable symbols can be mounted on the walls as a rapid means of keeping schedules and status up to date. A number of useful products of this type are on the market.

One ingenious scheme provides a means both for storage and for visual inspection of material on overhead projection transparencies. Fluorescent lights are mounted against a wall covered with translucent plastic. In front of this is a simple framework with horizontal holders spaced the width of an overhead projection transparency. The transparencies mounted in their holders are then put on the racks. When the fluorescent lights behind them are turned on, the transparencies make as effective and readable a display as printed paper mounted on the wall. In addition, whenever the data on it are required in a meeting or a working session, any desired transparency can be flipped out of its wall rack for immediate projection. The cost of such an installation is surprisingly low.

There are many other ingenious, low-cost ways of displaying data, for example, hanging charts from strings as from a clothesline. Whatever is convenient and useful is a good idea. Ingenuity should be encouraged in finding new low-cost ways to display information.

The project control room should have a place for storing project data that are frequently referred to during project meetings. It may also be helpful to provide a limited temporary storage space to each key member of the team; this space can be used as a mail distribution center for project material. If it exists within the organization, a microfilm capability is a useful means of storing data. A microfiche projector and a microfiche file take up little space and can provide a very convenient data storage capability.

For a large project that involves considerable activity in the project control room, it may be desirable to have a small adjacent room that doubles as a communications center, phone-answering station, place for data storage, workroom for preparation of graphic data, and projection support room. However, these supporting activities should clearly be subordinate to the main function of the project control room and should in no way interfere with it.

Data displays in a project control room

The needs of project management should determine the data displayed in a project control room. If graphic material is not used frequently by the team members, either in project review meetings or in working sessions, there is no point of going to the trouble and expense of posting it.

The project work breakdown structure is a good candidate for display on the project control room walls. It is fundamental to the planning and organization of the project and to scheduling and cost collection, and so is a useful reference document for most project discussions. The relatively extended horizontal dimensions of its display make it more suitable for a chart form than for a slide or overhead projection transparency.

The portrayal of the master project schedule status is another likely candidate for wall display. This can be a Gantt chart, a time-phased event network, or a line-of-balance chart—whatever is the most useful and best understood way of portraying project status.

A chart showing the overall fiscal status of the project is useful. It can display the typical comparison between budgets and actuals for rates of expenditures and cumulative values. The aforementioned displays are usually fairly sizable, and are preferably visible, at least in broad outline form, throughout the control room. However, there is no requirement for elaborate and expensive artwork. A project schedule and status chart done freehand on a roll of wrapping paper with felt-point pens of different colors can be a very effective display.

In addition to these larger displays, smaller displays, 8-1/2 × 11 inch or larger, may be put on part of the wall space. As noted above, it is easy to design a wall that will hold transparencies for inspection or immediate projection when desired; these are intended for reapy individual reference by members of the project team or for reference during working sessions.

The possible subjects for display vary widely from project to project, and indeed from time to time within a project's life cycle. Whatever is useful should be displayed. Among the subjects that can be covered are detailed schedules, detailed budget cost charts, graphic materials used in the last project review, list of delinquent items, action item assignments, technical performance of the project, organization charts, status assessment charts, critical path events, meeting schedules, travel schedules, lists of visitors, parts shortages, recent project events, test results, and relevant news items.

It is extremely important that data in the project control room be both current and accurate. Nothing works against the effectiveness of a data display more than misleading information. If a choice has to be made between slight degradation in currency or slight degradation in accuracy, it is usually better to opt for higher quality in currency. One of the greatest wastes in project management is perfect data too late to be helpful. However, there is really no need to accept compromise on either count. A sensible policy that encourages freehand marking up of graphic displays to reflect recent changes and the current situation will make it easy to have data that are accurate and up to date at all times.

About the only graphic standard that should be imposed on data displayed in the project control room is that it be legible. In the case of a few displays, sophisticated visual techniques may be appropriate and justifiable. For most displays, however, freehand or typewritten material highlighted by the imaginative use of colored felt-point pens is more than adequate, and is probably a better communications device than an elaborate professional presentation. A great deal of money can be spent and much time lost by unnecessary use of fancy graphic techniques.

Administration of the project control room

As in most project activities, the role the project manager plays is important in achieving a successful project control room. If he takes a keen interest in the room, so will the project team. If he uses the data in the room, the team members will be motivated to keep them accurate. If he holds significant meetings there, so will other managers on the project team. On the other hand, if he has his own set of data displays and shows up in the room only for a periodic project review, then the control room will be a much less useful project tool. The project manager must be responsible for the success of the project control room.

In a small-size project, the project manager can supervise the control room directly, with assistance from his secretary or a clerical employee. However, in a medium- to large-size project, it may be appropriate to assign the responsibility to one of the other managers on the team or to an administrative assistant. But under no circumstance should the project manager create the position of administrative assistant simply because he has a project control room.

It is common to assign the responsibility to the manager of project control. Since he has the responsibility for preparing unified costs, schedules, and related status data, he normally generates much of the material displayed. He is motivated to communicate these subjects effectively throughout the project, and so is naturally interested in an efficiently functioning control room. The control room must be operated for the equal benefit of the whole project team, not for the optimum convenience of the operating department.

It is easy to let a small bureaucracy grow up around administration of the project control room. As a general rule the room should be operated by project people who do this as a relatively small part of their total job. Employees obsessively dedicated to administering the room tend to raise graphic standards, thereby creating delays and unnecessary costs in data display. Charts are displayed for their esthetic value instead of their usefulness. Bureaucratic procedures discourage use of the room as a working facility. In some projects, upper management dissatisfaction with the whole concept of control rooms has stemmed from unnecessary expenditures on a large supporting staff.

A single person, normally a secretary, should maintain the schedule for use of the project control room. This should be done in accordance with a set of priorities laid down by the project manager. Conflicts or special cases regarding use of the room should be referred upward immediately to the manager in charge or the project manager.

It is helpful to establish a standard weekly schedule for periodic meetings and for updating material in the room; then other uses can be planned for the remaining available periods. Tight control should be enforced in ending meetings on schedule. Failure of team members to use the project control room may be symptomatic of arbitrary or unfair scheduling practices.

While the project control room does not need elegant appointments, it should be kept clean and orderly. Rules should be established to ensure that a group finishing a meeting leaves the premises in good order for the next group using it.

The manager in charge of the project control room must be assigned the responsibility for the overall timeliness and accuracy of the data displayed in it. It should be possible for him to delegate responsibility for certain displays to other managers on the team. For instance, the chief engineer might be responsible for data on project specifications and test results, the marketing manager for visit schedules, and the production manager for shortage data. Maintaining the accuracy and relevance of each piece of data should be the responsibility of a single individual.

Project team members should not be able willy-nilly to post data in the room. Standard data displays should be updated only by the individual concerned, and new data entered only with the approval of the person in charge of the room. However, in the interests of communication, it is appropriate to provide an area where material can be posted at the discretion of any team member.

At the beginning of the project, a short informal plan for the project control room should be approved by the project manager, after active participation by all key managers on the project team. As the project progresses, the data displays and the use of the room should be evaluated briefly, say every three months, to get rid of useless data bins and to make the room a more convenient working place for the whole team.

Communications efficiency from the project control room

The whole point of a project control room is to improve project communications. One way this is achieved is by timeliness in the distribution of data. If material in the control room is updated on a daily basis, then all members of the team can have immediate access to project data, thereby avoiding the inevitable delays in the mail distribution system or in document routing. This quality of constantly being able to display the latest nformation first is a great selling point for constructive use of the project control room.

If data are conveniently accessible in the project control room, a great deal of paper proliferation can be avoided in managing the project. First- and second-line supervisors as well as higher-level managers collect a great deal of status information and other reports, primarily for defensive purposes. If they are convinced that the material is there in the project control room when required, they can be dissuaded from producing much of the paper they might otherwise want to produce. Some projects have even gone so far as to eliminate all status reports except those displayed in the control room.

The concept of using standard data as a means of making better decisions has been discussed earlier. A key part of making this approach work is agreeing on what are "standard" data, and then providing ready access to them when required. A project control room can be a big help here. The rule can be established that the data in the control room are the standard data; then diligent efforts must be expended to keep them so and to make it convenient for all members of the project team to get them as needed. Thus the project control room makes the concept of standard project data workable and efficient.

PROJECT REVIEW MEETINGS

Responsibilities for the meetings

The project manager is responsible for the overall success of project review meetings, for they form one of his principal management tools. As leader of the project team, he is the chairman of each individual meeting and responsible for its success. He should always attend the meetings unless he is out of the area.

The project manager's position as chairman does not mean that he must lead all the discussions or ensure that all arrangements are made for a constructive session. It is better that he assume the role of the leader who is being briefed on project status. When facts are in dispute, or during a problem-solving discussion, he may assume the active leadership role, but he should not do so throughout the meeting. That would stifle communication. Best results are achieved when each project team member assumes leadership of the meeting while he is making a presentation of his views.

The manager of project control (or some organizational equivalent) should arrange the meetings and ensure that the right data are presented. Obviously he will not make all the presentations. He should be given the authority to ask any manager on the project team to discuss any particular subject. However, he should have control only over the general subject matter, not over what the manager says about it. He should arrange facilities, issue agendas as required, ensure that necessary supporting information is available, keep a brief record of the meeting, record decisions and action items, and generally feel responsible for the successful administrative conduct of the meeting.

Each manager and staff member reporting to the project manager should attend the project review meetings. They should attend on a regular basis and should miss sessions only when they are out of town. They should be obligated to do their homework, which consists in responding to action items from previous meetings, reviewing cost and schedule data distributed before the meeting, and preparing an ad hoc (unwritten) position on all project issues and the problems affecting them. They should also be prepared to give brief reports on any significant or interesting events that have occurred in their activities.

Other team members may attend at the discretion of the project manager. He may delegate this decision to his managers for meetings on selected topics.

Administering the meetings

The project review meetings should be held in the project control room. That is the place where project data are most readily available. Indeed, the meetings are a main reason for the control room's existence.

The meetings should be held at least weekly. Even if the project is proceeding stably, it is worth having a short meeting in which everyone agrees there are no problems. The meetings may be held daily if the project is in trouble or is going through a period when crucial decisions are being made frequently.

One useful format provides for a thorough review once a week with shorter meetings every other workday. Another provides for a review of a different part of the project each day: engineering, procurement, or some other aspect of the project, for example, costs, schedules, or performance. This is normally not a good idea, for it discourages participation by all the managers and inhibits the examination of interactions among different parts of the project.

When a project is going through a critical phase, the main review can be held outside normal working hours (a black Saturday meeting) so that key managers are not taken away from their workweek duties, and also because it demonstrates that special measures are in order. This practice should not continue too long or become standard practice, for it loses its psychological impact and may prevent the occasional relaxation that hard-pressed managers need.

Project review meetings should ordinarily be scheduled at the same time each week. This permits the attendees to organize their other work around the standard meeting time. It improves attendance and prevents irritation at having to miss or reschedule other activities. The start of the workday or shortly thereafter, when people are most alert, is the best time for meetings. Such an arrangement permits people to complete the meeting before becoming involved in their other managerial activities.

A standardized routing consisting of a meeting announcement, a formal agenda, and pseudo-parliamentary procedures is inappropriate for projects. However, the manager of project control should inform participating managers about the critical issues to be discussed at each meeting to allow them to prepare adequately for constructive discussions. The normal distribution of schedule status and actual cost data is part of this process.

Meeting minutes that discuss at great length who said what are inconsistent with the spirit of project management. However, it is helpful to give attendees an updated list of action items soon after the meeting begins. (The concept is discussed later in the chapter.) It is also helpful to give attendees paper copies of selected important transparencies that are used in presentations. This is a cheap but effective way to communicate. Since the project control room presumably contains readily accessible and updated cost, schedule, and performance information, it should not be necessary to distribute thick packets of charts after each meeting.

The manager of project control should be available and appropriately sympathetic to any manager who wishes to place an item on the meeting agenda. Failure to show this courtesy will stifle the salutary communications potential of the meeting. Even when an item is important only to its initiator, it is better to place it on the agenda and dispose of it quickly during the meeting than to exclude it altogether from consideration. The project manager should decide what is important enough to warrant discussion. A sigh of frustration, a call for help, or a cry of distress is worth hearing.

An agenda for a project review meeting

It is efficient to use a standard format for project review meetings. Not all items need be covered at each gathering, particularly if the meetings are held more than once a week. An agenda distributed in advance can list the subjects that will be discussed in detail. The following agenda is suggested:

General information
Items of general interest to the project team.
Visitors and meetings
A review of visitors expected during the next week and a list of major meetings, including those to be held by people traveling. This may permit a traveler to do some business for another team member.
Significant events
All major events that have occurred since the last meeting (or in the last week or last month); this includes the attainment of major schedule milestones.
Major decisions made in the last week or month
This ensures that everyone gets the word about significant project direction.
Review of product performance
Review of schedule status
Review of costs versus budgets
The order performance-schedules-costs is suggested because schedule difficulties often arise from technical problems and cost problems arise from both of them. Thus a problem area is reviewed before the areas where that problem will cause other problems. Detailed aspects of performance, schedule, and cost reviews were discussed earlier.
Review of action items
A quick rundown of action items assigned at previous meetings. Items that were not accomplished during the week should be rescheduled, but the original schedule date should be retained on the chart. Action items should be discrete actions, not general problems. They should not include events normally scheduled as part of the job.
Review of the ten biggest problems
A quick general look at the ten (more or less) biggest specific problems confronting the project. Any new information about the problems or their solutions is presented.
Detailed review of subjects needing attention
In-depth review and discussion about specific subjects needing collec-

tive project action. The subject may be one of the problems discussed above.

Decisions made at the meeting

A summary of any decisions reached after discussing problems.

Decisions required in the next month

A list of specific decisions that must be made within the next month, which focuses attention on the major issues the team members should address. They may be related directly to problems, but not necessarily.

New action items assigned during the meeting

Conduct of the meeting

The meetings should start promptly. This sets the right tone for conducting project business. The old routine of having tardy attendees contribute to a coffee (or other) fund may be a good idea. The meeting should be as informal as possible without letting it get out of control. Open communciation should be encouraged at all times.

Use of overhead projection transparencies makes meetings go much faster. All those who make presentations should be encouraged to use simple, inexpensive, typed or handwritten transparencies. Legible hand-printed charts are, of course, acceptable. The manager of project control should introduce each presentation. The manager making a presentation should lead any discussion that is part of his presentation. The project manager should lead any general discussion and may elect to take over any discussion of a specific problem. He should be the one to decide that a subject has gone on long enough.

The purposes of the meeting are best served if controversial issues are discussed openly and candidly. But if a discussion degenerates into a rancorous or repetitious argument, it is best to terminate it and arrange for a smaller meeting later to resolve the issue. Attendees should be free to question appraisals of the adequacy of the performance of specific tasks, but attacks on personal motives or competence should not be permitted.

Subordinate members of the team should not be put in the awkward position of having to discuss a subject on short notice without adequate preparation. Someone who makes an inept presentation may be told to come back better prepared, but he should not be ridiculed personally. The project manager should not yield to the temptation, often very strong, to criticize someone for poor decisions or unsatisfactory performance. It is all right to expose the deficiency in the meeting, but such a gathering is not the place for personal criticism or "wire-brushing."

The pace of the meeting should be kept brisk. Discussions of interest to only a few attendees should be deferred. However, this should not result in evading troublesome issues that need examination. The project manager should regard the meeting as a good opportunity to exercise his personal leadership and to promote cooperation among the team members.

Attendance of outsiders at the meetings

As a basic principle, the project review meeting is for the project team. It is one of their most valuable management tools in getting the project job done. Its effectiveness as a communications device is certainly lessened by outside participation. Even passive attendance by outsiders inhibits free communication, and active intervention constitutes interference. Therefore, the project manager and his directive authority should ensure that the majority of the meetings are only for the project team.

On the other hand, much is to be gained by inviting outsiders on a selective basis. If a particularly difficult technical problem confronts the project, there is no harm in bringing in technical experts from outside the project. The interaction between ivory-tower theory and rough-and-tumble project pragmatism may produce surprisingly helpful solutions.

In a major matrix project, it is a good idea to invite functional division heads to the meetings, perhaps once a quarter, or even once a month, if their organizations are heavily involved in the project, and particularly if they are personally responsible for project problems.

In one theory, meetings with visitors should be the same as meetings without them. In another theory, meetings should be polished performances that replay the previous rowdy meeting that was itself actually a dress rehearsal for the whole thing. The shrewd project manager—and surviving ones are that—will strike the right balance somewhere in between. It probably lies close to the real meeting unless the chartering or review authority calls for a different kind of meeting and a more carefully organized (but not censored) presentation than the utilitarian but highly effective weekly review.

In a project executed under a contract with the government or one of its major contractors, the customer may wish to participate in project meetings. Such meetings are a good mean of communicating with him. However, attendance by the customer's representatives should be limited. The customer is of course free to have his own review meetings with attendance by whomever he desires. Even if the customer attends some meetings, the right must be retained to limit the majority of the reviews to project personnel only.

If project work is subcontracted, the project managers and key managers of major subcontractors may be invited to attend meetings from time to time. They should have similar preparation responsibilities and be treated the same as the project team.

Project review meetings with subcontractors

It was noted above that subcontractors may attend in-house project review meetings. Periodically, the project manager directly responsible for subcontractor performance and a few selected people from the team should be given a review by the subcontractor project manager. It is usually best to do this at the subcontractor's facility where all his key team members are available for discussion if required and backup data are readily available.

The project manager should request the meeting sufficiently in advance to allow the subcontractor adequate time to prepare for it. He should indicate the items he would like to review, particularly those requiring special or in-depth treatment. The normal project review topics should be presented automatically. The project manager may request the subcontractor project manager to follow the general format used in internal project reviews.

The subcontractor project manager should chair the meeting and conduct it within his customary format. The project manager and his team should be free to ask questions and even to challenge data.

However, the meeting should not become a vehicle for giving criticism or direction. If needed, this should be given directly to the subcontractor project manager in a private conversation.

In DOD projects, the government project manager will sometimes wish to attend or be represented at project review meetings at the subcontractor's facility. This is a reasonable request. However, acceding to it should not preclude having meetings where only prime contractor and subcontractor personnel are present. Every effort should be made to avoid reviews of the subcontractor by the government project office without the prime contractor's participation. If there are resident government personnel in the subcontractor's plant, they properly will have reason to contact the subcontractor directly on routine project matters, but they should not intervene in project direction.

Results from project review meetings

Project review meetings are a most valuable tool for the project manager. He should never depart from the practice of having them, preferably at least weekly.

A primary use of the meetings is to bring the need for decisions to the surface and to be sure that all facets of a problem are highlighted. Not all problems should be solved in them. After a problem has been identified, a manager or some team members can be assigned the job of examining alternative solutions. Before a course of action is finally selected, the alternative solutions should be discussed at the review meeting to see that all their implications are understood and to give everyone a chance to voice views or concerns.

The meetings are an excellent communications device. They ensure that all the key players are working to common plans with a mutual understanding of each others' problems. Consequently, better decisions are made at all levels. A great deal of ad hoc direction can be given by the project manager without cluttering up the paper mill with needless memos. This does not mean that good practices for issuing direction can be abandoned, but rather that they can be restricted to the main issues, thereby promoting efficiency.

Project review meetings build esprit de corps in the project team. In the early stages of the project, they get people acquainted and accustomed to working together informally. As problems are faced and solved together, mutual respect and joint pride in the project are increased along with individual and mutual satisfaction at being on the team.

PROJECT CONTROL DATA AS A BASIS FOR REPORTING AND ACTION

In an ideal reporting situation, placing a one-page explanatory discussion on top of selected data from a project review would constitute complete fulfillment of all periodic project reporting obligations to the customer and/or the upper echelons of management. Unfortunately, real life is not that simple. However, the managers of the reporting function should work toward such a goal, both for effectiveness of communication and for economy.

A fundamental reality often overlooked by people in the midst of creating a project organization and its controls is that the customer himself needs controls over the project; and one of his principal control tools is the periodic report of project progress. If he requests that certain data be arranged in a certain way in a progress report, that means he considers such data a useful control on the progress of the project.

Detailed reporting requirements are occasionally capricious or random; in such cases an effort should be made to get them changed. But the main idea is that if the customer thinks particular data are important, then the project manager should consider them important too. By incorporating these requirements into the content and format of project control data, material generated for the project managers will be suitable for reporting project progress without additional unproductive processing.

In addition to the information required by the customer, project reports should include summaries from the key data systems used to manage the project. If PERT is the principal method used to measure project status, then the customer should get PERT status reports so that he understands how project management is looking at the problem.

Thus project reporting procedures should be based on the data used to manage the project. They will primarily be determined by the control methods selected by the project manager, but modified to include special reporting requirements imposed by the customer.

Necessity for honest reporting

Honest reporting is absolutely necessary for good project management. First of all, good business ethics requires it. However, situations eventually arise where the reporting, while not illegal, fraudulent, or literally dishonest, is less than completely honest in the picture it gives of what is going on.

This occurs most often when future problems are evident in their earliest symptoms. The project manager either is not sure of the implications of the problem or is confident that a solution will be found to make the whole matter go away. He therefore ignores any mention of the problem in his reports. Sometimes the problem does go away, but when it does not, confidence in the project manager is lost and completion of the project becomes more difficult.

This does not mean that every project difficulty need be proclaimed loudly for all to hear; confidentiality about project problems is sometimes appropriate. But it does mean that the project manager should give candid assessments of all project problems to his key customer project manager and his own immediate superior executive.

In projects that deal with the customer according to a negotiated fixed-price contract or on some other arm's-length basis, it is obviously inappropriate to give him all available data about the project. The point is that whatever data are promised should be reported honestly and candidly. No commitment should be made to provide data that should not be provided.

On a detailed level, failure to report data honestly leads to operating inefficiencies—for example, an increase in the amount of data demanded. Worse, it can lead to withholding delegation authority, which slows down the decision-making process and contributes to project inefficiency.

Quality of data in reports

Given the premise that reports should be based on project control data and not very much else, then all the attributes of good data discussed above should also apply to data contained in reports.

Project reporting should be based on data from the set of books that is used to manage the project. There should not be a separate set for the customer. Past cases have indeed existed where project managers insisted that all departments working on the project use common data, but then blithely kept a second set of books for their customer project manager. Hopefully, this breed is vanishing.

Data in customer reports should be accurate. Discrepancies between data in different sections of a report, for example, engineering development schedules versus master schedules, should be resolved as part of the internal project review process. Permitting their inclusion in project reports is not in itself a major problem, but it does create a lack of confidence that leads to additional data requirements and audit requests from the customer and additional useless effort by the project team.

Periodic project reports should be completed and delivered soon after the end of the subject period. If the report is really based on project data, it should be possible, and indeed convenient, to meet this requirement. A long time lag between activity completion and activity reporting is a symptom of less than optimum management. It may indicate a long period of "massaging the data" for the customer. This suggests that the real project data are unnecessarily and undesirably being converted for customer use and are no longer real project data. Another possibility is that no adequate attempt has been made to incorporate customer needs into the project control data scheme, or to reach agreement on appropriate modification.

Open project data—minimum project reporting

An economical approach to reporting may be described as "open project data—minimum project reporting." This is not a term in general use, but it expresses the idea fairly well. Under this concept, reporting is confined to the summary statistical data needed to maintain records in the customer organization. Information is provided to comply with any legal or policy requirements, and a report by exception is submitted on any significant events or problems that have occurred or are forecast.

Trends and events are reported on an exception basis; that is, they are reported only when they depart from plan. In return for this minimal reporting requirement, the project manager makes available to the customer, on request, any data used in managing the project. Normally, this consists in making the data available for inspection, but it can involve transmittal of reports or copies of data. These procedures are subject to the usual exception of specific data excluded in advance, or deemed not appropriate for transmittal because of arm's-length commercial dealings.

This is really the approach used in companies with enlightened methods of providing general management surveillance of their projects. Senior executives attending periodic project reviews require little additional data beyond those fed into the summary reporting system for the whole organization. Within the organization, this approach is particularly applicable in meeting the requests and needs of staff specialists.

Government agencies that previously required extensive and highly structured reports from their projects, largely in the name of adequate surveillance, are now turning to the approach just described. They have recognized that these voluminous reports create large costs while making small contributions to true project control. Joint government-industry association teams are continuing to explore this issue constructively and effectively.

Making this approach work requires good faith and good judgment on both sides. The agency generating reporting requirements must control requests by people in its organization, particularly staff or technical specialists. Some highly structured reporting systems were designed originally to control—not to expand—the number of reports. An unsupervised use of the system described above can actually result in more rather than fewer reports. However, management control of data requests, made with an eye on the costs involved in generating the data can result in a low-cost system that satisfies everyone's needs.

On the other hand, the project must be responsive to requests to view data on an exception basis. Data should be made available promptly and with no attempt to filter out uncomfortable facts. They should be furnished on a timely basis that does not cause inconvenience to the requester. When opinions differ about whether some data ought to be withheld or released, the matter should be promptly referred upward, to the project manager if necessary, rather than be permitted to persist as an irritant to the working echelons of the disputing organizations.

The manner in which the project manager in a matrix organization obtains data from functional organizations supporting the project was discussed elsewhere in a somewhat different perspective. The general approach here applies equally well in that situation.

7

Personnel Management of the Project Team

An earlier chapter discussed the special aspects of the project environment and the effect that they have on people assigned to the project, and indeed to those elsewhere in the organization who come in contact with it. This chapter discusses the policies, techniques, and procedures that are useful in accomplishing personnel administration for the project.

The first key task is to select the project manager. Then the other key managers on the project are chosen. After this the entire team can be recruited and selected and all members informed of their status on the project. Issues of promotion, salary review, reassignment, disciplinary action, and dismissal are addressed, and, finally, consideration is given to the all-important matter of satisfactory reassignment of people at the end of the project.

As a general rule, the organization's existing personnel policies should be followed as closely as possible. This is particularly important when union personnel are involved in the project. However, because projects are created to cope with unusual situations, changes in personnel policies may be required. Also, the "two bosses" situation requires special treatment, but this should be looked on as an extension of existing policies rather than a fundamental departure from them.

As a corollary to the retention of existing policies where possible, maximum use should be made of the personnel organization. It is usually appropriate to assign someone from personnel to the project with the prime responsibility of supporting it. However, he should be one of the last members of the team to be placed on the payroll of the project manager. This in no way lessens his obligation to be responsive to the project manager.

Any personnel policies that are changed for the project should be documented clearly and issued in the same form used for normal personnel policies and procedures. It is essential that the project personnel matters not be managed by a set of verbal agreements or sub rosa departures from standard policies. Such an approach inevitably leads to maladministration, hard feelings, confusion, and inefficiency.

SELECTING THE PROJECT MANAGER

One of the two or three most important ingredients of a successful project is the right project manager. Selecting him is a particularly formidable task because each project has a unique set of circumstances that tend to demand a unique set of qualifications in its manager. In addition, the job has many more dimensions than most managerial posts. Where the project is large and involves many different parts of the organization, the task of finding the right leader approaches in complexity the filling of a general management post. The factors to be considered involve personal characteristics, expert knowledge and skills, experience, and reputation.

Selecting the right project manager should not be a job of paralyzing subtlety: a number of definite traits and qualifications usually required for success were examined in an earlier chapter. But before examining them, let us first look at some of the wrong reasons for selecting a project manager.

Some wrong reasons for selecting a project manager

We need somebody mature like Joe in such a complex job.
You need someone mature, all right, but not someone overripe like Joe.

Availability is a key factor in selecting a project manager, and John is available now. We shouldn't let the problem of assigning a project manager affect our ongoing operations.

With an attitude like that, the project isn't likely to be one of your ongoing operations. Besides, the factors that make John "available" are exactly those that will guarantee his failure as a project manager.

Bill would be a good choice because he belongs to the executive vice president's country club and could get his attention whenever the project needs it.

If the project really needs the attention of the executive vice president and the only way you can guarantee that it will get it is to appoint one of his golf buddies to head the project, you might as well forget it right at the beginning.

We need a hard-nosed project manager in this matrix environment, and Sherman really fits that description.

Sherman is hard-nosed, all right; so much so that he can hardly run his functional department, despite his expertise in that function and the fact that everyone in the department is on his payroll. He'll have generated a social crisis on the project by the time he's been on it three months.

Pierre would be a good choice as project manager; he did a great job of keeping everybody happy on that last committee he headed.

Pierre will keep everybody happy about this project, too—that is, for about six months, until management inquires about progress. A project isn't a committee and a project manager isn't a committee chairman.

Sam is one of our most competent engineering managers. If we make him project manager, this will broaden his experience in several new fields and have a marked effect on his career.

To be sure, it will have a marked effect on his career—it will stunt it, probably permanently. He will fail in the job because he doesn't have the breadth of experience to cope with it.

Why don't we make Ralph the project manager? He has been in at least five different divisions.

Yes, and he has left each one with the encouragement, or at least the silent relief, of the division vice president. When he comes back as project manager to deal with the divisions he left, they'll get an initial impression of the project that will make its success unlikely in the long run.

What justifies the choice

The best project manager is the one who is most likely to get the project job done well. This obvious premise is sometimes forgotten at one end of the spectrum in learned discussions about the best mix of talent for success, and at the other end in calculations about internal political expediency. But the main idea must never be lost.

First of all, relative importance must be assigned to the various "good" characteristics evaluated in the context of the project at hand. Even then, the man with the best personal qualifications may not be the best selection, for reasons to be seen below; selecting too good a man for the project should be avoided; the man should be matched to the job. That is why phrases like "select the best man for the job" have been avoided; "best" may realistically be too good for some projects.

Not only should the project manager have the qualifications for the job, but his fitness should be readily apparent. If at all possible, he should be known to potential team members as a proven manager, a dynamic leader. He should be known to the other executives of the organization as a prudent executive willing to explore complicated issues on a rational basis to get at the best overall answer.

A superior manager who is unknown to most of the key players concerned may not be as wise a choice as a competent manager who is well recognized by everyone. Strangers, particularly when they are imports, have a difficult time as project managers. When, even considering all the difficulties, it is still the best idea to bring strangers onto the scene, more careful preparation and more visible manifestations of top management support will be necessary.

Since many projects are carried out under continuing contracts to a customer or are sought under competitive conditions, the preferences of the customer in general and the customer's project manager in particular are most important. A proposal may become a winner because the designated project manager has a long history of honest and successful work with his counterpart on previous projects. Or a government project manager may feel that a particular technical issue is the key to project success; the competitive proposal that designates a project manager who is an expert in the critical field is surely in a preferred position, at least for that area.

One subtle criterion for project manager selection may be derived from examining the value of project success and failure in both the long and the short run. In some projects, to achieve success is excellent, and to achieve great success is only a little better; to fail is a disaster. For this environment, the solid citizen and proven performer is the natural selection.

On the other hand, success may not pay if the product does not come in first; in this case, great success will be magnificent, for the winner takes all. Here, the brilliant project manager is the right choice, for if he botches the job he is no worse off than the competent plodder who comes in second; if he wins, the selection is a success.

Looking at the time dimension, one would want a program manager who would succeed in the short run and leave behind him a constructive atmosphere for future projects and related interpersonal relationships. However, some projects require so much urgent attention for successful schedule performance that the brilliant, heavy-handed driver is the right choice. Alternatively, the clear-thinking manager who can optimize costs and schedules and technical performance may not be the right choice, whereas the big spender will get the job done better or faster under conditions of great urgency.

Participation by functional executives

It is a very ticklish matter to decide how much the senior functional executives should participate in selecting the project manager. Any ideal management appointment puts the best man in the job, with maximum concurrence and acceptance by his peers. But these two conditions are not always compatible.

On the side of concurrence, it may be impossible for a project manager to be effective if he is unacceptable to one or more key functional executives. This is particularly apt to occur in the matrix environment. It may also apply to the project management mode, for project success depends on being given good people from functional divisions.

On the other hand, the very needs that led to establishing a project may make any really good project manager unattractive to functional executives. Consensus is achieved, but "lowest common denominator" managers too often fail. Certainly selection of a project manager should not become a subject of politics, nor should it be done in a contentios way that creates some enemies for the new project manager no matter who he may turn out to be.

Because of the many opportunities for selecting badly, it should be done by general management—and very carefully. It is advisable to keep all communications verbal and informal: The running dialog will discourage people from taking rigid positions that may be difficult to modify. One way to go about this is to announce general management's intention to organize a project and to appoint a project manager. Key functional executives are then invited to submit nominees for the job. In awkward, highly political situations, this may result in a nomination list whose occupants are distinguished by their weak knees and strong personal ties.

Perhaps a better solution is to submit a list of candidates to each functional division head and to ask him to comment on how well he might work with each candidate—but no statement is to be made on that candidate's suitability. It should be made clear that the process is an information exchange, not an election. To reiterate, the survey should be made in a low-key, conversational mode. The principal risk lies in the implied suggestion that the functional executives are "more equal" than the project manager, an illusion ripe with possibilities for future problems.

An even more subdued approach might be to announce the imminent appointment of a project manager and to wait for voluntary comments from key players. But this gives the vocal and the brash executive a larger say; it may also evoke positive statements while discouraging hostile ones that would be more productive of a correct selection.

If general management knows its people, it may be best simply to announce the appointment and get on with the job. Or the normal management style of the chief executive will seem the best way to handle the matter—but he must realize he is making an especially sensitive decision, one that permits a very small margin for error.

An important general management responsibility

Selecting a project manager is a significant event in the life of an organization. General management should take an interest in it, even if the project manager reports not directly to the top but one or two levels lower in the hierarchy. There are particular reasons for this.

- A project manager is given license to cut across several organizational lines. His activities, therefore, take on a flavor of general management, and must be done well.
- Project management will not succeed without a good project manager. Thus, if general management sees fit to establish a project, it should certainly see fit to select a good man as its leader.
- A project manager is far more likely to accomplish desired goals if it is obvious that general management has selected and appointed him.

SELECTING THE PROJECT TEAM

General management direction for selecting the team

Selecting the project team can best be done in three phases. First, the project manager is selected by general management, usually after consultation with heads of the divisions that will play a key part in the project. Second, each functional manager to be assigned to the project (for example, the project chief engineer) should be selected by joint action of the project manager and the head of the corresponding functional division. At the same time, members of the project staff who will report directly to the project manager in jobs having no affiliation with any function may be selected during this phase if they are to be drawn from functional divisions. Third, the rest of the project team can be selected by joint action of the project functional manager, the functional division head, and the project manager.

It all sounds so neat that one might infer that general management's job is done once it has established the project and appointed the project manager, but this is not the case. General management must remain directly responsible until the entire team is selected and approved. A reasonable set of policies for selecting the team should be established. One such set is discussed below, but whatever the policies may be, it is most important that they be communicated clearly to the project manager and the functional heads.

Elaborate or formal written policy directives can be dispensed with where verbal direction will suffice; it is essential only that all concerned get the same message—whatever it is. Even if written directives are issued, it is desirable that preliminary discussions include the general manager and all key executives so that everyone will interpret the document properly. In addition, these discussions should emphasize that selecting an adequate project team is everybody's responsibility, not just the project manager's.

Priority guidelines should also be established. These need not be very formal, but some projects may have higher priorities than others, and various activities within a project may have varying priority rankings relative to functional objectives. All these conditions should be acknowledged.

General management should remain available for decision making in cases of appeal or disagreement throughout the entire selection process. Further, it should ensure that the process is proceeding amicably. This is the first real opportunity for disagreement between the project manager and functional heads, and if conflict does arise it should be taken care of quickly. A project that starts out in an atmosphere of hostility among key executives is working with a crippling handicap.

Finally, it is good practice that the general manager announce the appointment of the key managers of the project team—and of the project manager, of course, if this has not been done earlier. In a smaller project it may be sufficient to announce the senior participant from each division, but in a large project it is best to announce two or three echelons of managers for each major division. In so doing, general management declares its support for the whole project, not just for a few top men; this may encourage wavering functional managers to give enthusiastic support to their counterparts on the project. Furthermore, by placing its seal of approval on the appointees, general management can help mend rifts that may have been opened during the selection process.

Development of project requirements for people

One way to staff a project team calls for the project manager to develop his own requirements for people. With these in hand, the functional executive proposes appropriate candidates and the project manager either accepts them or negotiates a change. Such a process works quite well at one end of the spectrum, where the project is well outside the normal business of the organization.

For example, something esoteric is being attempted; the project manager has studied the matter in depth for some time and is the only one who fully understands both the problem and the people and technologies he will need to solve it. A possible instance is a study of some new social, organizational, operational concept, the application of a new technology, or an examination of the possible sales penetration of a new market.

The same approach will also work at the other extreme, in the perfectly routine program. The project manager knows he needs a good architect, a good chief engineer, a good construction superintendent, and a good project control manager; he need only state these requirements and the functional heads will respond by listing several qualified candidates to fill each slot. The best person is picked, given the current situation. The fact that similar requirements have risen many times before in an organization accustomed to using project management makes it easy to communicate requirements for people.

Yet in the great majority of cases the best results are obtained when the project manager and the functional head work together in this endeavor. A functional head can be a big help in defining the key technical issues in his field and the kinds of people who will be needed to solve them. He can identify the high-risk areas that will require either particularly talented people or a sufficient number to cope with the magnitude of the problem.

In all cases there are advantages in having the functional heads aboard during the definition process. Participation in early project planning develops a positive attitude toward the project among functional heads rather than the negative one that might develop if they felt excluded. These all-too-human feelings exist in even the top executives. Furthermore, delay or confusion in making selections can be avoided because the functional heads have more time to plan the necessary moves to release the people who are best suited for the project jobs.

It should be stressed that project personnel requirements should be agreed upon before each phase of the selection process is started. Often an apparent selection disagreement really turns out to be a symptom of a deeper disagreement about the degree of competence or the special skills required for project success.

Selecting key project functional managers

Several executive actions should be completed before the actual selection of project functional managers begins. First the project manager is selected and formally appointed, or at least his identity is made known to the executive team. Next the organizational arrangement for the project is spelled out—whether it is to be project management, matrix, task force, or some combination of these. In particular the operating mode of each functional manager is clearly specified— what direction he receives from the project manager and what direction comes from the functional head.

An organization chart is then prepared and the division of responsibility and authority among managers on the project is clearly defined. Personnel policies for the project need to be worked out, at least on the basis of significant exceptions, and finally the requirements for project personnel are worked out by the project manager and functional heads and approved by general management.

As in so many aspects of a fast-moving project, these events need not be carried out strictly in sequence; parallel activity and iteration will increase speed and efficiency. Nevertheless, these key decisions should have been made before discussions are begun with the key managers about their project assignments.

The selection process can now begin—preferably with a private conversation in which the project manager reviews personnel requirements with the functional head and expresses any preferences he may have for a particular manager he knows personally or by reputation. He should also state any negative feelings he has about possible candidates; it is far better to bring out reservations early so that they can either be dispelled or taken into consideration in the selection process.

The functional head should then present his nominee for the job, or perhaps better submit a list of several candidates. He should give a candid appraisal of their strengths and weaknesses, along with the rationale that led to their selection for the job. It is always good practice to require that the functional manager appraise and rate each candidate relative to other candidates and peers; and on a project of any length it is well to have a joint review of personnel folders, management-by-objective results, and performance appraisals.

A key executive policy statement, completed before the selection process begins, concerns the persons and procedures involved in deciding who will be picked for the job. The following guidelines, which are not necessarily mutually compatible in all organizations, are offered:

• In the absence of other considerations (several are suggested below), selection of project functional managers will follow the normal personnel policies of the organization.

• Where there are special reasons for organizing a project (for example, to work around deadwood), exceptions to normal policy will be clearly specified.

• Reasonable requirements and qualifications established by the project manager will be met; utopian, unreasonable, or nit-picking requirements will not.

• The functional executive will select the project functional manager after reasonable dialog on his choice. This ensures that top executive's continued commitment to, and responsibility for, the success of the project.

• As an exception to the rule just formulated, the project manager may veto any candidate proposed by the functional head—but for stated cause only. There is no point in starting a project with a major lack of confidence in key project personnel. However, veto of all candidates will normally be regarded as a lack of good faith or judgment on the part of one or both parties—and this should be made clear in advance.

• A fast decision-appeal route to top management should always be available when there is a disagreement. However, its excessive use should be discouraged.

• Selection dealings will be kept confidential (but not be made a cloak-and-dagger secret) unless pertinent specified and approved reasons call for their disclosure.

After agreement has been reached on the nature of the selection process and on the person to be chosen, recruiting may begin. This consists primarily in ordering, informing, pleading with, intimidating, cajoling, and/or reasoning with the selectee in order to persuade him to join the project. This process is examined in a subsequent section. If the selectee is permitted to decline his prospective good fortune, the whole sequence may begin again.

In a small project, where elite skills are required for success, key professionals and staff executives should be chosen with at least as much care as is given to selecting project functional managers. Indeed, in the small but important project requiring high intellectual capacity or perhaps pronounced innovative tendencies in all members of the task force, selecting the right professionals may be even more important than getting the right functional managers would be on a much larger project.

Selecting project personnel

After the project functional managers have been selected, the rest of the project team, or at least those needed to begin the initial work, should be selected immediately. However, in practice the whole thing is complicated by the presence of the project functional manager as a new third party in the process.

First the three parties should review the project requirements for manpower. On a larger project the detailed manpower needs may not be identified until the project functional manager has participated for a while in the planning phase. More often than not, the functional head and the project functional manager should identify the problems the project will encounter and the people to be assigned to solving them.

It is probably a good idea to grant the project functional manager the right to veto any candidate he finds unacceptable (a right to be used thoughtfully and usually sparingly). However, it should be clearly understood in advance that if the project functional manager feels that any of the people offered cannot do the job, he is required to so inform the functional head and then report this to the project manager. At this point the disagreement can either be resolved between the project manager and the functional head, or placed in the appeal process.

It may seem that the project functional manager is being placed on the spot unnecessarily early in the game, but in a sense he will be on the spot whenever there are project-functional differences of opinion, and it is just as well to work out the communications and decision-making format right away. Indeed these early exercises in collective decision making, if pursued constructively, can actually build up a happy three-way relationship strong enough to endure throughout the project.

It should be emphasized that selecting the project functional manager before selecting the rest of the team is most important; this puts him immediately into his new role of having to find a way to reconcile the individual views of two bosses while at the same time he is learning to make honest recommendations on the better course to follow when the two points of view are neither compatible nor susceptible to compromise. As in so many other situations, the quality of his judgments and his ability to communicate them are key ingredients of project success.

RECRUITING AND ASSIGNING
PROJECT PERSONNEL

"Recruiting and assigning" is the name given here to the process that takes place between the time an individual is selected for the project and the time he is actively employed on it. Since this phase provides the first contact most people will have with the project, it can have a lasting influence on their attitude toward the project. It is therefore important that this process of getting the project team aboard be especially well thought out.

A number of guidelines for accomplishing this task are suggested.

- Unless some other condition is paramount, project recruiting policies should be as similar as possible to those normally used in the organization for assigning people to new jobs.

- Everyone should be given the same briefing about the project, its benefits, and any special policies related to it. For a sensitive project, this rule can be modified to permit different amounts of information to be given to different managerial levels, but at least everyone in the same general classification should get the same briefing. It should be complete and accurate.

- Any commitments made to members of the team about treatment at the end of the project should be approved in advance by general management. No other commitments should be made.

- Every individual selected for a project should be told why he or she was chosen.

- A similar degree of freedom should be granted all people, or at least all those within a given job category, in the matter of accepting or declining a project assignment.

This last is a major consideration in the recruiting process: How much discretion is to be given to the employee concerning the proposed assignment? Several degrees of permissiveness appear possible:

- The project is explained and the individual is asked to join it. He is given complete freedom to decline, no questions asked.

- The individual is told he will be assigned to the project. However, he is invited to bring forward any reservations he may have about joining. Any sensible reason he offers will excuse him from the assignment.

- The individual is told he is assigned to the project. Only a significant personal or career preference is accepted as a reason for excusing him from joining the project.

- The individual is assigned to the project as he would be to any other work assignment. Only an emergency can excuse him from serving on the project team.

In most cases, the third alternative is the best. If management has done its homework, it should have picked the right people for the right reasons, and assignments should be accepted as made. In the case of a high-priority task force that will operate for only a limited time after which the members can return to their original jobs, the last, the most mandatory, form of assignment is appropriate. For projects that involve relocation, or that have permanent career implications, the second approach may be best. In projects requiring a high intellectual capacity or a very strong personal commitment, for example, a research or study project, the first approach is probably the best. In any case, the policy to be used should be applied as uniformly as possible.

Information required for recruiting discussions

It is important that every individual who is approached about a project assignment be given full and accurate information about his prospective role. The list of pertinent facts is longer than one might expect. It should include general information about the project, how it will be organized, the individual's own specific assignment and compensation arrangements, any special policies that apply to the project, and what sort of assignment the individual either will be promised or can reasonably expect at the conclusion of the project.

As a general introduction, the reasons that led to establishing the project should be identified, along with the goals it is expected to achieve. The kind of work to be done should be described, and the expected duration of the project and the number of people to be involved in it should be given. Any special feature, such as remoteness of location or involvement with another organization, should be covered.

At this point it is appropriate to brief the prospective team members on the organizational aspects of the project. This can best be done by using an organization chart of the entire project and, if the particular department under discussion is large, a chart of that department. The prospect should be told the name of his immediate superior, the name of the superior above that, and, in the case of a supervisor or manager, the names of all the people who will report to the same person he reports to.

The responsibilities of his superior's department should be clearly delineated. Then his own authority and responsibility should be described. Whatever the organizational form may be, it should be defined in some detail; in particular, if a matrix organization is to be used, the exact authority of the project manager, the functional division head, and his immediate superiors should be spelled out. The expected extent of communications with the individual's old functional organization should now be discussed.

Next, the individual's specific job duties should be outlined. Any special technological or professional challenges that must be met should be pointed out. It is often as important to define what is not involved as what is. If a project has top management visibility and seems to offer exciting opportunities, it is easy for people to picture more stimulating activities and more profound professional problems than they will really encounter. While such misunderstandings may help the project get off to an enthusiastic start, the ensuing frustration will be unfair to the people concerned and destructive of their long-run performance.

Next, the individual should be told why he has been selected for the assignment. If his general qualifications and current availability were the only considerations, this is worth stating. It eliminates any chance of paranoia on the one hand or false feelings of annointment on the other.

Compensation questions should be discussed. For example: "Do I get a raise immediately? If not, when? Who will decide?" While the first of these questions may be of greatest interest, the last is no less important, particularly for the person moving into a matrix environment. Also, any changes in job classification should be clearly identified, and any job title should be defined along with its level in the hierarchy—a particularly sensitive point in an organization where prerogatives and fringe benefits (for example, carpet or no carpet in the office) are closely tied to job titles.

Next, any special administrative arrangements with members of the project should be covered. Of particular importance are issues related to moving, travel, or special working hours and overtime. And finally, the policy regarding assignments at the end of the project, or promotional reassignment during its course, should be stated. If the project has no specific policies or commitments, this fact should be established.

The foregoing is a formidable list of items to cover. Since the information will be communicated to project members by supervisors or managers who may themselves be recent recruits to the team, it should be well organized and written down. Such a set of fact sheets covering the widely applicable subjects provides uniformity of information and avoids ambiguities and misunderstandings. Careful planning pays off in this important exercise.

Conducting recruiting and assigning interviews

After adequate policies have been developed and combined with other pertinent information into a set of fact sheets, the process of interviewing may begin. This complex job will be easier if:

• The project is announced as soon as possible, consistent with considerations of competition, unmade decisions, or special sensitivity.

• The head of each organization announces what its involvement will be in the project, and what individual job opportunities will exist. (On small but important projects requiring special professional skills, this practice and the next are not useful, for the small number of the right people needed should be simply drafted.)

• People interested in being assigned to the project are invited to state their interest, without any implication that desires will be accommodated. (The practice of asking someone whether he would like to express interest in or volunteer for a project is not the same as asking him whether he will accept an assignment on the project.)

• Discussions about project assignments are made with different people on the same basis of confidentiality. Preferably all discussions should be conducted in an open atmosphere, but if secrecy is right for some then it is right for all.

After these preparations are complete, the important task of actually interviewing candidates can begin. How well this is done can have an impact not only on immediate decisions but also on long-range attitudes of members of the project team and on interpersonal relationships between project and functional managers. Some useful points to keep in mind while recruiting may be mentioned.

• A person selected for a project should first hear of it from his own immediate supervisor or manager. Later it may be appropriate for a higher-level manager to discuss the matter with the selectee at greater length, particularly where professional people are involved and implications of career direction are present.

• In general, any information about the impending transfer, the selection process, and the long-range career implications of the new assignment should come from the present manager. Information about the project, its administrative arrangements, and the new job assignment should come from the new manager.

• The exact nature and amount of the individual's choice in the assignment must be covered by his present superiors. The new manager must not be put in the position of giving his new subordinate direction, probably made higher in the organization, that may have career implications.

Where a number of people are to be involved in project assignments, time can be saved by a preliminary joint briefing. First each person should be told individually by his present superiors that he has been selected for the project. Then the group can be given a briefing by someone from the project, preferably the project manager. It is extremely helpful to have the functional heads attend the discussion, and perhaps take part in it. Their presence contributes greatly to an impression—hopefully true—of executive solidarity in support of the project.

It is particularly desirable that the general manager kick off the meeting. In a large organization where this is not practical, a short film clip containing his comments is useful. A carefully prepared information sheet about the project can be distributed at the end of the presentation. Thereafter individual interviews between the selectees and their new managers can begin.

When the project work is to be done at a remote site, and particularly where family movement is involved, the briefing schedule may be more complicated. In this situation, the selectees are more likely to be given a choice of whether or not they wish to accept a project assignment. It is desirable to show them a number of colored slides of the new work and living environment; colored motion-picture films are also helpful. However, a lot of money should not be spent on an unnecessarily elaborate promotion; a good orientation, not excessively professional, may be put together very cheaply in a short time by managers who are good communicators.

Both the good and the bad features of the new location should be honestly presented, preferably in a session attended by both the employees and their spouses. The presentation should then be followed by a question period. Such activities are worth the extra effort, for they ensure that everyone will get the same story.

This may seem like a somewhat complex business; it is, if it is done well. However, it need not take a lot of money or a long time to accomplish. If management has done its planning well, and if the new team of managers is on its toes, very little preparation is needed beyond that required for an orderly project startup. Moreover, good execution at this stage will eliminate many of the downstream personnel problems.

BUILDING THE PROJECT TEAM

Teamwork, esprit de corps, and success

Sometimes a collection of warring departments can somehow accomplish desired tasks, or a shapeless collection of uninspired organizational entities can muddle through to a marginally acceptable conclusion, but how much more could have been done, and how much more efficient it could have been if the collected talents had been a team! In today's demanding world, modern management cannot afford to operate its enterprise too far below potential effectiveness. By any fair measure, teamwork is necessary for project success.

Building the project team is a prime responsibility of the project manager. He must have the gift of leadership and he must use it. A big part of this job is to inspire his subordinates. They, too—and particularly the project functional managers—must be leaders and must inspire their people. One of the greatest satisfactions a manager can enjoy, personally and professionally, is to observe talented people from varied backgrounds and with different aspirations being transformed from a motley crowd into an efficient and dedicated project team.

The term *esprit de corps* implies that extra camaraderie and pride that come from experiences shared not only at times of success but during difficult periods as well. It cannot be simulated; gimmicks and flamboyant promotions are to be avoided, for they may assault the individual's sense of dignity and may work against the intended result. A project manager can provide an atmosphere favorable to the development of esprit de corps by his positive thinking, good communication, and can-do attitude. Good leadership, fair treatment, and a sharing of glory are the best ways to build the spirit. Then people will work better together, take more pride in their accomplishments, and have more fun on the project. These personal benefits are not only good intrinsically, but contribute to project success as well.

Project ties and functional ties

Project personnel will have loyalties both to the project and to their functional organizations. In a newly staffed project it is entirely natural that such ties are strongest to the functional departments. In his efforts to build a project team and develop esprit de corps, the project manager will quite properly try to develop enthusiasm for the project and a sense of identification with it. However, an astute and constructive functional executive will be proud if his people continue to communicate well with him while gaining the reputation as the most enthusiastic group on the project team.

Loyalty to both the project and the functional organization is possible, desirable, and the only path to full job satisfaction. It is the path to optimal project performance as well. The crux of the matter is that both the project manager and the functional head must understand this and behave accordingly. They must not indulge in clandestine conversations intended to build one loyalty at the expense of the other. Nothing is worse for the morale and success of a project than this kind of struggle, whether it be sly or overt. Whoever of the two key executives may be at fault, such a conflict is a sure sign of trouble on a project.

These principles must be recognized by all members of the team. The project manager will give operational direction to project personnel and be largely responsible for their immediate future; the functional head will give them technical and policy guidance and be responsible for their long-range prospects; but loyalty to both parties is expected, is reasonable, and is necessary for success.

A central location

Locating project people together is the easiest step management can take to ensure the rapid and effective formation of a project team. It is also necessary. It involves locating the people really close together; the offices of key managers should be near each other and near their people. Everyone should be within walking distance of everyone else.

Working together in the same geographical area inevitably ties people together. Perhaps the group is experiencing a special form of the territorial imperative, but the project area, the scene of shared trials and successes, may in time become a major element of the growing esprit de corps. This is true even on projects of short duration.

There are also very practical reasons for locating project people together, most of them associated with good communications. A walk two doors away is more effective for discussing a controversial problem than the more impersonal phone call that would occur if the other person were ten minutes away. Informality is also encouraged by direct contact with one's colleagues. In addition, the proliferation of paper is minimized, and this is most desirable. Important plans, specifications, directions, and reports must be documented precisely, but these constitute only a tenth of project communication and coordination paper. Most of the rest can and should be eliminated by locating the team together. Also, fully successful use of a project control room as a communications center requires that people be near each other and near the room itself.

Locating people together is a key feature of successful "skunk works" for development projects. Empirical evidence is slow to appear, but the principle of locating people together has presented itself as a major key to project success. Project managers have often observed that they would rather run a matrix project whose elements are grouped together than a project management organization whose units are scattered in odd locations.

Communications efficiency from the project control room

The project control room is designed to improve project communications. If material in the control room is updated on a daily basis, every member of the team can have immediate access to project data and thus avoid the inevitable delays in mail distribution or document routing. The great advantage of the project control room is its capacity to display the latest information first.

If data are always conveniently accessible, the production and accumulation of paper can be minimized. First- and second-line supervisors as well as higher managers collect a great deal of status information and other reports, primarily for defensive purposes; knowing the material can be found in the project control room whenever it is required, they may be inclined to abandon much of the duplicate paper they might otherwise want. Some projects have even gone so far as to eliminate all status reports except those displayed in the control room.

The concept of using standard data as a means of making better decisions has been discussed earlier. However, a key part of making this approach work is to reach agreement on what "standard" data are and how to get them when required. Here a project control room can be a big help. The data in the control room are defined as "standard"; diligent efforts are made to hold to that definition. If such a facility is administered so that the project team has convenient access to the data they require, the concept of standard project data is both workable and efficient and is a big help in achieving project teamwork.

General management attention and applause

In a project, as in most situations, the general manager can make good things happen better and more quickly by the selective use of a little bit of his time. Visible attention to the project team is a case in point. People in an organization take for granted that general management is interested in the major functional areas; after all, that is the way things are organized, and therefore general management must be interested in the functions that are assigned to the big divisions.

In the case of a project, senior management attention is not so obvious. A general manager may have given considerable thought and attention to planning, organizing, and staffing a new project without having been at all visible to the project team, but the obvious fact of his interest in project success is a great morale builder. His constructive concern in difficult times is just as important as—and is perhaps even more likely to be required than—his positive attention to successes.

The general manager's alert attendance at a project review meeting is a great boost for everyone. Acknowledging that a milestone has been reached is a good incentive to move forward to the next one. His conversations with the project manager, later reported to the team, help create spirit, although the name dropping should not be used by the project manager as a mere ego-building exercise. A note from general management to the project team, or any expression of its interest, is good for the project.

Similarly good results are achieved when a senior functional executive takes a similar interest in the success of his own people on the project. Also, by extending his positive recognition to other departments on the project, he helps build cooperation and team effectiveness.

ADMINISTERING THE PROJECT TEAM

Personnel paperwork

In the area of personnel paperwork, standard forms should be utilized whenever possible. Procedures should also be standard except where project procedures explicitly call for a variation, for example, salary increases that require the usual approval of the functional head but now require the additional approval of the project manager. This is not to say that special policies are not appropriate for the project, for flexibility in dealing with special situations may have been one of the main reasons for setting up a project. But even with these individual variations, it is almost always possible to use the usual forms and most of the same practices and procedures.

Personnel administration is a typical example of an activity that usually can be carried out most efficiently in functional departments and in the personnel division. A matrix operation can be made to function very well, with very little increase in cost directly attributable to the existence of the project, whereas project management leads to creating a whole new personnel department and interfacing functional administration. Although its special problems may require the best professional personnel support, the project may not be able to duplicate the expertise of the main personnel staff. Permitting the project to design its own personnel practices is an invitation to union problems and long-term chaos.

The project manager need not control the personnel administration function. All he needs is the clearly delegated authority to make project decisions and the assurance of a strong voice in the compensation, promotion, and reassignment of project people. He does not normally need to be saddled with all the time-consuming details of personnel administration, an area where he is least likely to have special competence.

In a matrix organization, the personnel administration function can best be carried out by the personnel department and the functional divisions, with project functional supervision playing the role normally assigned to supervisors and the senior functional head playing his usual role. Even under a largely project management mode, the personnel department may provide necessary support to the project without transferring anyone to it.

Job classifications for project people

Standard managerial, professional, and hourly job classifications, with their accompanying rate ranges, should be used wherever possible. However, the very reasons that led to the formation of a project may call for new classifications. This subject is complex and should be addressed early on with the aid of personnel executives.

Often an organization oriented to production will establish a project to develop a new product involving new technology and calling for a very special kind of experimental shop. Many different skills are required to do the job; more union job classifications are needed for the work than are covered by the actual workforce.

An imaginative solution can be negotiated with the union to create new job classifications in the top labor grades or even above these, but with the proviso that all people in such special classifications be permitted to do work covered by any and all of the lower job classifications. That way everyone gains. Flexibility in work assignments is achieved without numerous union grievances, skilled people are well paid, and an exciting form of job enrichment takes place.

On the professional level, new job classifications may be needed to get the right people for a complex advanced-study project. There may be a mismatch between job classification and the professional talent required. An example would be the professional classification of statistician—intended to describe an individual of modest education and talents who can extract economic data from voluminous government reports and use them to compute means, standard deviations, and fitted curves. When the project needs a really brilliant econometrician to help uncover what economic factors really influence the industry, it may have trouble hiring this "statistician" because he can be hired only as a statistician "A". Project success demands executive action to change situations like this; they abound.

Circumventing managerial job classifications may be the toughest challenge of all. General management may have crossed the divide and named a project manager who is on an appropriate level with functional heads, considering the size and urgency of the project. (He may be a vice president, a director, or a manager.) Lower-level management jobs are left to be arranged by the project manager, the functional heads, and the staff.

Now the project manager finds that he needs two key subsystem managers, one to manage the program of a major subcontractor, another to manage the efforts of several technologies within the organization. Clearly, they should be at the organizational level below the project manager; perhaps they are to be managers. All is well until it is discovered by an organizational purist in personnel that these people will supervise no branch managers—and even no section managers! True, they are responsible for managing project work whose costs are ten times those incurred by departments managed by others in the organizational peer group, but there are no lower-tier managers to supervise!

Unenlightened management solves the problem in several ways. It caves in to the personnel specialists and calls these key managers "coordinators," "specialists," "advisers," or some other innocuous title guaranteed to distress the managers or even make it unlikely that they can do their jobs. Or management may rise indifferently to the occasion and create enough unneeded branch managers to satisfy the criteria for appointing the subsystem managers.

Of course, the problem has not been solved because the bureaucrats will eventually discover that the branch managers supervise no section managers! That oversight will in turn be corrected—until it is found that the section managers have no sections! Then some unneeded people will be grouped perfunctorily together to form sections, and all is well. Except that an unnecessary, unfunctional overlay has added gross cost increases to the entire enterprise. The federal government is sometimes a conspicuous victim of this problem. In a project environment, well-meaning regulations, intended to prevent the growth of a top-heavy bureaucracy, actually create one.

Special compensation for project people

Though people assigned to a project should normally be compensated on a par with everyone else in the organization, special arrangements are appropriate in several cases. Projects at remote or unusual locations offer especially difficult problems in this regard; the matter is given special attention below. Or a project may require long work hours, and very erratic ones as well. Administering overtime or additional compensation for irregular schedules becomes an administrative burden that is both costly and irritating to the people concerned. Also, the few who always try to take advantage of potential overtime may exploit project urgencies by working at a pace that makes scheduled overtime inevitable.

In such circumstances it is good practice to build into the salary rate a percentage increase of, say, 20 percent, with the understanding that people will work whatever hours are required to get the work done. Under this arrangement, administrative procedures must be relaxed so that people need not work the normal day's or normal week's work schedule when there is no need for their services. While this is a good policy, it needs review to ensure that the extended workweek compensation does not become merely a bonus for people on the project.

When a project warrants special compensation to any or all of the people assigned to it, the reasons for each increment should be clearly spelled out. Not only should care be taken that all the rules are stated as formal policies, but they should also be communicated effectively to all the people concerned. A person assigned to a project may receive different types of additional compensation for a number of different reasons:

- A salary increase because he has been doing a good job and would have received one anyway at about the time of his assignment to a project.
- An increase in basic salary because he is being promoted to a more responsible position in the normal hierarchy.
- A higher salary because he is being transferred to a special job classification appropriate only for work on the project.
- A percentage increase to account for long hours, accepted in lieu of more exact overtime payments.
- Periodic compensation to cover higher out-of-pocket living costs at the project location.
- A special salary increase intended to compensate for the undesirable working conditions, remote or unusual location, or other drawbacks of the project.
- A pure salary bonus just for joining the project, perhaps as an inducement to take a chance on its uncertainties, or as a concurrent bonus for expected ultimate success.

It will be noted that only the first two of the aforementioned increases will persist after the individual leaves the project, and perhaps only the first one. It is therefore important that everyone on the project understand exactly why he is receiving additional compensation. This is necessary as the project progresses, in order to avoid unhappiness about imagined inequities. It is doubly important at the end of a project, for people are inclined to regard most of their special pay as a benefit that will continue long after the project is over.

Compensation for projects at strange locations

All the things that have been said about special compensation apply to the special case of an unusual location, which may be remote, different, full of hardships, foreign, distasteful, or all of these. Here particular attention must be paid to advance preparations, for once people are moved they are deeply, if not irreversibly, committed. Corrections to policy can be made and inequities righted, but losses in schedule, morale, or efficiency may never be regained.

Projects carried out at remote locations or under conditions of hardship often warrant additional pay. In many cases a simple cost-of-living adjustment will be the equitable solution, but the increment should be scaled to some widely accepted index and not used as a thinly veiled bonus designed to attract people to the project. Special payments must be appropriate for such things as clothing in a very cold area or educational allowances in a very remote one, but in all instances care should be taken to make the extra compensation equal to the actual extra expenses.

It is easy to make a flat payment or a percentage salary increase, but these tend to be unfair to married people, particularly those with children. On the other hand, if an increase is intended only as a recruiting inducement, a flat payment may be the best solution. Or in special areas where the organization must assume some responsibility for the well-being of the families of its personnel, a flat payment or a percentage increase may be desirable in that it encourages single people and discourages heads of families, especially heads of large families, thereby easing the administration difficulties of supporting people off the job.

When a project at a remote location will last for some time, employees and their families must be moved. A policy for purchasing the houses of people leaving on a semipermanent assignment must be developed if none exists. A particularly troublesome situation occurs when a project will last too long to permit full per diem treatment. Or it may last long enough to justify moving families but not long enough to warrant the compensations for a full semipermanent move. In such cases, policies must be developed that provide compensation sufficient to permit families to live in reasonable comfort at the new location without compelling them o incur unreasonable costs.

In addition to paying additional money, the organization may be required to provide a number of special services. Personal tax advice to employees may be desirable. In remote or undeveloped areas it may be necessary to arrange for a host of supporting services such as supplies, transportation, and housing. Special forms of salary payment may be needed to comply with local regulations and to get the best tax treatment. Policies regarding paid leaves should be considered for many foreign locations.

If an organization is unaccustomed to operating at remote locations, a great deal of close executive attention is called for. Nothing is more demoralizing to a project than an unhappy lot of workers, dumped at a remote location, living miserable home lives with families that are even more miserable. The problem is more critical by an order of magnitude when a foreign site is involved. Certainly the wise executive will seek out the experience of other organizations that have been active in the area, most notably the large construction and oil companies.

Employing an experienced administrator familiar with the area is often a good solution, provided that he is given adequate direction by someone who really understands the policies of the organization. Here assistance on a consulting basis may be the best solution.

Salary review and administration

People assigned to a project should be given essentially the same basic compensation that they would have received in an ordinary functional assignment at the same professional or managerial level. This is in accord with the "equality principle" discussed earlier. When salary increases are contemplated, good practice calls for inputs from both the project manager and the functional head.

An individual's compensation is determined by several factors. A simple tally of his accomplishments is of course very important, but it is also necessary to consider the difficulty of the tasks involved. It is obviously unfair to give a low grade to the best technologist available, who because of his superior skill was assigned to a difficult and perhaps impossible project task, and who has performed well, but who has not yet solved the problem. It is equally unfair to give a high grade to a technologist who is succeeding in a relatively easy task assigned to him because it matched his modest level of ability.

In such situations the project manager is best equipped to assess the zeal and orderliness with which the job has been approached. However, because he is oriented toward results, he may not be qualified to judge the reasons for a good or bad performance and may rate the successful solution of an easy problem higher than the near solution of a difficult one. The functional head, on the other hand, has a far better perspective on the difficulty of the challenge and on the quality of the professional and technical effort expended in meeting it.

The ability to function as part of the team is desirable in all cases, but in a project it is essential. Stable functional environments can tolerate aberrations in behavior that are unacceptable on a project, where failure to work as part of the team may negate most of a person's fine technical contribution. The project manager is in the best position to make an evaluation of this aspect of job performance.

In addition to these short-run influences, there are important long-run salary concerns as well. A highly promising young man may be put in a job because he has the imagination to solve a difficult technical problem. When he succeeds brilliantly but in a rather inelegant administrative way, the project manager may remember the inelegance while only the functional executive will appreciate the brilliance.

Also, because of overall manpower demands, a talented person is sometimes given an assignment that does not challenge his capabilities to the fullest. If he figures in the long-term staffing scheme of the functional division, his unspectacular performance in the temporary assignment should not work against the normal increase of his salary. Finally, some people are paid well, not for what they do today but for what they give high promise of doing in the future. The functional executive is by far the best judge of all these situations.

Administrative procedures should reflect the facts of administrative life just discussed. Both project and functional viewpoints must be considered. Also, since functional divisions normally have stable and efficient procedures for salary reviews, it is well to use them as fully as possible, adding only the inputs from the project manager that may be appropriate. The following format may be used for salary review in all projects but those most strongly organized in the project management mode.

• The project manager evaluates functional personnel in general terms; for example, no raise, a modest increase for good performance, a generous increase for excellent performance, or the highest increase consistent with policy.

• The project functional manager makes his own evaluation, which need not be consistent with that of the project manager. He recommends a specific amount of increase.

• The recommendations of the project manager and the project functional manager are processed through the functional salary review mechanism. Recommended salary increases are determined for each person.

• Recommendations for or against increases are returned to the project manager for approval. An explanation is given for any divergence from his recommendations, preferably in a meeting. In the happy event that good faith persists between the project and functional organizations, the best and most efficient procedure is to explain to the project manager only those cases in which his judgment was not followed.

• The project manager approves the salary actions that he accepts. Nonconcurrences are solved by negotiation if at all possible. Stalemates should occur only infrequently, and these should be referred to a predetermined higher authority.

• After all approvals are completed, the salary review action is processed through the functional administrative machinery.

In a large project it is cumbersome and inefficient to have the project manager submit recommendations for all project employees. A better policy is to agree in advance on the level of project people the project manager will review. The list would reasonably include managers, supervisors, and key professionals, and it is a good idea to let the project manager participate in any other person's review when he expresses a specific desire to do so.

In a project strongly organized in the project management mode, salary review is one of the two or three areas where a functional head should still play a major role. The process described above is still appropriate, but if the project has its own salary review mechanism, the functional heads should have the right to provide inputs and to veto the final results in a manner similar to that described for the project manager.

In sum, salary review procedures and personnel selection are the most important personnel activities in a project environment, and deserve careful general management scrutiny and direction.

Promotion of project personnel

In one of its applications, the equality principle states that people on a project should be promoted for the same reasons and with about the same frequency as their equally competent peers assigned elsewhere. Two special cases occur, however, when the promotion is to a higher position either within or outside the project. Two quite different sets of decision-making policies are appropriate here. Failure to recognize the difference has been an underlying cause of much needless friction between project and functional executives.

An opportunity for promotion within a project usually arises because an unexpected turn of internal events creates a minor crisis: a key manager quits, or becomes ill, or is discovered to be incompetent; or a particular technology or function is perceived to be far more critical in the scheme of things than was originally anticipated. When a competent manager or professional has been with the project for some time, has learned a great deal about it, and is obviously the man most qualified to fill the higher-level vacancy or to head his special function at a higher organizational level, then he is the man who should be promoted.

Whatever the case, project needs should be given much greater weight than functional preferences. The situation is vastly different from the one that prevailed at the onset, when it mattered little that hardly anyone had any specific project-oriented experience; now it may be necessary that the newly promoted manager really understand the details of what has occurred to date in technology or in organizational relationships.

The functional head should be consulted on his nominee for the promotion, but he no longer is in the position he was in at the beginning, when the project and functional executives met on a negotiating basis and the latter held the prime decision-making power, subject to appeal. Now the project manager should be the key decision maker, with the functional manager given the right of appeal. (In analyzing an appeal, when the functional head does not want his nominee promoted, it is fair to ask why he assigned a nonpromotable individual to the project. This may not help the functional head in solving the problem at hand, but it may be useful in guiding him in making future assignments.)

When the promotional opportunity occurs outside the project, the decision making should be done quite differently. Every senior functional head should be held responsible for constantly improving the average competence of his executives; and since one of the best ways to do this is by judicious promotion of competent professionals and managers, that senior executive should have almost unilateral authority to promote and reassign even a key man on a project.

The project manager should of course have a large say in the change, primarily in seeing that the functional manager provides a satisfactory replacement, often by promotion from within the project. He should also be satisfied that adequate time is allowed for "passing the baton," for properly orienting the new manager, for assuring the orderly transition of authority and responsibility, and for introductions to colleagues and customers. (Here again guidance is appropriate for a functional head who has not provided adequate backup for a key man whom he assigns and soon wants to promote.)

Unwise promotions can create long-term problems in any organization. On a rapidly growing, perhaps glamorous project, these can be the product of an unsuspected collusion between the project manager and a functional head. As the project expands and opportunities for promotion abound, a project manager may push for promotion of functional people who may not necessarily be irreplaceable, but who have proved themselves on the project. Secretly he thinks, "I know how to pick a good man, these men have done well, and I don't need anyone untried from the functional organization." The functional head, on the other hand, thinks, "In my own organization I would never condone promotions of such men, but let them go ahead and promote their favorites; they don't deserve as high a level of competence at a managerial level as we do."

Two results, one immediate and the other long range, will ensue from such immature decision making by rather senior prople. In the short run, the best people have not been assigned to the job and the project suffers. Expansion of the project has been viewed not as an opportunity to bring in more and better talent, but rather as a time to elevate the mediocre—a course destined, if not to failure, at best to muddling through. In the long run it means that some promising people were deprived of an opportunity to gain stimulating experience on the project and to grow in managerial stature.

To add to the inefficiency, at the end of the project a number of overpromoted, underqualified managers will be waiting for reassignment; many of them will be of lower competence than their nonproject peers. The situation can be corrected by a rather messy set of decisions, but several remaining human relations problems will take some time to heal. People who are advanced too rapidly and then demoted through no fault of their own will be demoralized; a subtle rift is also likely to be opened between project and nonproject people.

Transfer of people from the project

In general, the decision to transfer someone out of the project should be made in the same way as the decision to assign him to the project. There are, however, a few pertinent elaborations and exceptions to this rule.

Some decisions for transfers will emanate from the project, for example, when the need for manpower diminishes and the number of people on a project must be reduced immediately. In this case, who goes and who stays will be negotiated, and reasonable notice should be given to permit the functional managers to do adequate advance planning for reassignment.

When a functional executive wants to transfer a person from the project, he has the obligation to provide an adequate replacement. In the case of a promotional opportunity outside the project, the decision of the functional head should be essentially unilateral. However, when the transfer is intended merely to improve the overall pattern of assignments from the point of view of the function, then the matter is negotiable; its advantages should be weighed against the loss of continuity that will occur when an accepted and knowledgeable individual is removed from the project. In any case, adequate time should be allowed for making the transition and getting the new man up to an acceptable level of competence on the project job.

Problems of transferring people to and from the project can be minimized by careful advance planning on the part of both project and functional managers. Thereafter, a periodic meeting, perhaps quarterly, can be held to consider changes in manpower needs. In addition to reviewing the overall numbers of people required, individual cases can be discussed. People who are doing well enough to justify promotion can be identified, along with those whose marginal performance may make them candidates for reassignment. Such dialogs eliminate surprises and foster a climate of mutual understanding.

Dismissal from the project

The project manager should have nearly absolute authority to dismiss anyone he wishes to separate from the project. Projects move fast and are subject to pressures that amplify the usual organizational social strains; nothing is gained by retaining a man whose contribution is clearly counterproductive in the eyes of his project manager. Even if the man is somewhat unfairly judged, his further presence is unlikely to be profitable to him, the project manager, or the project.

On the other hand, dismissal is a serious course of action that should never be taken lightly. Presumably project managers have the good judgment not to make rash decisions about people. Also, the project manager would normally be well advised to consult with the functional head before making any such decision, not only as a matter of courtesy and good executive communication, but because in this as in all matters, an appeal is possible and executive reversal of the decision can be made in exceptional cases. The project manager is placed in a particularly awkward spot if he has to reaccept someone he has dismissed.

Dismissal from the project does not imply dismissal from the total organization. The fate of the individual should be referred to the head of the functional organization from which he came. His future will be decided on the merits of his project experience and his skills, in comparison with those of others in the functional organization.

However, dismissal of an individual does not guarantee an instantaneous replacement of high quality; negotiations for a successor should follow the same rules that govern initial recruitment. Consideration of an available replacement should be part of any decision to proceed with dismissal.

Giving the project manager the right of dismissal is a strong delegation of authority to him. It is, however, a useful and necessary part of his managerial toolkit. In extreme cases it helps ensure rapid decision making and execution on a fast-moving project where lengthy haggling and appeals cannot be tolerated. It also gives the project manager some defense against being staffed with incompetents by order of an unenlightened division head. And if the right man is selected as project manager, it is unlikely that this potent prerogative will be misused.

Disciplinary action

Disciplinary action taken within a project should conform to policies that apply throughout the organization. This complex administrative task is best carried out by the functional organizations without the involvement of the project manager and, as a matter of fact, it clearly demonstrates one of the advantages of a matrix organization.

This policy is not inconsistent with the previous recommendation that the project manager be delegated the authority to dismiss people from his project. The dismissed person should be given the normal disciplinary treatment warranted by his behavior. This may be merely a routine reassignment based on the conclusion that his unsatisfactory performance on the project was the result of a failure to match his skills with the job requirements. Or it may be termination of employment because of a serious violation of rules. In any case, the disciplinary action is kept separate from the dismissal from the project.

Sometimes special disciplinary action must be taken. Where handling classified material is involved, strict discipline must be enforced. Also, at remote or unusual locations, special provisions may have to apply. Normally an organization is unconcerned with the private behavior of its employees outside working hours, but in remote locations where housing is provided on customer premises, or where there is a very intimate relationship with a small community, it may be necessary to prescribe certain rules governing conduct off the job. Communicating these rules and the procedure for dealing with violations should be generally accepted as part of the normal personnel function.

Incentive compensation for the project team—and others

The highly structured nature of project events makes them particularly suited to the use of incentive compensation. Key project events are precisely defined and the schedule for completing the job is clearly visible. Many projects have an end product whose performance can be measured quantitatively. Others are concerned with completing a contract where profit margins or incentives are measurable. It is possible to tie incentive compensation to all such well-defined project events.

One caution, however. When a project is dependent on support from other divisions of the organization, appropriate incentives should be extended to managers there as well. Nothing will dry up support for a project faster than providing generous incentives for the project team without extending comparable opportunities to the functional managers. Furthermore, a scheme that makes incentive compensation depend in part on the success of the project is a very potent managerial tool; it reminds key functional executives that management is serious enough about the project to reward their active and genuine support of it.

Communications about project personnel

For projects of any length, a cardinal administrative rule should state that all communications about project personnel be made available to the project manager, the functional head, and the appropriate level of functional project managers. Managing people is obviously a very serious part of managing a project, and no part of the procedure should be conducted in a clandestine or ambiguous atmosphere.

Of course, such a policy does not mean that every piece of paper involved in personnel administration should cross the project manager's desk, but it does mean that he should see anything important or controversial. This principle also applies to verbal evaluations of project personnel by project functional heads; long verbal assessments should not be given to functional chiefs without also being given to the project manager, either at length or, if he prefers, in summary form.

These remarks apply specifically to a matrix situation, but the identical principle applies in reverse to project management organizations. There the functional head should have full access to all information about people in his area of responsibility who are fully assigned to the project.

When a task force or a project is of short duration, the above principle should be applied realistically. In this case the project manager does not need to take part in the details of personnel administration or have access to information about salaries and performance evaluation. Any effort to involve him in such matters is unlikely to gain anything and will arouse resentment against the project. He should, however, be shown all communications about how well people are performing on the project.

PERSONNEL MANAGEMENT
AT THE END OF THE PROJECT

Honor all commitments

When a project is concluded, whether in success or failure, all previous commitments made to people on the project must be honored scrupulously, both in letter and in spirit. There are several important reasons for doing so. First, an organization should maintain an ethical stance in all its commitments to its employees, including its project commitments. Second, common sense dictates that available managerial and professional resources be deployed as efficiently as possible; the better people should be in the more responsible jobs and should rank higher in the managerial hierarchy than the less competent.

Finally, future attempts to use project management and to recruit people for projects will be greatly influenced by how people have been treated in the past projects. If they have been rewarded for excellent work by being left to fend for themselves at the conclusion of the project, thus making them obviously worse off because of their project assignment, then people will be very reluctant to accept new project assignments. Similarly, functional managers will not volunteer their best people. The whole organization will view these cold personnel reassignments as a negative message about how management really feels about projects.

On the other hand, if people are all treated according to the equality principle, then everyone will regard a project tour as a healthy experience in progressive career development. Project assignments will be regarded positively and will be readily filled with good people.

Personnel assessment at the end of a project

Near the end of a project an assessment should be made of overall project personnel policies and individual performance. This can be integrated with an overall examination of project success by the senior executive group of the organization. Such a review is a valuable long-range control on staffing and organizational planning.

Personnel policies should be evaluated primarily by the project manager and the senior personnel executive, but with considerable participation by other senior functional executives. They should address several questions.

- Were the people on the project generally happy with the personnel policies? Did they feel they were fairly treated, particularly in comparison with their peers in functional organizations?
- Were any special policies equitable (for instance, relocation reimbursement)?
- Was the personnel administration convenient and economical or was it cumbersome and costly?
- What improvements should be made in future similar projects?

In this assessment, all the key managers should be interviewed and selected people should be asked to give their views. The latter group should be a reasonable cross section of project personnel and should be augmented by all those who have been conspicuous or vocal in expressing their dissatisfaction with things; one can learn without complete belief in all one is hearing.

In addition, the performance of each individual on the project should be thoroughly evaluated. Even in the lower hourly classifications, it is important to determine who performs well in a project environment and who does not. Without such a review, the simple fact that a person has been assigned to one project may lead to his selection for the next one; whereas a full assessment of his previous performance might well indicate that he should never be assigned to another one.

In general, the assessment of a project staff should be conducted by the same people who participated in its selection. The project manager and the functional division head should meet to discuss project functional managers; the functional division head and the project functional manager should discuss the functional people at lower echelons.

Since the functional executive is responsible for future personnel assignments, he has the most to gain from the process and naturally plays the leading role; but the project manager should nonetheless be an active participant and his views should be given appropriate weight. More often than not, this participation is easy to obtain, for a project manager usually has the leadership qualities to see that his key managers are properly rewarded for their performance by good subsequent assignments.

Equitable reassignments

Reassigning people at the end of a project is a challenging and important task. Top executive attention is necessary to see that it is done both equitably and with minimum disruption to the organization. Of course, with a short project whose members are on loan from their regular departments, the matter is straightforward. But when a project lasts a year or more, and affects many people, the task is formidable.

The first key to placing project personnel fairly is a long-range plan. Where a major project is concerned, each functional executive should prepare a plan for reassigning his people and restructuring his existing organization a year before anyone actually leaves the project. In this way he will be able to integrate shifts of project personnel with the normal changes resulting from attrition, rotation, and promotion. This is a good idea even in a project management organization that has made only limited commitments about returning its members to their old departments. Surely the functional executive will want to provide places for the most talented people, those who are better than many he currently has.

When a project comes to an end rather rapidly, the functional executive is faced with difficult decisions. He may want to replace an adequate department head with an even better man from the project. An appropriate assignment must be found for the man replaced. One solution is to move the new man in as chief and retain the other as his deputy. That avoids a dominolike disruption of the organization, permits an orderly transfer of know-how about the job, and creates a situation in which either man can be reassigned when the right opening occurs.

Sometimes the demise of a project results in an excess of personnel, both from the project and in other areas of the organization. In this case everyone should be put in a single pool from which the people needed to do future work can be selected. Thus merit and the requirements of the job are the criteria, not whether or not a person was on the project.

All this decision making requires considerable effort on the part of the functional executives. It also demands a great deal of courage. General management should oversee the process to ensure that both the tenderhearted (whose first love is people) and the hardhearted (whose first love is the status quo) give fair treatment to everyone and achieve the best staffing for future operations.

8

Making Project Management Work

EXECUTIVE DECISION TO ORGANIZE A PROJECT

Recognizing the implications of project management

A project environment is a different kind of management environment. If it is not different, then a management cosmetic has been applied under the name of project management, but with little hope of achieving results different from "business as usual." Project management is successful because its principles are better suited to meet a certain class of challenges. It uses a different set of techniques and gives rise to a new set of problems. By recognizing all this, general management takes its first step in assuring a project's success.

A project environment emphasizes transience rather than continuity. For this reason it is particularly well suited for one-shot, one-of-a-kind endeavors. Business and government activities normally take place in an atmosphere of periodicity; each year is like every other year, and each spring quarter is like every other spring quarter. True, things vary from year to year, hopefully with a long-term trend of improvement. Less-than-average results in a quarter are undesirable but not catastrophic. Moreover, there are cyclic trends; opportunities may be lost in one period, but can be exploited in the

269

next one. Policies may be changed to meet changing conditions, but on an orderly, reflective basis.

All this is different in a project environment. Only one chance is given to meet the performance requirements of the new product on the predicted date. Failures can be corrected and projects are good vehicles for applying corrective action, but the atmosphere is dominated by the feeling that there is one best time—"Here today and gone forever"—to make things happen as planned. One bad failure to reach an important project milestone may result in project cancellation, and there will be no next quarter for a better performance.

Effective project planning requires establishing clear cost, schedule, and end-product performance goals. A project is an ideal environment for management by objectives. But a manager of a forward-looking development project who narrowly misses achieving clearly defined goals is at a frustrating disadvantage when this effort is superficially compared with that of a functional executive who ambles along with no clear goals, no innovations, and no mistakes, and who meets his budgets by working with the same old crew beneath the same old comfortable manpower ceilings.

Because of pressures to meet clearly defined, short-term goals, so that every second chance given creates the increasing appearance of ineptness, the now-or-never project environment is a reasonable by-product of efforts to solve immediate project problems. On the other hand, panic that results from poor planning or sloppy controls is not acceptable.

Project management creates new organizational alignments. A new player has appeared in the power structure—the project manager. Particularly in the matrix arrangement, new interpersonal and organizational stresses and new opportunities for creativity appear; but this is also true in the projectized organizational form. More decisions are appealed upward—not because of incompetence from below, but because of organizational intent from above. These factors can lead to better results, but they require a new dimension of general management interest and decision making.

All this creates an aura of impermanence that correctly reflects the finite duration of the project. Here today—gloriously, objectively here—but gone at the end of next year. Concrete successes are more important than abstract policies. The project team has been given the project goals. A carefully run routine that will produce mildly better results is of little interest to it. An imaginative, creative, vigorous scheme to meet the goals is the thing. Success happens now or soon; absence of failure is not success. This is a different view of the world. General management must recognize all these differences before it can make project management succeed.

Project management for smaller projects

A special point needs to be made about the applicability of project management to smaller projects. A decision not to use project management should never be made just because the project is small. The ratio of benefit to cost is often at its highest in small projects.

All the principles of project management apply just as well to small projects as to large ones. Most of the complex management tools and systems developed for large projects are not needed for the smaller ones, but this does not invalidate the principles concerned with organization, planning, and controls.

It is usually much easier and less disturbing to the organization to implement a small project than a large one. Often a committee or working group is established to address a task and one may expect the floundering, the relaxed debates, and the ineffectual compromises that often characterize such committees. If the same people are organized into a project with appropriate delegations and discipline, then actions will be more efficient and the results will be much better.

Assessing the costs and benefits of a project

Project management produces better results in the execution of many complex tasks. It permits an organization to cope with a class of challenges that could not be handled efficiently by normal practices. It increases the probability that a new product or activity will be completed on schedule and within budget. It reduces the chances that the work will be performed untidily, or even chaotically, with poor end results. All these factors were discussed at length in the first chapter.

Establishing a project creates changes in an organization. These in turn create interpersonal stresses and strains. Inefficiencies arise because of modifications to well-understood and smoothly working internal practices. It is difficult to place a dollar value on these changes but their existence should be recognized.

The cost of employing a project manager and his staff usually ranges from 1 to 5 percent of the total project cost. In addition there may be costs for developing adequate information processing and control systems.

In arriving at a decision to implement project management, a general manager will certainly want to consult all the members of the management team reporting to him, even if a decision to have a project will not affect them greatly. The consultations should be on both an individual and a group basis. Everyone's views should be heard.

Excellent results in a wide variety of organizations and with many diverse jobs strongly indicate that good project management saves money and improves performance. However, each case should be evaluated on its own merits.

WHEN TO USE PROJECT MANAGEMENT

General management's first decision about project management is whether to use it at all. For the majority of organizations, a good opening presumption is that project management will *not* be necessary. Then the case at hand should be examined on its own merits to see if there is any compelling reason *for* using a project approach.

Exceptions to this positive approach exist in the aerospace and construction industries, in some segments of the electronics industry, and in a few other cases where particular circumstances almost always dictate the use of project management. In these instances one may as well start with the presumption that project management will be used, but this is no contradiction. It simply suggests a more general rule, that one begin the decision-making process with the most likely outcome, then test that assumption against the special circumstances of the case at hand.

Project management is not a panacea. Often, when the problem is with an activity or a product, establishing a project will not solve it at all, and indeed may delay the ultimate solution. If the fault lies with incompetence in one or more line departments, a project manager should not be expected to correct the matter. Such difficulties should be resolved through normal line management channels. In fact, the appearance of the project manager on the scene complicates the organizational structure, creates a potential scapegoat, obscures the real source of trouble, and can delay the correction of a simple line management problem.

Often general management does not want to hear bad news. A product line may be unprofitable with no hope of recovery; or the terms of a contract may be based on a mistaken initial judgment, with no hope of profitable completion; or a research project may have been directed down a path leading to a technical dead end; or a study may have been undertaken to solve a problem that is not currently solvable. When management begins to realize the facts in these situations, it may appoint a project manager to provide insulation from the bad news, thus postponing the day of reckoning and transferring or diffusing the blame.

Such a course is bad management. A project management approach can salvage a viable activity that is in trouble, but it cannot save a basically losing proposition. When a project manager is appointed in such a situation, he should be given an honorable option to recommend scrapping the effort.

One-of-a-kind activities

Any time an organization undertakes an activity that is out of its normal line of business, it is confronted by a special set of problems of adaptation. Project management is a uniquely useful tool for coping with these.

For example, an organization may embark on a venture that is the first of its kind in its experience. If the activity is to be repeated in the future as a normal part of the business, it can be done the first time as a project to solve all the start-up problems. If there are no other reasons for continuing to manage future similar activities in the project mode, then part of the initial project mission may be to develop the capability to manage them in the normal functional manner, and one of its final tasks may be to convert the activity to this mode.

Or say a company moves its factory. Nearly all departments from public relations to facilities are affected in one way or another. General management is not and should not be willing to take on the many details that must be coordinated successfully to ensure an effective move. No department already in existence can conveniently be given the responsibility for the move; assigning the job to a project team is therefore the logical solution, one that is used more and more often by companies aware of the technique.

First, detailed integrated moving plans must be prepared, requiring inputs from a number of different departments. All tasks must be closely scheduled to minimize disruption in operations. Minor conflicts will abound—matters that must be settled immediately to avoid slowing down the move. The project manager can make all such decisions and thereby ensure that progress is not impeded by petty arguments. He can alter the plans to correct unforeseen disruptions. All this ensures an integrated operation without the necessity of constant petty decision making by general management.

The above rationale applies to any number of one-of-a-kind situations where the need is to accomplish an activity outside the function for which an organization was designed. The whole job will be done with less organizational friction, it will cost less, it will be far closer to originally planned schedules, and it will be done better if project management techniques are used.

Organizational complexity

Project management is particularly useful in projects involving organizational complexity when a number of separate divisions of an organization are required to work together, or when a number of subcontractors are involved in a project and completion of a major task involves the carefully sequenced completion of subtasks to be performed by these different divisions. Before the first step is taken, every step must be planned so that no task is begun before the required preceding tasks have been completed.

Perhaps even more important is replanning to accommodate a delay in one of the subtasks. A rigid interpretation of "I can't start until he has finished" will result in needless new delays, whereas a work-around plan that permits further subtasks to begin after most of the earlier task is finished will produce the proper results. It is the project manager who must be constantly alert to these problems and ready to provide solutions. This is the feature that has made project management productive in the construction industry.

Often an organization is called upon to make procurements for a project from a number of subcontractors on an integrated schedule. The procurement department is perfectly able to procure these goods and services and to administer the subcontracts. However, in cases where several alternative courses may be taken, each of which involves changing the scope of work of several subcontractors who may vary considerably in their ability to react to changes, the project manager can evaluate the alternatives and choose the solution that optimizes the effort of all the subcontractors in light of total project goals and criteria.

Another task of the project manager is to control changes in requirements to subcontractors. Engineers are well known for their pursuit of product excellence, and this involves changes that can be made relatively cheaply if made internally but would be expensive if passed on to a subcontractor. Many a poor bid was predicated on "getting well on changes," and only the project manager can provide the proper controls of changes in subcontractor requirements.

Government tasks involving many departments benefit particularly from project management. This fact, recognized years ago in the Department of Defense, is now widely accepted throughout the federal government and in some state and local governments as well. Regulations designed to protect the public can add great complexity to a relatively simple project task. Project management can achieve the coordination necessary for success and still comply with other regulations, which is a prime reason for its adoption in government.

In summary, project management adds greatly to the success of endeavors involving a number of organizations, particularly when their activities are intertwined throughout their execution of the required tasks.

Projects involving several technologies

Some of the first successful applications of project management occurred in projects involving advanced technology. In research laboratories and development organizations, project management principles were used long before the name for the discipline appeared. The titles *project engineer* and *project leader* preceded the title *project manager*, and in more than one case these older jobs evolved directly into the newer one.

In a laboratory or an engineering department, people are organized according to their technological specialities. The technology group is the long-run organizational home for the scientist and engineer, and it is here that his professional status with his peers counts the most. The same situation exists in organizations devoted to the study of economics and the social sciences. Research and development in such specific technological areas fit naturally into the normal line functional organization. Most of the important skills and resources are under the control of the technology manager, and those few that are not can be readily obtained on a consultative or support basis from other technology organizations. Very good results are attainable within the normal organizational structure.

However, when a project involving several different technologies comes along, the situation is far more complex. First of all, in many instances no one technology is dominant in the new project or in its desired end product. Therefore a project leader must be named, a person oriented not toward his own specialty but toward the right combination of technological efforts and the optimal performance of the project's end product.

In such a case it is difficult at first to determine the effort that will be required from each technology group. In fact, some project decisions may involve a comparison of and selection from two technologies, with one subsequently playing a major role and the other a minor one; for example, should a hydraulic power source or an electromechanical device be used?

Also, where technology is pushed forward on several fronts, it is not always easy to spot the tough problem at the beginning. One technology may make its required advance rather easily, while another runs into considerable difficulty that requires far more resources to solve than originally anticipated. Here, a project manager is needed to continually review the status of the project and reallocate resources to areas that need them most. It is not realistic to expect managers of technologies, or their representatives working on the project, to do this on a voluntary committee basis.

Another challenge to a project leader is optimizing the project end product according to its own criteria and restraints. A product that is the sum of suboptimization in each technology is usually not optimal. In other words, few products need the best of all technologies. Usually two or three technical problems, or perhaps only one, will demand the best performance available; whereas for cost or other reason, other problems can be handled best by a relatively unsophisticated technical approach. The project manager must direct the resources applied to technology in a way that achieves the best and most economical overall results for the project.

Project management also meets the need for constant updating of the project plan and schedule. Often an original test plan requires that a number of pieces of hardware be available at the same time. When trouble appears in one area, the plan must be altered to avoid a situation where most of the project team is employed inefficiently (and is squandering project funds) while waiting for that one problem to be resolved.

It is worth remembering that many highly competent people in both the physical and social sciences are oriented almost exclusively toward technical excellence—and properly so. Their contributions will be fundamental to project success, but the project manager is the only person who should make the final project decisions.

In summary, project management is a most useful and often indispensable tool in the management of study, research, and development projects that involve a number of different disciplines.

Unusual personnel situations or the union environment

Some projects could hardly survive in a normal environment of personnel administration, and would never be undertaken in the first place in a business-as-usual environment. A complex technical development or test program may need a different mix of people during each of several phases. Everyone works about forty hours a week, but not always the same forty. Some schedules may require fifty hours one week and thirty the next. Calls for support may come on short notice and at odd hours. Engineers ork at consoles that are normally the prerogative of technicians; technicians do the assignments of test engineers. Perhaps twenty different job classifications are required to do all the required tasks, whereas there is really enough work to keep only ten technicians busy. Everything is different from the normal industrial relations environment, and yet people would like to work under these conditions because of the excitement of participating in something new and promising.

An attempt to manage such a program with all the agreements existing in a large manufacturing facility would be doomed from the beginning if all the rules were followed. Costs would rise out of sight and scheduling would become a travesty. Even worse, attempts might be made to operate under the table and violate a labor contract. Justifiable grievances would soon bring things to a halt.

An imaginative solution is to establish a project and insulate it physically and administratively from the rest of the organization. Union leaders and management personnel can work together in establishing new job classifications that permit work in several old job areas at a pay scale comparable to the highest then in effect, or perhaps at a higher level as a recognition of multiple skills. Blanket premiums for overtime and odd-shift work can be arranged with no premium or reduction for actual work schedules that differ from the assumed standard. Determination of true requirements for different roles can best be made under a project management arrangement, in which a project manager is supported by an experienced and constructive personnel manager assigned to the project team.

Some companies that manufacture a complex product have experimental shops with special streamlined procedures. (These shops are informally called the "skunk works.") The project management approach is used to manage the skunk works successfully.

Remote locations

Principles of project management are especially applicable to activities at a remote location. The subsidiary organization is a smaller version of the parent, and many of the usual operating problems exist alongside new ones caused by remoteness.

It is easy enough to set up a separate independent organizational unit and consider the matter solved. However, all the aspects of a project are present: the activity is usually of a definite scope, limited in duration; it may be one of a kind with many special problems not readily solved by normal policies and procedures.

At one end of the spectrum is the enterprise in which each department is permitted to operate under the normal policies and remote direction of its home organization. The senior official on site will have only limited authority to issue direct orders. This usually results in failure to cope with special local problems effectively and in a timely manner. Production comes to a halt while interdepartmental conflicts are being resolved at home. This kind of arrangement is inefficient, damages morale, and often leads to a deadly overall paralysis.

At the other end of the spectrum is a completely autonomous organization set up under a manager given most of the authority of general management. This can work when an unusually talented field manager and supporting management team are available, but it is expensive to provide all the required expertise on site, and even then the operation may run into trouble without the guidance of the senior functional heads at the home organization.

The most efficient approach is usually to organize the remote location like a matrix project, giving the remote-site manager well-defined operating authority, while providing support and surveillance from senior functional division heads. Project management principles are a ready solution to this type of complex operating problem.

Customer influences

The federal government spends a great deal of money in the private sector, and a large part of that goes to projects. These are one-time efforts that usually call on several technologies or disciplines because of the complexity of the problems that must be solved. They range in monetary value from less than a hundred thousand dollars to more than a billion, and whereas the Department of Defense is still the largest spender, other sophisticated government agencies in the non-defense area will have more and more money to spend in this way.

Contracts are usually awarded to organizations that understand how to accomplish project management effectively and economically. The successful recipients cover the spectrum from the mighty corporation with its stable of blue-chip subcontractors to the talented university academic with his two postgraduate aides, but most of the winning bidders owe their good fortune at least in part to their proposals to use good project management techniques in spending public funds.

Government procuring agencies prefer to select a contractor with a successful record of project management in large part because nearly all successful projects in the recent past, at least those of any size, have used a good project management approach. On the other hand, a large number of failures are attributable to poor project management, or what in practice amounted to a lack of it. This high correlation between good project management and success has not been lost on procuring agencies.

Another reason for preferring a project management approach stems from the plight of the principal government procuring agent, perhaps himself a project manager. He wants to feel that someone out there is responsible for how the funds are spent. He needs a focal person to contact for vital information. Providing this liaison is one of the major functions of a project manager. Without that contact the customer faces a miserable time trying to find out what is happening. He is told by the contract department that all milestones have been reached, but is given no account of technical status. Sent to the engineering department, he receives a knowledgeable report of the technical problems but no true budget or schedule status. He is given the same treatment in the control department, and so on.

His problem is particularly acute when a small contract is being executed in a large company. A study or research contract with an academic institution presents the same generic problem, exacerbated by even looser communications between technical and business-oriented people. After an experience like this, the government procuring agent may well resolve never to award another contract to anyone not proposing a genuine project management approach.

Government agencies are not alone in wanting good project management from their subcontractors. Companies needing to subcontract critical project tasks, even though these are small in dollar value, will have exactly the same attitudes for the same reasons.

Urgency

Occasionally an organization is faced with the need to accomplish a particular objective as fast as possible. Cost is not a primary consideration in the short run if immediate execution will reap high gains in the long run. When a government agency on a very tight schedule requires practical, coherent answers to complex questions involving many divisions, it must often mobilize the best thinking of the total department; its skill in coming up with good answers can influence the future success of the department. The department head may detach first-class executives from their regular duties, give them free access to all available information, and ask the team for recommendations affecting personnel in the whole organization. In all such cases, in which faster first-class results produce greater payoffs, project management principles are the best tools for success.

One must remember that project management principles do not necessarily require using the whole stable of project management techniques. The strong application of sound procedures for delegating authority, streamlining operations, and improving communications is the essence of project management. In cases of urgency, only the most streamlined version of planning and control techniques need be used, if they are used at all. A special framework for mobilizing resources, getting information, making decisions, and ensuring their fast execution is the key contribution of project management.

In urgent situations, project management may best take the form of a separate group dedicated to the special goals at hand and operating as a temporary unit. Equally effective is an overlay of project management planning, direction, and control; such overall authority over the normal flow of operations allows activities to proceed in parallel in different divisions, or in sequence from one division to another. But wherever the project is concerned, the decision of the project manager comes first. This may be likened to racing an excellent automobile that has been optimized for commuting: the car can be made to perform as superbly as a racer, but only if driven properly. General management gives the project manager the wheel—for a while.

The point here is that an organization needing an excellent immediate solution to a challenge can enjoy the benefits of project management in the short term without making unwanted changes in long-run operations. Project management is a weapon that can be brought out of the arsenal, fired with great success, then put away until it is needed again. It is a weapon worthy of consideration in all urgent situations.

The best way to do the job

A number of opportunities for the effective use of project management have been examined. Actually the categories are not mutually exclusive, nor were they intended to be. Certainly a project may be one of a kind, may involve several technologies, and may be urgent. Rather than being rigidly separate categories, however, any one of the attributes described above might be sufficient to call for project management. The idea is not to propose a rigid test for the appropriateness of using project management, but rather to provide a checklist that will ensure that project management won't be overlooked when it is the best logical management solution.

Whenever a complex set of tasks needs to be accomplished, an executive should ask himself if project management is the right approach. The answer is "yes" if he believes it is the best way to get a job done, whether best means cheapest, earliest, with the least chance of failure, with the highest-performing end product, or a combination of these. Nor should he require a perfect fit for one or more of the attributes to feel safe about using project management.

LAUNCHING THE PROJECT

After the decision to establish a project is made, the general manager should communicate this visibly and positively to the entire organization. He should announce it personally to his entire executive team, ideally in a staff meeting. He should also discuss it privately with each executive who will be significantly affected by the project. He should indicate that he expects that executive's full support of the undertaking.

Finally, he should announce the decision in a written form that will be read by managers and supervisors in every part of the organization to be affected by the project. This can be combined with an organizational announcement that designates the appointment of the project manager. It is usually better to announce the formation of the project as soon as possible to get everyone's support in working out the other arrangements.

Selection of the project organizational philosophy

The various forms of project organization and their respective advantages should be reviewed thoroughly by the general manager in consultation with his key subordinates. The selection should be made and announced in much the same way as the decision to establish a project. As noted, the two announcements may well be made together.

It is very important that the organizational responsibilities of the project manager and the functional division leaders be spelled out clearly and in some detail. If this is done early and decisively, it will prevent a host of subsequent bickerings and appeals. It will improve the chances that the project will get off to a good start.

Definition of project goals and ground rules

Early in life of a project, its goals and ground rules should be stated briefly and approved by general management. They can always be expanded, updated, and revised as the project progresses. After the decision is made to establish a project, it is tempting to proceed directly with its organization and staffing. It is much better to define the goals and ground rules first, for they may well influence the decision on how to do the job and who the best people are to do it.

First, the overall goals of the project should be stated in clear and simple terms. For example, "The X Project is established for the purpose of winning the competition for the design and construction of a new factory for Ace Corporation, and for subsequently completing the job profitably and to the customer's satisfaction." Or "Project Y is established to develop and install a new computer-based accounting system that will meet the information requirements of the vice president of finance, and that will lower accounting costs."

Second, the performance requirements of the end product of the project are described. They should be stated in terms of specified performance rather than the type of development effort required to achieve it. For example, "The accounting system should apply the most modern technology available consistent with a high level of cost effectiveness. It should be designed so that it can be processed at a single location. Terminal communication should be considered for those transactions where such an arrangement best meets the needs of the accounting department at reasonable cost.''

Third, a statement should be issued concerning any project constraints (as differentiated from product requirements). For example, ''The project should be completed in thirty months. Total cost of systems analysis, programming, and machine time during development must not exceed $1.5 million,'' or ''All systems analysis work will be done internally but programming may be procured from an outside agency.''

Fourth, broad criteria for making tradeoff decisions should be established without attempting to account for all contingencies. For example, ''If lower production costs can be achieved by increasing expenditures on development, this should be done, provided that the payoff is obtained within three years after operations begin. Cost expenditures to avoid schedule slippage will be evaluated in terms of relative cost payoffs over a five-year period from the start of development.''

Initially providing it with clear guidelines will start the project off in a well-defined direction. ''Everyone is singing off the same sheet of music.'' A desirable byproduct of issuing such direction is the thought and attention that will be given to it by the top management team and their consequent increased understanding of the project.

Organizing the project and delegating authority

Establishing the right kind of project organization is one of general management's two most important responsibilities in project management. Making the correct selection is the hardest part of the job, but there is still much to do. The organizational task may be accomplished in two phases: in the first, the project manager and a few of his key subordinates are brought aboard; in the second, they are allowed to work out further aspects of the organization, which will be announced later. General management should continue to participate in the organizational planning and should approve all decisions to see that the desired principles are carried out.

When the nature of the organization is announced, it is not enough to issue an organization chart. Specific delegations of authority to the project manager should be made at this time.

Selecting the project team

The importance of staffing the project team with excellent people—and the right people—was discussed at length in Chapter 2. For emphasis, a reminder is given here. This is the other of the two most important responsibilities general management has in project management.

Allocation of resources to the project

The key project resource is people, but other allocations must be made. The project should start out with either an actual assignment of resources or the authority to acquire them. The project manager should not be put in the position of having responsibility for the job without the ready means to see what is needed for execution.

A budget should be established immediately for the project. When the project manager is to rely on general support from other divisions using their existing resources, he should be given adequate priority. Adequate facilities should be made available immediately. He should have a way of getting laboratory and production work accomplished quickly.

Even in the absence of initial authorizations and allocations, these matters will be worked out by a competent and energetic project manager. However, there is no point in creating a head wind for the project when the difficulties can be avoided by initial executive direction.

Provisions for management systems

When initiating a project, general management should consider what sort of management control philosophy it wishes to use for the project. This matter can usefully be considered when the organizational philosophy is being developed. Early definition of the control philosophy avoids friction between the project manager and functional divisions.

An organization accustomed to project management usually has all the systems it needs for adequate controls. The decision merely consists in selecting the particular systems desired for the project along with the depth and frequency of their application. However, a new project management organization usually requires new reports, new ways of slicing and presenting data, and even completely new information systems. Here again the project manager must be provided adequate information and access to the systems that generate it, or be given the authority to procure the service.

Requirements for planning and review

When the project is initiated, general management should give firm direction to ensure that project plans will be prepared before the bulk of project execution begins. It is a good idea to require a formal review and approval of certain plans before funds and authorization to proceed with the project are provided. Approving plans before beginning project work gives a strong incentive to complete and integrate high-quality plans early in the project.

Direction should also be given on how often the project will be reviewed by general management or the review authority. It is well to build in control thresholds that require a project review whenever these thresholds are exceeded. For instance, general management may wish to review a project quarterly, or at any time that forecast schedule slippage exceeds one month, or whenever the annual budget is expected to exceed 10 percent in any major WBS element. The project manager should be given the opportunity to request a high-level review when he feels it to be important.

EXECUTIVE DECISION MAKING
AT KEY MILESTONES

General management needs and wants to know what is going on in projects. It does not want to spend an excessive amount of time on them or exercise too much control over them. A good approach is to divide the projects into phases. At the end of each phase, top management thoroughly reviews the progress of that phase and the plans for the next. If the project is going well, an executive decision is made to proceed to the next phase; funds and resources will be provided.

Periodic reviews may be made, but the project does not wait for specific reviews or decisions until the next phase comes up for review.

A project that is not going well may be canceled, given instructions to complete additional work, or told to do more validation of the planning of the following phase. A decision to proceed is withheld until another review shows that the problems have been corrected.

This management scheme sharpens the decision-making process. General management retains control over major decisions about the project. At the same time, the project can be managed in each phase without the delays that result from a ponderous approval process. A number of progressive companies use this approach. The Department of Defense follows the policy in its DSARC reviews.

The phased approach is equally suitable for small projects. The only difference may be that phases are somewhat shorter. The chartering authority may exercise adequate control by reviewing the project only at the proposed start of a new phase, leaving the directive and rreview authorities the task of keeping track of the project in the interim.

Phases should be adapted to the project. For the development of a major information system, the phases could be as follows:

Development of a concept and a cost validation procedure
Statement of requirements
System design—development of specifications.
Program development
System test
System operation

The phases for development of a hardware product could be:

Concept development
Market survey and program planning
Key technology verification
Prototype development and test
Production program
Commercial introduction and product support

A well-defined set of end products should be defined for each phase. This makes the planning crisper and the review process more efficient.

How far in the future should one plan?

It is difficult to determine just how far into the future the project should be planned and in how much detail. Enough planning should be done to allow the entire project to validate the overall concept, schedules, and cost estimates. On the other hand, trying to make detailed and complete plans for work to be done three or four years in the future is likely to be wasteful and an exercise in futility. Several Department of Defense procurements in the sixties required an excessive amount of detailed planning information for work scheduled for years in the future, a practice that gave the whole planning process a bad name, much of it undeserved.

The idea of project phases is a good framework for a realistic approach to planning. When a project is nearing the point of deciding on entry into the next phase, detailed plans should be available for that phase. However, only broad planning sufficient to update and validate the concept is necessary for subsequent phases.

For instance, a project preparing to enter a design and development phase should have firm and detailed development plans. A less detailed plan will be required for the actual production. The details can be filled in more realistically as the design progresses. Plans for operational support can be even less detailed. However, the operating concepts must be defined well enough to have the appropriate influence on design. Only the detailed plans for execution can be postponed.

TRADEOFF DECISIONS
DURING PROJECT EXECUTION

The main reason for using project management is that as a project progresses, things rarely go as planned. As problems arise in product performance, costs, or schedules, corrective action will be needed. As a first step, vigorous management action can be taken to try to get the project back on plan. However, a brute force application of attention and effort may not be the best solution for the overall project. The best approach is usually to examine the options that exist to revise schedules, costs, and performance for an optimal project solution. Skill in making such tradeoffs is a required attribute of a good project manager.

After the tradeoff analysis and decision are made, project planning must be revised. Direction to implement is given in revisions to specifications, work authorizations, budgets, and schedules. General management should monitor major tradeoff decisions and the resultant implementation.

Tradeoffs within a single parameter

Earlier discussions have alluded to tradeoffs within each of the parameters of performance, costs, and schedules. For completeness, the possibilities will be summarized here.

The essence of systems engineering is the tradeoffs among different subsystems and components to achieve the optimal total system and project. All design work involves such tradeoffs at different levels.

Tradeoffs in schedules occur when one event in a series is estimated to take longer than planned. Other events in the series are then scheduled to be done in less time. Or events planned for series execution are done partly in parallel.

Budgets are transferred from one WBS element to another or from one department to another. If it is not the policy to move budgets, at least projected overruns are matched against each other for planning purposes.

In major systems development efforts, tradeoffs are made between development costs and operating costs. Often additional money is spent on development to generate savings during future operation. On the other hand, immediate funds for development may be limited, and so the solution actually makes for greater total costs in the long run.

Tradeoff decisions in each of these areas are much more complex than suggested here. The really complex decisions come when the interactions between the areas are considered in decision making.

Product performance and schedule tradeoffs

Performance and schedule tradeoffs usually happen when a part of the project gets into technical difficulty. This typically occurs when a test shows that a component fails to meet performance requirements. Then it becomes obvious that a redesign is necessary to attain the specified performance.

If the problem is such that a redesign is necessary to get the product to function at all, then there is no alternative but to go ahead with the redesign. One possibility is to accept the delay required to complete the redesign, modify the hardware, and slip the project schedule by the amount of time required to conduct the test again. A second choice is to reduce the amount of testing required and complete the engineering and test program on schedule with an increased risk of future problems.

A third choice is to slip the completion of the engineering and test program and make up the slippage by an equal compression of the tooling and manufacturing program. A fourth choice is to slip the completion of the engineering and test program but to permit no slippage in the tooling and manufacturing program; this increases the concurrency of two project phases and the likelihood that changes will be required after the product is released. Fifth and other choices are combinations of the first four.

If the failure to meet the specification is simply a lower-than-specified value of some parameter, then all the alternatives above are available. In addition, one can consider accepting the product performance degradation. Or one can accept it temporarily and plan to fix it at a later date.

Sometimes it happens the other way around; schedules drive performance, and great advantages appear to result from advancing a project completion date. This leads to reviewing what relaxation in performance specifications can contribute to an earlier product delivery date. Sometimes problems in a nontechnical aspect of the project or changes in project requirements lead to slippage in the project end date. The development program can be examined to see whether the extra time can be used to produce a product with better performance.

In the discussion on product performance measurement, the interrelationship of product performance verification with scheduled events was shown to be a part of the control system. It will bring early attention to problems such as these.

Admittedly some of the solutions described above have major cost implications. These were passed over in this discussion to stress the relationship between performance and cost. In some projects, delivering a product with desired characteristics on schedule is so important that cost is really not a prime factor in decision making. In others, development cost is relatively insignificant compared with ultimate production costs, schedules, and profits, and so development cost does not dominate development decisions.

Product performance and cost tradeoffs

Product performance usually drives cost upward when technical difficulties are encountered during development. More designers than anticipated are required to solve the problem, and tests may have to be repeated. When problems appear, it is often prudent to proceed in parallel with several design solutions, of which only the most successful or the first to succeed will be selected. This obviously costs more than a single effort. Sometimes the initial design solution was selected for its low cost, but when its deficiencies become evident a switch is made to a better but more expensive design.

Sometimes a design is created to optimize the solution to a set of requirements, and a cost estimate is made that exceeds the available funds. The design is reviewed to see how costs can be reduced by accepting a lower level of product performance. As an example, an information system was critically designed to have exclusively n-line inquiries. It turned out that the cost of programming was too high, and so only the most frequent inquiries were put on line, with other information being supplied in batch reports. This substantially reduced the costs.

Product performance, schedule, and cost tradeoffs

The majority of project tradeoffs really involve product performance, schedules, and costs. In analyzing project alternatives, it is usual to select two of the values and explore the relation between them, identifying several alternative pairs of feasible values. A value of the third parameter can be assigned to each pair; feasible alternatives are then available for comparison.

It is most common to look at the relation between product performance and schedules, to determine sensible alternative courses, and to analyze the cost of each one.

Efforts have been made to develop three-dimensional analytical models for simultaneous consideration of all three parameters. However, they are difficult to follow. Keeping the model up to date is nearly impossible. A simpler analysis based on specific cases is still the most practical way to proceed.

Making good tradeoff decisions requires the efforts of the whole project management team. It requires strong leadership and substantial involvement by the project manager. Properly done, it makes large contributions to project success.

Schedule and cost tradeoffs

Costs and schedules usually are reviewed together. Some of the interrelationship is portrayed by looking at time-phased budgets and actuals along with project schedules. In good practice, the budget loadings are based on these schedules. Earned value controls give additional insight into cost-schedule relationships.

Schedule difficulties can be caused by shortages, tooling problems, design deficiencies, and many related problems. Additional costs may be expended to recover schedules. Overtime or an additional shift may be instituted. Substitute but more expensive material may be used. Production may continue in accordance with a plan to modify the hardware at a later stage. All these unplanned additional activities incur costs higher than available budgets.

Some development projects are started with overly optimistic estimates about the simplicity of the task. Schedules may be maintained for a while but in a very hectic and inefficient environment. A new look at the whole project structure may show that the total project cost will be lower if schedules are extended to permit a more orderly execution of project tasks.

Occasionally, things go exceptionally well on a project. Allowances for contingencies are not needed. A number of fixed costs are always associated with a development phase or, indeed, with the whole project. It may be well to take advantage of the favorable situation and shorten the schedule for project completion. This will lower total costs by reducing the time during which fixed-level costs are expended.

Prompt decision making is important

In complicated project situations it is nearly impossible to make the tradeoff that is exactly the best, but it is very possible to get quite near this goal. A well-thought-out analysis of the problem with full participation by members of the project team who are affected by the decisions can make for successful tradeoffs and can develop a coordinated change in project plans and a short implementation time.

A great deal of time can be spent in developing lengthy analyses to demonstrate that the proposed solution is indeed the best. Additional time can be spent in haggling over how to increase the efficiency of the plan by 2 or 3 percent. Such practices should be avoided. Nothing slows down the momentum of a project, destroys morale, creates additional costs, and causes schedule slippages more devastatingly than drifting indecisively when the project is in trouble. That is why active, decisive people turn out to be better project managers than their more precise and deliberate colleagues. Prompt decision making and vigorous implementation are marks of good project management.

GENERAL MANAGEMENT SURVEILLANCE AND SUPPORT

Review of project progress

It is important that general management keep track of project progress. Even a very good project manager can use guidance from the top. It was noted earlier that project management is an extension of general management in that it manages the activities of many functional departments. The general manager will want to look at the project now and then to ensure that all team members are playing well together. He is the one who can detect developing hostilities between the project manager and the functional division heads and eliminate them before they adversely affect the health of the organization.

Project reviews need not be long or frequent. But periodic concentrated attention of upper management is required.

General management support

Projects with outstanding records of success have always had general management support. One form of support to the project manager is consistent decision making. A project manager who is given major delegations of authority at the beginning of a project may run into trouble with functional executives when he tries to exercise that authority. The general manager should support the project manager, affirm the delegation, and require performance by the functional executive. If the project manager consistently issues poor direction or uses his delegated authority improperly, the solution is to get a new project manager.

Another form of support is availability. Occasionally, a project manager will encounter an immediate problem that only the general manager can solve. The general manager should make himself available to the project manager for the required help. A project in a critical phase suffers when it is on dead center with no solution in sight.

The general manager can help a project greatly by a visible display of interest. Attendance at a project review meeting is a great morale booster. A compliment to a project team member who does something particularly well is a positive help. Acknowledging that project milestones have been reached is desirable.

Finally, the general manager must let it be known that he supports the idea of project management. His continuing positive attitude will be felt throughout the organization and will lead to project success. In many situations, project management is very valuable to general management and, if the technique is used, it is worthy of support.

Index

decision making (cont.)
 in matrix environment, 60–61
 new framework for, 10
 in personnel selection, 235
 policy conflicts and, 3
 in project initiation, 269–272, 282–283
 project management and, 49–50, 63–64
 in project personnel, 50–51
 in project planning, 104–110
 standard data in, 249
 in tradeoffs, 292–293
 types of in project establishment, 13–14
Defense Department, U.S., 7, 54–55, 91–92, 154, 159, 279–280
 change management in, 165
 configuration management in, 169
 cost optimization in, 114
 Cost Schedule Control System of, 179
 decision making, 287
 earned value measurement in, 203
 Instruction 7000.2, 53
 PERT-COST requirements of, 179
 planned earned value in, 200
 planning in, 288
 project management in, 4, 275
 project review meetings at, 222
 training programs of, 55
Defense Systems Management School, 55
deputy project manager, 84–85
design changes
 product performance measurement in, 196
 project manager and, 174
 unneeded, 197
design reviews, 171–172
development plan, 149
development tests, review of, 175–176

direction
 budgetary, 158–159
 general operations, 160
 procedural, 159–160
 schedules, 157
 technical, 156–157
directive authority, project manager and, 82–83
disciplinary action, 262–263
dismissals or transfers, 261–262

EACs, see estimate at completion
earned value concept, 197
 overruns and underruns in, 201–202
 in project management, 203
 in variance analysis, 200–203
earned value curve, for WBS elements, 200
earned value measurements, 197–203
 case examples in, 201–202
 milestone dates in, 198
 parameters in, 201–202
 project earned value baseline in, 199–200
 tasks and subtasks in, 198–199
 usefulness of, 203
 variables in, 202
 variance analysis in, 200–203
earned value systems, computer and, 206
efficiency, improvement in, 28–29
electronics industry, project management in, 272
end product
 configuration of, 176–177
 iterations and, 109
 test results for, 175–176
energy, as qualification in project manager, 48–49
engineering technology, in systems engineering, 115
entertainment expense accounts, 163–164

304

project (cont.)
   objectives in, 3, 9, 16, 20, 38–
      40, 283
   operational phase of, 12
   organizational independence of,
      66–79
   organizational phase of, 12
   organizational philosophy of, 283
   organization charts for, 96–98,
      242
   organization requirements for, 2,
      10
   organizing of, 13–17, 34, 269–
      272, 282–286
   perceived need for, 40
   performance requirements in, 3,
      190–192
   personnel assessment at end of,
      265–268
   personnel management at end
      of, 265–268
   personnel problems at beginning
      of, 34–35
   phases of, 287–288
   planning of, see planning; project
      planning; project plans; see
      also integrated quantitative
      planning
   product performance as measure
      of, 189–192
   progress review in, 293–294
   project control room for, 207–
      215
   psychological implications of, 36
   recruiting for, 45, 240–246
   reporting of, 25–26, 293–294
   resource allocation for, 285
   rumors and resentments in, 40
   scope of, 16, 19–20
   sequential phases in, 12
   short-duration, 264
   staffing of, 16, 34, 45, 240–246
   steady state of, 36
   success of, 9
   systems engineering and, 110–
      120

   task statement in, 20
   team for, see project team
   technical performance require-
      ments for, 190–192
   technology stage of, 46
   time required for organization
      of, 14–15
   tradeoff decisions in execution
      of, 288–293
   transfer from, 261
   urgency of, 280–281
project autonomy
   concept of, 67–68
   unique aspects in, 77
   see also organizational auton-
      omy
project baseline, documentation of,
      160–161
project budget, 140–145
   cost estimating in, 142–144
   project plans and, 148
project changes
   administrative systems and, 167
   control of, 91
   see also change
project charter, outline for, 97
project control, in unique project
      functions, 90
   see also control
project control data
   quality of, 224–225
   reporting and action based on,
      223–227
project control manager, 215
   meeting agenda and, 217
   schedules and, 139–140
   schedule status review by, 180–
      181
   work breakdown structure and,
      133
   project control meeting, pace of,
      220
project control room, 207–215
   administration of, 212–214
   communications in, 209, 214–
      215, 248–249

data displays in, 210–212
maintenance of, 213
need for, 207–208
physical design of, 208–210
posting of data in, 214
visual aids in, 209–210, 219
project control systems
data for, 178–179
fundamentals of, 178–180
planning and direction in, 178
project costs, control of, 186–189
see also cost (adj.)
project decisions, criteria in, 16
see also decision making
project direction, 21–22, 151–177
administrative direction and,
161–165
depth of, 22
design reviews in, 171–172
general operating direction and,
160
planning and, 104
principle of, 151–154
procedural direction and, 159
special systems in, 153–154
systems for issuing, 152–153
work authorization in, 154–156
project earned value baseline, 199–
200
project end products, defined, 106–
107
project engineer
defined, 7
as title, 276
project environment, 162–163
changing nature of, 38
encounters in, 58
special features of, 33–40
transcience vs. continuity of, 269
project evaluation, 23–24
controls in, 113
project execution, 22–23
project experience, 41
learning through, 58
as professional and managerial
development, 57–58

project functional activities, 85–
87
project functional management, in
matrix project organization,
72–74
project functional manager, 37
budget development and, 145
charter of, 86–87
nomination of, 238
promotions and, 259
qualifications for, 51
salary review by, 257
schedules and, 139–143
schedule status review by, 180
selection of, 237–239
work definition for, 131
see also project manager
project functions
supervision of, 86–87, 131, 139–
143
unique, 87–94
project goals, 3, 9, 16, 20, 38–40,
283
project inefficiency, planning process and, 151
projectization, 66
projectized management or organization
complete vs. incomplete, 68–70
controls in, 180
project leader, as title, 276
see also project manager
project location
examples of, 84, 162–163
in organization, 80–84
project management
academic courses in, 53–54
activities in, 8
adoption of name, 11
in aerospace industry, 272
applications of, 29, 272–282
authority levels in, 81
bad management in, 273
in ballistic missiles program, 27